Where did I go wrong?

By Michael A. Obenski, VMD

© Advanstar Communications Inc.

Published by Advanstar Communications Inc. 641 Lexington Ave., 8th Fl. New York, NY 10022-4503. Website: www.advanstar.com.
All rights reserved. None of the content in this publication may be reproduced, stored in a retrieval system, or transmitted in any
form or by any means (electronic, mechanical, photocopying, recording, or otherwise) without the prior permission of the publisher.

First edition
Printed in the United States of America
ISBN 13: 978-0-9794343-1-0
ISBN 10: 0-979434-1-9

10 9 8 7 6 5 4 3 2 1
First Printing March 2007

FORWARD: When did I go wrong? vii

CHAPTER 1: Flights of Fancy

Inter-galactic hijinx garners 'A' 2
Twilight Zone, The Phone Call ... Unfortunately, it's not a prank 4
Hokey Awards: Client theatrics, originality should be rewarded 6
Talent abounds at 2005 Hokey ceremony 8
The high cost of veterinary brain power has aliens outraged 10
Time flies in Wonderland... 13
DVMs purge tubular menace... 15
If only dogs could talk; the things they would say about clients 17
Cumulus rains on Brutus' parade 19
Why your filing system suffers to this day 21
Rustle up some techs and head on down to the rodeo..................... 23
Dream day is just that—a dream 25
OSHA inspector takes top prize in daytime comedy awards 27
'Wrong Way' Obenski's brain declined for advancement of science 29
Prune Juice left in dust as DVM hero rides into the sunset on white bronco... 31

CHAPTER 2: Fables and Friends

'Old Fogysaurus' rears ugly head..................................... 34
Veterinary terminology: Sometimes the meaning can go awry 36
Real science, real jargon 38
Fake stethescopes are more than a novelty.............................. 40
Dr. Hardway no match for rugrats 42
Answer: All of the above.. 44
Rebates: Dumb, dumb and dumber................................... 46
'Love Training:' This book report long overdue......................... 48
'Ninth pin' ruins otherwise good day.................................. 50
Dr. Hardway can only plead 'temporary insanity' 52
Long IRS fingers reach Arnie 54
'Abe's Practical Practice Scripts' destined for bestseller list 56
Fail-safe client bait delivers jolt 58

Chapter 3: Dr. O's Diary

Medical genius or ice cream delivery driver; too close to call for some clients . . 62
Bankers test relationship between me, myself and Michael 64
Good old days getting a little blurry 66
Pet psychics bridge gap in medical knowledge. 68
Aren't we lucky we don't have to deal with people?. 70
Bad college habits catch up with you after all 72
Daisy pulls quick one on Mike. 74
Arnie tries contest 'end run' 76
Granny's cookies as 'natural' as Arnie's stories 78
Good fences make good neighbors 80
The Terminator 82
Client translation an acquired skill 85
Ahoy mateys! 'Thar he blows! 87
Howdy, Jake and Binky? Nah, more like Larry, Curly and Mo 89
Nowhere to run, nowhere to hide. 91
Nourishment-challenged clients pose portly problems 93
Drugs on rugs? $2,000 for a ticket to a football game? Who's dumber?. 95
Old dogs can teach new tricks 97
First interactive column has Dr. O looking for the blue cup. 99
Reckless ways catch up with Dr. O. 101
Watch out for abductions when looking for that 'extraterrestrial' vehicle 103

Chapter 4: Dumb

'Dim Bulb' competition heats up. 106
Telephone a mixed blessing 108
'Blue pill' cures variety of ills 110
It's déjà moo all over again. 112
Secret second opinions sought in Mr. Nomad's clandestine city tour 114
Bad things come in threes. 116
A toast to Chablis. 118
Cats age, but owners seldom mature. 120
Stereo's incessant chatter leaves out small diagnostic detail: What's wrong? . . 122
Mrs. Bedlam's offspring know how to keep office visit calm 124
'A veterinarian afraid of a little kitty?'. 126
You're fired!. 128

Chapter 5: Dumber

One clear thought deserves another.................................. 132
Know when to call in specialist 134
Sock-pilfering pooch uncovers hanky-panky........................... 137
'Wallet lockjaw' found to be contagious.............................. 139
Client talking doesn't necessarily guarantee information.................. 141
Home diagnoses add new dimension to medicine....................... 143
Hugh Betcha, Augusta Wind blow in with helpful hints 145
Can anyone explain pet owner economics?............................ 147
Dreams of retirement fleeting.. 149
You can't win in pill stampede....................................... 151
Hey, what's in a name anyway?...................................... 153
DVM degree just doesn't cut it....................................... 156
The customer is always right 158

Chapter 6: Dumbest

'Just one more thing, Doctor...'...................................... 162
Idiots, grass rolls cause logjam 164
'Hooked' on human/animal bond.................................... 166
Why eat only one foot when you have two?........................... 168
'Sticker shock' almost kills Purstring and Dr. O 170
Ow! Ooh! Ouch! Nothing hurts as much as a rubber check............... 172
Flip-flop syndromes invade clinic.................................... 174
Guy Macho turns to Tinkerbell 176
Racket hits exam room... 178
A lesson in counterintelligence...................................... 180
Bungling Bundles botch office visit—twice 182
Hey, doc, Izzy Dunyet?... 184
Mrs. Bungle's lager-loving pooch still has those pesky fleas 186
Does anyone lease pets? Client Izzy Worthitt may be in market 188
... Because the clients helped....................................... 190
Mrs. Lotsavets proves plenty of 'stray' clients still roam streets............. 192
Mechanical Cesarean cures cat carrier dystocia 195
Client monkeyshines leave a doubting Arnie.......................... 197
Queen of the Clueless takes defective reasoning to new heights 199
Time on their hands, trouble on their minds, a mess in their wake......... 201
Mr. Punster wears out welcome; Dr. O would like to just 'barium' 203

Chapter 7: The World We Live In

How do you treat acute pet owner stupidity? 206
Politics in the exam room can get heated 208
Computers: friend or foe? 210
Do-it-yourselfer redefines medicine 212
Enough blame to go around 214
Old habits die hard 216
Just how far can you stretch a dollar? 218
No such thing as a simple question 221
Computers = Hula Hoops and other passing fads 223
Procrastination rears ugly head 225
Dr. O is in deep doo-doo 227
Veterinary 'dream team' gets Gator by the tail, has the last laugh 229
'Emergency calls' foster beeper blues 231
Too bad sloppy baking can't be blamed for these animal 'crackers' 233
Machines that go nowhere and other inducements to shape up 235

Chapter 8: A Runaway Train

Safety's cardinal rule: Just don't get hurt 238
Ghost of veterinary future delivers ultimate reminder 240
Road to recovery still requires a toll 242
Ingenuity, imagination can lead to ultimate equipment bragging rights 244
What's wrong with catalog drug sales? 246
Post-Seminar Syndrome has Dr. O re-examining old habits 248
What the heck is wrong with you? 250
Bout of temporary sanity stymies Dr. O 252
Where is the on-ramp to the information superhighway? 254

Chapter 9: My Corner of the World

Mrs. Blastaway takes aim at those 'high' exam fees 258
Consider a 'not my problem' department 260
Losing clients can be ... satisfying 262
Cookie batter's ingredients raise concern 264
Wanda Sample spurs spurious ethical dilemma 266
Beware of grass moles 268
Axioms guide, as well as rule, veterinary life 270
Smooth-talking Dr. O fells unsuspecting Arnie 272
Let's set the record straight, please 274
Blockhead Hall of Fame competition fierce 276
Two rules to deal with salespeople; 'just say no', 'don't pay attention' 278
The dreaded Double Whammy 280

v

Forward

When did I go wrong?

Long, long ago, sometime after the extinction of the dinosaurs (it was 1958) in a remote corner of an obscure galaxy (Hatboro, Pa.), there came a time of great decision.

A young lad of 11 (that's me) chose to pursue a career in veterinary medicine.

Having been born into a family where all males were expected to become mechanical engineers, the decision made me the "ebony ovine" (black sheep) of the clan for quite a while.

Nonetheless, I remained steadfast in my career goal even though it meant suffering through 14 more years of formal education. I never wavered from my choice though, and have been content with it to this day.

In the late '60s and early '70s, during my years in veterinary school, I met many of my fictitious colleagues within this book. Some of them include:

• Arnie, the greatest genius to ever practice my profession

• Juan Armup, the dedicated large-animal practitioner

• And of course, Leonard D. Hardway, the burned out practitioner who now resides in the Cold Ember Home for burned out veterinarians in Ropes End, Wisconsin.

Over 1,800 Thursdays have gone by since those carefree days of higher education. Darn near 400 of those Thursdays found me mailing in my monthly contribution to *DVM Newsmagazine*. The pages of this book are made up of a decade's worth of these columns.

This writing career came to me out of the blue. You see, as an active veterinary practitioner, I met so many notable people and witnessed so many strange events that I felt compelled to record my observations and eventually share them.

All these stories are true. Of course, the names have been made up, but the events happened. (That's my story, and I'm sticking to it.)

Perhaps, as you read one of these columns, you will recognize yourself or a client or two. Well, as they say: If the shoe fits…

If you do recognize yourself, please don't be insulted. I assure you that it was someone else I was thinking about when I wrote it.

It's true; veterinarians have a wonderful sense of humor. Because of these columns, I routinely hear words of appreciation from colleagues who take pleasure in my work. To stop would be to let them down, and I can't bring myself to do that.

So, enjoy this compilation of stories. I hope they bring a smile or a chuckle, because, frankly, we deserve it.

— *Michael A. Obenski*

CHAPTER 1:
Flights of Fancy

Where did I go wrong?

Inter-galactic hijinx garners 'A'

In a distant corner of an obscure galaxy, there is a little building with a big mortgage. It's my office.

If you had been there last Friday, you could have heard first-hand the exciting news that Mrs. Alpha stopped in to deliver.

"Doctor, I just can't believe how well my cat is doing. After our last visit to you, those horrible seizures just stopped. It was like magic. Do you think that hairballs may have been causing the problem? The reason I ask is that I bought some of that Lube-a Cat Gel hairball medicine when we were leaving last time and the seizures have been gone ever since. I thought I'd pick up some more while I was here today and, by the way, I need a refill on those phenobarbital tablets, too."

Several of my staff members who overheard the conversation were politely choking back the laughter as I asked her if she didn't realize that the medicine was supposed to stop the seizures.

"Well, of course I knew that, doctor," she said. "But, I didn't think it would actually work."

Meanwhile just a few miles down the road, Mrs. Beta was talking to my friend, Arnie, about her dog.

"Don't try to tell me there's nothing wrong with Astro, doctor," she said. "He's been losing weight for six months. I don't care if all your X-rays and blood tests say he's normal. I know that something must be causing his weight loss."

Arnie tried to assure her that the dog appeared to be in excellent health and was, in fact, in better shape now that he was no longer obese. Still, she insisted on being given a specific reason for the weight loss and even following an extensive battery of tests, Arnie didn't have the answers she wanted.

Moments later in a third location, Alpha and Beta, along with several other students, met to discuss their veterinary office visits with their instructor G'zork. They were exactly 50,000 miles above my clinic in a huge mobile artificial asteroid. It had strange markings on the side which you and I will never see. However, if we could see them, and if we could translate them, they would say, "G'zork's Traveling College of Inter-Planetary Astro-Psychology."

G'zork would not start the class until each student's dog- or cat-simulating android was put away properly. Then, reports were given one at a time. The subject of the day's research was: "The Response of Earth Veterinarians to Illogical Situations."

Student Delta went first. He told the group how he had set his dog simulator on the vicious setting and then let it lunge at the veterinarian. When the test subject jumped away from the pseudo-hound, Delta squealed with delight and did the best he could to imitate an earth laugh. In theory, the veterinarian should have been surprised by a pet owner's attitude that viciousness is funny. Such was not the case, however, and G'zork gave Delta a C-minus, calling his work trite and unimaginative.

Next, B-12 told how she attempted to complete the assignment. She pretended to be an important client who not only owned lots of dogs, but was also a breeder. Then, she scheduled a routine appointment near the end of the day for one puppy, but showed up late with four sick dogs. G'zork's response was predictable.

"Trite, unimaginative, C-minus," was the verdict.

Alpha's report concerning the subject, Obenski, was well received. The veterinarian had managed to maintain a straight face, but the laughter of the hospital staff had not gone unnoticed. Alpha was awarded a B-plus.

Back on the home sphere, Arnie and I were discussing some recent cases while, high above us, Beta was getting up to give her report. She had decided to complete the experiment in front of the whole class. And so, moments later, Arnie's receptionist informed us that a Mrs. Beta wished to speak with him on the phone.

"This is the lady I was telling you about, Mike," he said. "The dog was in perfect health. All the test were normal. There has been some degree of weight loss, but we can't figure out why."

Arnie put the call on the speakerphone.

"Hello, Doctor," Mrs. Beta said. "I've been thinking about Astro's weight loss and I think I might know the reason for it. I put him on a diet a few months ago and have been feeding him half as much as I used to. Do you think that could cause it?"

Arnie pushed the mute button as we both burst out laughing.

Beta got an A. I'd have given her an A-plus.

October 2001

Twilight Zone, The Phone Call … Unfortunately, it's not a prank

In the 1960s, Rod Serling came to my house each week. He took me, along with millions of other Americans, to a place he called The Twilight Zone. His television show, for which he wrote and hosted, featured half-hour stories with strange and bizarre endings. Many years later, Mr. Serling's format for entertainment was revised into a somewhat different form. It was called Twilight Zone, The Movie.

To this day, I still enjoy a crazy ending. Luckily, we have an occasional occurrence in my office that satisfies this craving. We call it Twilight Zone, The Phone Call.

My last conversation with Mr. Dubious serves as a perfect example. "Doctor, I'm concerned about my cats," he said. "Snorty has a bad cold. His nose is stuffy, and he won't eat. I thought those vaccinations that you veterinarians recommend were supposed to prevent stuff like this."

I explained that annual vaccinations might not protect against every type of virus. Although Snorty had respiratory symptoms, they could have been much worse without the vaccination.

"That doesn't make any sense to me," he argued. "What you're saying is that those shots didn't protect Snorty. I suppose that means this could spread to my other cats. If the vaccines aren't effective, you veterinarians should warn people before they spend all that money for something that doesn't work."

A glance at the records revealed that we had never given any vaccines to his cats. Foolishly, I mentioned this to Mr. Dubious. "Your records wouldn't show it, of course," he said, "but we give them the vaccines at home. We get them through the mail from the Polyp & Carbuncle Catalog. We don't know how to give shots though, and my wife read all about those tumors that vaccines cause. So, we just squirt the vaccine in their mouths."

It was later that same day when another wacky ending phone call came in. Miss Nomer was called to clarify my instructions concerning her cat's diet.

"He is absolutely, positively not allowed to have any seafood," I emphatically told her. "Check the ingredients on the back of the label when you buy canned food because he can't have any seafood, even if it isn't the main ingredient."

"I understand perfectly, doctor," she said. "I just have one question: Is he allowed to have fish? You know, most people don't consider fish to be a seafood."

I was tempted to point out that although it may not be considered seafood on her planet, here on earth fish does tend to fall into that category. It was easier to just change my recommendation to exclude both fish and seafood from the diet.

These episodes of Twilight Zone, The Phone Call happen just frequently enough to keep practice interesting. Rarely, however, do they occur twice in one day like these two did. In fact, part of the fun is that you never know when the next one will occur.

Allow me one more example. It happened several years ago when Ann Biguous called about her dog, Puddin.

"He has diarrhea again," she announced. "He feels bad and hasn't eaten for two days. Can I try giving him some milk? Wouldn't that help to give him both fluid and nourishment?"

I explained that milk might not be the best thing to give during an episode of diarrhea.

But doctor, he has to eat something, and he won't touch his regular food. Milk might be just the thing to get him feeling better," she said.

Against my better judgment, I gave in and told her that she could try offering him some milk to see if she could get his appetite started. "Oh, that won't do any good," she retorted. "Puddin hates milk."

There are, of course, many other examples of strange phone calls from my career, and I'm sure yours as well. They lead us to this simple conclusion: Back in the '60s, Rod Serling may have been the master of the tricky ending, but if he were alive today, he'd have to take a back seat to many of our clients.

January 2006

Hokey Awards: Client theatrics, originality should be rewarded

Will Mel O'Drama upstage Wanda Barf?

Mr. Mimic was crawling across the exam room floor yelling, "He does this. He does this." Actually, you wouldn't describe what he was doing as crawling. He was actually sitting down on the floor, but dragging himself along using his hands for propulsion. Yes, in an effort to show me how his puppy was behaving, he was "butt surfing" like a dog with an itch. It was quite a performance.

Watching it, I couldn't help but think that such theatrics should not go unrewarded.

So, in the tradition of the Oscar, Emmy and Tony awards, it is time for me to present the nominees for this year's Hokey Awards.

Please join me now for the fictitious awards ceremony. Imagine if you will a large theater filled to capacity with a crowd of several thousand excited drama fans.

Along one side of the magnificent stage, there is a table with this year's Hokey Awards on display. By the end of the ceremony, each Hokey winner will have earned his or her award by virtue of an outstanding dramatic performance in a veterinary hospital.

A Hokey Award itself is not difficult to visualize. Just think of one of those joke items of fake dog poop that you can buy in a novelty store. Change the color from brown to gold, and you have an accurate mental image of the Hokey.

Be quiet now! The ceremony is about to begin. To the sound

Chapter 1: Flights of Fancy

> Other prizes will be awarded for dumbest question of the year and the coveted lifetime of stupidity award.

of thunderous applause, the master of ceremonies walks to center stage. It's me. Dressed in a rented tux, I looked pretty good (either that or the black coat and tails made me look like Mickey Mouse).

It is no wonder the crowd is excited. Many of them remember the controversy that developed last year when Mel O'Drama was presented the Hokey for Most Hysterical Phone Call. His performance titled, "My dog just passed a worm" narrowly beat Wanda Barf's presentation, "I think I saw a tick."

Now, just be patient! Before naming any of the winners, it is up to me to list the categories for this year's Hokeys.

First, there is the Hokey for outstanding performance in pet owner ventriloquism. This will go to the person who does the most ridiculous job of talking in a squeaky voice and pretending to speak for their cat or dog. (They do this because the pet cannot speak for itself. I usually find myself wishing that the owner couldn't speak either.)

Next, we have the award for exam room charades. This is the category in which Mr. Mimic was nominated. The winner will be the person who does the most laughable physical impersonation of his or her pet. (Butt surfing has a good chance of winning, but several clients who do good hairball imitations are in the running as well.)

The Hokey that I most look forward to each year is the vocalization award. This is presented to the person who, by howling, growling, barking or meowing, does the most irritating job of pet noise imitation.

Other prizes will be awarded for dumbest question of the year, worst client suggestion, and the coveted lifetime of stupidity award. (The lifetime award can only be presented to someone who has won four previous Hokeys.)

An impartial panel of experts selects nominees. (That's me.) Voting is done by me also. So, when I say, "May I have that envelope please?" I already have a pretty good idea of who the winner will be.

You won't see a list of winners until next month. However, just to give you a hint, I have a pretty good idea that I am in the running for best host of an imaginary awards show.

June 2005

Talent abounds at 2005 Hokey ceremony
Walking the red carpet: Mel O'Drama, Alexander Graham Bellow rally for top honors

Mr. and Mrs. Bicker were just about screaming at each other. Apparently, I had started the argument by asking a simple question: "How old is your dog?"

He was absolutely certain that they had gotten their dog while they still had the 1978 Jeep and Aunt Betty was still alive. She called him an idiot and pointed out that she distinctly recalled that the puppy threw up on a Bob Dole for president brochure. Amazingly enough, none of these important facts did me any good.

I asked if the pooch had been eating. He said, "Sure, I just saw him eat breakfast this morning." She said, "My husband is a moron. This dog hasn't touched a bite in two days."

You guessed it! It was a case of dueling histories. They couldn't agree on anything. Even the dog's name was left in dispute.

"We call him Little Guy."

"His name is actually Prince Little."

"Nobody calls him that."

"Well, I do."

I had to stop them, or I'd still be standing there listening to them quibble. I'm not sure actually why they even came to see me in the first place. (They couldn't agree on that either.) However, when they left, they seemed satisfied with our services, even though I'm not sure what it is that I treated.

That visit earned them a nomination for this year's Hokey Award in the Dueling Histories category. You see, following in the tradition of the Oscars and Emmys, the annual Hokey Awards are presented for best dramatic performances in a veterinary hospital.

Last month, we were in the middle of the fictitious ceremony for the presentation of this year's Hokey awards when space ran out. (You may want to check your

bird cage for last month's column.)

The imaginary ceremony is hosted by a handsome and skilled master of ceremonies. (That's me.) The impartial panel of judges (me) has evaluated the choices of the nominating committee (me again) and chosen the winners.

During the ceremony, I am assisted by a gorgeous blonde model who brings me the envelopes containing the names of the winners. For the sake of family harmony and self preservation, let me note that the gorgeous model looks exactly like my wife.

At this point, several awards already have been presented. For a realistic imitation of his puppy, Scooter, butt surfing, Mr. Mimic won the Hokey for Exam Room Charades.

This year's Telephone Relay Award went to Alexander Graham Bellow for his performance entitled, "I don't know. I'll have to ask my wife." Six times during just one phone call, Mr. Bellow had to yell to his wife in the next room to find what it was he was calling me about.

The 2005 Hokey for most irritating performance in the Ventriloquism category is up next. This award goes to a person who, speaking in a squeaky voice, pretends to be their pet talking. There are two nominees. Mr. Pinenoggin's performance entitled: "Put me down. I don't like needles," was very good. However, it paled in comparison to Mrs. Oaknoodle's rendition of "I don't like that mean old doctor. Mommy, don't let the bad man hurt me."

Mel O'Drama went home with a Hokey again this year. You may recall his win in the Hysterical Phone Call category based on the panic that ensued when his dog vomited up a worm. This year, he took the Vocalization Award for the most annoying job of imitating animal noises. Mel did a great imitation of the way his dog howls and growls whenever he sees the mailman. In addition, based on those noises, he concluded that the pooch is in pain whenever mail is delivered. As a result, he was also up for the Twisted Logic Award.

Well, we are about to run out of space again. So, we will present just one more award. It is the Hokey for best performance at an imaginary awards ceremony. There are two nominees; the master of ceremonies and the beautiful blonde model.

And the winner is ...

... the beautiful blonde model. (Yes, I'm going for family harmony again.)

July 2005

The high cost of veterinary brain power has aliens outraged

Byar checked his speedometer and was thrilled to find that he was making good time.

Having just passed the star that the earth people refer to as Betelgeuse, and maintaining a speed of 8.0 Astro-zippies, it was clear that they would make it to earth in time for lunch.

This knowledge came to him as a great relief. Being the proprietor of the galaxy's largest culinary resort and starship was an awesome responsibility. He knew full well that his passengers would not be pleased if he failed to deliver on the special lunch treat that he had promised them.

Down in the lounge where the good news was received telepathically by one and all, a dozen anxious tummies began to anticipate the upcoming meal. (There were only seven passengers, but several had more than one tummy.)

Amylase was the first to speak.

"Let's do something to kill some time," he said. "There's still a two durble time delay before lunch."

"How about a game of Call the Veterinarian?" asked Galactose. "That's always fun when we're in the proximity of earth."

All but one of the group heartily agreed. Methionine was the hold-out.

"Just a minute," he said. "Call the Veterinarian is only fun if you establish certain rules before the game. First of all, you have to talk directly to the veterinarian and not to any of its ancillary earth beings. Secondly, you should never make sense. The last time we played, Amylase said something logical and the veterinarian became suspicious."

"Don't be ridiculous," was Amylase's response. "If these earth vets had any brains they

> "You have veterinarian brains priced at 86 coinders an ounce."

would realize that many of the stupid phone calls they get must be coming from outer space."

Nonetheless, all present agreed to follow the rules as proposed by Methionine and the game began.

Peptide, who had never played before, went first. He managed to get Dr. Bovine on the phone.

"Doctor, I hope you can help me," he said. "I have an emergency. My dog might be sick."

The group could hear Dr. Bovine's response over the speaker phone.

"You don't understand, sir. This is a large animal practice."

"That's O.K.," said Peptide. "He's a large dog."

After a good laugh was had by all, Esterase asked to go next. She chose to call an earth time zone that would ensure hitting her victim with a night call.

"Doctor, I hope you can help me," she said. "I've called several veterinarians and none seem to be able to answer a simple question. My cat just isn't himself. He's been very quiet and nostalgic lately. Furthermore, he hasn't eaten one bite of his food for four months. I think he might need an operation. That's what I'm calling to ask. How much do you charge for an operation?"

The veterinarian was unable to come up with a simple answer and the group received a mild chuckle.

"Let me show you losers how the game is played," said Galactose. "I'm putting in a night call to that Obenski character. He's usually good for a laugh."

The call went through.

"Hello, Doctor, this is Otto Space calling," he said. "I used to bring a dog to you in 1993. Could you drive over to your office and check the record? That dog got sick once and I'd like to find out what he had. My neighbor has a dog that got sick tonight and I thought it might be the same thing. Check under the name Fifi. It was a Poodle that belonged to my old girlfriend. I don't remember what her last name was."

All seven players had a good laugh at this one and were still chortling at the gullibility of those earth veterinarians when the waiter arrived to take the lunch order.

The special repast of the day was to be fresh brains of earthlings. The good news got all 12 stomachs growling. The waiter explained that each diner would be able to select his entrée from the menu, after which the shuttle craft would descend to the planet's surface to abduct the appropriate earthlings and harvest their brains.

Unfortunately, one glance at the menu

brought a complaint from Methionine. He demanded to speak to Byar at once.

"What's the trouble, sir?" Byar asked upon coming down from the flight deck.

"It's these prices," said Methionine. "The brains of politicians, businessmen and housewives are all reasonably priced at three to five coinders per ounce. But this last one here is ridiculous. You have veterinarian brains priced at 86 coinders an ounce. That's outrageous!"

"My dear sir," said Byar. "Do you have any idea how many veterinarians we have to abduct to get an ounce of brains?"

July 2001

Chapter 1: Flights of Fancy

Time flies in Wonderland

I discovered something very interesting about myself this week.

The realization came after a few typical veterinary office telephone calls.

The first was from Mrs. Frets. She had an important question.

"Doctor," she said. "When I got up this morning I found that my puppy had chewed the cord on the telephone. Well, at first, I yelled at him. But then I realized that he was probably trying to tell me something. So I waited. And, sure enough, he bit the cord again as if to say, 'Call the vet.' Apparently, he requires medical attention. What do you think is wrong with him?"

I explained that he probably just wanted to warn her of the potential danger that electrical cords can represent and that it would be wise to remove them from his reach. She marveled at the intelligence of her puppy.

The next call was from Mr. Colon. His cat had been constipated for more than a week and the treatment that he read about in his cat book had, so far, failed to produce results. He wanted to know if I could suggest a treatment that might be more effective than putting mineral oil in his ears every day.

I seem to be mired in the silly and often illogical world of veterinary practice. How did this happen? It seems like only yesterday that the world was less complicated. In fact, it was 1964 to be exact. Thinking back, I have a clear recollection of cruising the roads of rural Pennsylvania on my Harley. My buddy, Frankie, and I took off right after high school let out at 3 o'clock. We both road motorcycles which had been "retired" after long police department careers. They were massive machines with the old style stick shift mounted on the left side of the gas tank. Let me tell you, in the winter months that big chrome shift knob was colder than a witch's handshake.

At any rate, it dawned on me after those phone calls, that I am now a middle-aged veterinarian. What happened to the kid on the Harley? More importantly, what happened to the 36 years? I certainly don't remember that much time going by. That kid must have made a wrong

Where did I go wrong?

> *She marveled at the intelligence of her puppy.*

turn and followed Alice right into Wonderland. That would explain the crazy things that are always happening.

Just today, the Tweedledum Veterinary Supply Co. sent me one bottle of eye drops in a box big enough to house a child's tea party. The shipping cost was three times the value of the drops.

Then, Mrs. Heart called about her dog, Queenie. It seems that the pooch was not eating and she wanted to know if it would be all right to try giving the dog some milk. She figured that it would be a good way to provide some nourishment as well as fluid at the same time. I told her that it would be OK. She replied, "That won't work, Doctor. Queenie hates milk and won't go near the stuff even when she's well."

No sooner had she hung up than Mrs. Cheshire called about her cat, Smiley. It seems that he disappeared and she wanted to know if it was his distemper shot that made him run away.

"When we got back from your office, I put Smiley outside and he ran away," she said. "Does the vaccination cause that type of reaction?"

I asked if Smiley had ever shown any tendency to roam before this.

"I don't know, Doctor," was her reply. "I never put him outside before."

Later in the day, I called Mrs. Hatter about her dog, Madonna. She was late in scheduling her appointment for follow-up blood tests. Now that the dog had been under treatment at home for two weeks, I felt that it was important to check the progress of the condition. Mrs. Hatter did not agree.

"Why didn't you people take extra blood samples while my dog was there?" she asked. "You could have kept them in the refrigerator and you'd be able to check the progress now without me having to make another trip over there."

Now, don't get me wrong. I enjoy practicing in Wonderland. But sometimes, I think it might be nice to find the exit and go on a short visit to my old world. In fact, I have a sneaking suspicion that tomorrow may be the day it happens. You see, tomorrow is a special day for me. It's my unbirthday.

December 2000

Chapter 1: Flights of Fancy

DVMs purge tubular menace

Recently, during a routine office call, I happened to mention to Mr. and Mrs. Panic that their cat might have worms.

The news hit them like a ton of bricks. They were horrified. Mr. Panic became unglued and had to sit down for a few minutes while the initial shock of my statement sank in. His wife was terrified. The look on her face reminded me of one I had seen before. I was in a horror movie when a lady was confronted by a character wearing a hockey mask and carrying a chain saw. Apparently, the lady in the movie was almost as scared of being hacked to death as Mrs. Panic was of facing the worm diagnosis.

Their reaction came as no surprise to me, of course. We veterinarians are used to witnessing the occasional petrified over-reaction on the part of our clients. I have often wondered why Hollywood tries to scare people with chain saws, monsters and airplane crashes, when they could do a more effective job with things like worms. You may recall that I have proposed such horror movies on these pages before. My favorites were: *The Flea* (May 1983) and *Hairball* (October 1984).

Well, it's time to try again. Our newest attempt to see movie patrons paralyzed with fear will simply be called *Worms*. Or, for those of you who prefer something a little more catchy, *Helminths from Hell*.

In our opening scene, we are treated to a picturesque view of some sewer workers sitting around a manhole enjoying their lunch. All is peaceful until one of them happens to look down and sees a worm float by. He trembles with fear. By the time he has calmed down enough to tell his friends what he saw, the creature has drifted away.

Soon, we are treated to other scenes of sporadic sightings from different locations throughout our country. Rumors begin to spread and, before long, America finds itself gripped in the icy fingers of vermifobia.

Now it's time to shock the

audience, so we hit them with a surprise close-up in which one of our tubular devils fills the entire silver screen. Though actually only three inches in length, the worms in our sewer systems cause people to be

> *The tubular menace is purged from our country.*

so "grossed out" that America founders into a state of helpless ineptitude.

Politicians scramble for a solution. Local governments consult chiropractors to see if their pipes need realignment. In a nationally televised news conference, the president asks each citizen to call his or her grandparents to ask if they know a good home remedy for worms. Some, such as a dose of gunpowder or garlic, are tried, but to no avail.

Meanwhile, the supermarket tabloids are reporting that the worms are actually from outer space and cannot be destroyed. Furthermore, several people claim to have communicated with them and are sure that they are a superior life form. This does not ease the panic.

The Department of Health, Education and Welfare, urges all 10 year olds to scan their encyclopedias for a solution. The Surgeon General surfs the Web looking for an answer. At the same time, the Secretary of the Interior writes letters to several newspaper advice columnists seeking a way out of the crisis.

Finally, after all else fails, Congress passes a special appropriations bill which allocates the expenditure of $30 to consult a veterinarian. Using a regulation Olympic diving tank to run a giant stool sample on our nation's sewage systems, our hero diagnoses the problem and prescribes the appropriate medication.

Every veterinarian in America dispenses pills to the people in his area and, at a prescribed time, everyone in the country simultaneously flushes the medication. The tubular menace is purged from our country. The people rejoice. The economy becomes stable once again. Best of all, the veterinarians are not only seen as heroes, but also manage to make a tidy profit on the deal. I love a happy ending.

January 2000

If only dogs could talk; the things they would say about clients

I have thought of my friend, Arnie, as the greatest creative genius ever to practice veterinary medicine. However, last Thursday, it was my turn to have a brilliant idea.

The morning had promised to be one of the busiest in recent memory. We were over-booked and, with two staff members away on vacation, we would have to put in a record-breaking performance with a skeleton crew. Still, I knew we could do it as long as none of my morning office calls turned out to be people like Mrs. Factless, the lady who can talk more while saying less than any person on this planet.

You guessed it. At 8 a.m. I saw Mrs. Factless and her dog, Stranger, waiting for me in exam room #1.

"Doctor, I hope you can help us. Stranger hasn't been himself for a few days now. When he doesn't act right like this, I just know that he's trying to tell me something. I wish he could talk. Don't you wish he could talk? Then, he could tell us what is wrong."

Mrs. Factless was exhibiting the Lassie Syndrome. This is often seen in people who watched too many episodes of the old *Lassie* television show in the 1960s. They are convinced that any dog behavior from striking an unusual pose to passing gas has some message behind it. The messages could be that a storm is coming, there is a baby duck caught in the rain gutter or Timmy is trapped in an old mine shaft.

In this particular case, she was convinced that Stranger had a diagnosis, prognosis and proposed treatment regimen to report to us, but, was hampered by his lack of speech. Hence, her constant lament, "If only he could talk. I know he's trying to tell me something."

Personally, I knew what the dog was trying to say. In fact, he and I were on the same wavelength. Though we were each restricted from doing so for different reasons, we both wanted to say the same thing, "Shut up, lady!"

When I got a chance to squeeze in a question, I asked if Stranger had been drinking more water lately. This set her off on a long tirade concerning other animals, types of dishes, her neighbor's opinion and several other matters that bore no resemblance to an answer.

I began to daydream and leave reality behind.

I could see what would happen if anyone had to get useful information out of Mrs. Factless.

I imagined her on a plain wooden chair in a darkened room. Several detectives were shining a bright light in her face. Dick Tracy was there, but after two minutes of an attempted interrogation, he was so frustrated that he left the room without his overcoat.

Sherlock Holmes tried next. Unfortunately, Mrs. Factless gave him such a headache that he went to see if Dr. Watson could give him something for it.

Sergeant Friday was next in line. He tried his famous line, "Just the facts, Ma'am." He was subsequently barraged with so many facts that his brain was numbed. After that session, he started to let his hair grow long.

My mind returned to reality just in time to ask another question.

"Bleeding? Why no, doctor. There hasn't been any bleeding that I am aware of. Although, there was some vomiting. Other than that he seems OK, except for the blood I saw this morning."

There you have it. The old give and take routine. Conflicting statements right in the same paragraph no less. Then, as she continued to spew forth a continuous stream of non-information, it hit me, my brilliant idea.

This lady would make a great spy. In the event of capture by the enemy, she would not be able to divulge any useful information. She would certainly be a natural talent if ever called upon to play dumb.

It seemed my patriotic duty to leave reality once again, and head over to the imaginary CIA headquarters where I would share this flash of brilliance with the guardians of our national security.

Much to my surprise, the government was already working on the project.

I was introduced to agent Dewclaw who was in charge of Project DataScooper. He informed me that numerous experiments were being conducted using babbling dog owners for spy work.

"Our initial experiments with these people were very successful," he said. "When they fall into the wrong hands, the bad guys are literally unable to get any useful information out of them. Unfortunately, the government has decided to drop the project."

"Why would we do that?" I asked.

Agent Dewclaw proceeded to point out the flaw that made my brilliant idea completely worthless.

"Because the good guys can't get any useful information out of them either."

That certainly brought me back to reality for the rest of the day.

January 1999

Cumulus rains on Brutus' parade

How far will I go to get a free meal? Well, speaking for myself, there is no limit. In fact, I recently traveled some 20 centuries into the past just to attend a veterinary association meeting. Yes, you guessed it, I've been time traveling again. This time, it was to observe a get-together of the ancient Roman Veterinary Medical Association.

Upon my arrival, my host, Magnanimus, informed me that I'd have to wear a toga so as not to stick out like a sore thumb. He then proceeded to instruct me in the proper way to put one on so that nothing else stuck out, either.

The meeting place was a beautiful outdoor amphitheater. Along the southwestern wall, where they would have the advantage of the afternoon shade and cooling breeze, the association officers were preparing for the meeting. The president, Peristalsis, had a reputation for being able to keep a meeting moving right along. His vice president, Cumulus, was a real drip. Seated at the opposite end of the forum and somewhat downwind (by popular demand), was Odiferous. The rest of the members were scattered about waiting for the discussion to begin.

I was seated next to a gabby fellow named Gregarious who informed me that the purpose of the meeting was to discuss the association's position regarding low-cost vaccination clinics.

As Peristalsis got the meeting under way, Cantankerous was the first to speak.

"I'm tired of the way we coddle the public," he said. "They want emergency service at night, low cost vaccinations, spay and neuter clinics! I say enough is enough! If they can't afford to take care of a pet, they shouldn't have it."

Magnanimus was quick to disagree. He spoke elegantly.

"Friends, as I drove to the meeting today, I couldn't help but notice that the view from my chariot reminded me of our colleague, Cantankerous. You know, the southern end of a north-bound horse. We, as veterinarians, have pledged to alleviate animal suffering. Sometimes, that means giving more of ourselves."

"Perhaps I can shed some light on this matter," said Lumonous, who was well-known for his reflections on matters of great importance. "The general populous contains many people who would not seek veterinary care if it were not for these charity functions. Therefore, we must support them. Only the poor people attend these clinics. Since citizens who can afford proper veterinary care would never go to such things, our businesses will not suffer in the least."

"Get real, you Bozo!" shouted Brutus, who was quick to disagree. "Have you ever worked one of those shot clinics? You should see some of the fancy chariots that pull up outside. Why, the last time we held a low-cost clinic, Caesar himself brought his dogs, Romulus and Remus, for shots."

Everyone was shocked to hear such a thing.

"That Caesar has a lot of Gaul," said Gregarious. "Showing up at a shot clinic that was planned for the poor is one thing, but naming your dogs after our great founders, Romulus and Remus, is even more tactless. How would he like it if anyone was ever to name a dog Caesar?"

His statement managed to break down the tension which had been mounting since the beginning of the discussion. Everyone chortled at the ridiculous thought that anyone would ever name a dog Caesar.

This led to a whole new discussion. Some of the members felt that Caesar should be asked to change the names of his dogs.

"He is insulting our heritage and should be reprimanded for it," said Bacillus, who was not one to spare the rod.

Brutus disagreed.

"We should never, under any circumstances, encourage a client to change the name of a pet. They do it too much already. A name should be forever!" he emphasized.

Then, something unusual happened. Cumulus asked to address the group.

"Friends," he said, "I feel that Brutus cannot be trusted in this matter and when you hear the shocking news that I have to reveal about him, you will no doubt agree with me."

The group waited anxiously for his next words and so must you until next month's column, when I plan to reveal how Cumulus rained on Brutus' parade ...

November 1998

Why your filing system suffers to this day

You may recall that, by turning this page last month, you left me stranded at a meeting of the Ancient Roman Veterinary Association.

Using my ability to time travel, I had taken a little jaunt back some 20 centuries or so just to get a free meal by attending a routine get-together of that average, small town veterinary group.

As fate would have it, I wound up witnessing one of the greatest debates in history, the outcome of which would have an impact on our profession even up to the present day.

It all started when Brutus mentioned to the group that Caesar had named his dogs Romulus and Remus. Since this seemed to be somewhat disrespectful of the legendary founders of Rome, several members of the association felt that Caesar should be asked to change the dogs' names. Others felt that people change the names of their pets too often and should be barred from ever doing so. This simple disagreement led to the great debate.

Lumonous, who was known to be very bright, was the first to speak.

"If we encourage people to change the names of pets, we will louse up the filing systems of veterinary hospitals for generations to come. I would propose that we require each animal to have one name, and only one name, which would never be changed throughout its lifetime."

"I certainly can't agree with that," said Cumulus. "Our citizens have certain rights, and one of them has always been the right to change their dog's name every time they get a new boyfriend or become enamored with a new fictional character."

"You're all wet, as usual, Cumulus," Brutus said. "A name should be a permanent thing, never to be changed!"

As the debate raged on, the association became split right down the middle. Half the members sided with Brutus, the other half with Cumulus. Each person present had the chance to speak whether he had anything important to say or not.

Flatus, a real windbag, spoke for 20 minutes. When he was finished, no one was sure which side he was on.

Celsius had no opinion, but he felt compelled to express a desire to hold the meetings later in the day when it was cooler.

Ravenous wanted to know if we could break for lunch. He thought we might be able to send Marco Polo out for pizza. Being the only experienced time traveler in the group, it was up to me to point out that Mr. Polo would not be born for another 12 centuries.

Finally, the association president, Peristalsis, decided it was time to get things moving along. He called upon Cumulus to sum up the arguments for his side.

For a man who seemed to be in a fog most of the time, Cumulus spoke eloquently.

"Friends, our colleague, Brutus, says that a name should never be changed. Can we trust his opinion? Is he not the same Brutus who was a well-known public figure long before becoming a veterinarian?

You see, Cumulus was reminding the group that Brutus had, at one time, been quite well known throughout the Empire due to his long-standing rivalry with a legendary Roman sailor. Although he was a man of immense physical stature and strength, Brutus never seemed to be able to get the better of his scrawny looking, seafaring rival. It was said that the smaller man possessed unparalleled strength, most of which was concentrated in his massive forearms, each bearing a tattoo in the likeness of an anchor. Furthermore, legend had it that when faced with great danger, the sailor could increase his strength at will, even to the point of defying the laws of physics, simply by chewing on some spinach that he always carried with him. Yes, Brutus' rival was none other than Exophthalmos the Sailor.

Cumulus continued, "How can Brutus tell us never to change a name when many of us know that he has done it himself? Many of you here today are old enough to remember that, in the early days of his rivalry with the great Exophthalmos, his name was not Brutus, but Bluto."

That did it. The outcome of the debate favored Cumulus and his opinion that name changes should be allowed. Consequently your filing system and mine suffer to this very day.

December 1998

Rustle up some techs and head on down to the rodeo

Howdy, pardner! Before you mosey on down to the exam room for your next boring office call, I want you to set a spell and think on somethin' important.

I reckon' you may have noticed that veterinary practice can get a mite dull at times. Well, if you've got a hankerin' for some adventure, I've got good news. It's time to start training your staff for this year's technician rodeo.

That's right, those poor souls who make a living by assisting veterinarians will soon have the opportunity to show off their skills. For some it will mean the thrill of victory, for others, the agony of defeat.

Of the four events chosen this year, dog wrestling is the first.

Each contestant must restrain a 98-pound hyperactive dog for a toenail trim. In order to make the event a true challenge, the dog's owners will be allowed to help. Only those contestants who accomplish the task successfully will be allowed to move on to the second heat. They will have the opportunity to immobilize a Boston Terrier, Pekingese or other noseless breed of dog while a new, graduate veterinarian attempts to draw blood. The final score in dog wrestling will be based on performance in both the nose and noseless categories.

Second on the agenda of events will be cat catching.

Each competitor is presented with a vicious cat in a homemade carrier.

He or she must lift the 40 pound box to the exam table, figure out how to open the darn thing, and then get the cat out. At this point, anyone receiving a tracheotomy from the cat will be excused from further competition. Those remaining must restrain the cat for an intramuscular injection, and put him back in the box.

Judges will watch carefully as the cat's owners then announce that he must come back out because they want his nails clipped. Anyone aiming an obscene gesture in their direction will lose points.

A lunch break will be scheduled to take place immediately following these first two events. However, contestants will be told, "We are too busy to stop for lunch today," and the competition will continue.

Those whose bleeding has stopped will be paired up for team penning, the only event in the competition where two technicians get to work together. In preparation for this event, four children between the ages of 8 and 10 are each given a bowl of chocolate frosted cereal and a large cup of coffee. They are then let loose in a veterinary hospital. The technician team is given the simple job of finding them and getting them all into one room while simultaneously minimizing damage to the hospital and its equipment. Ropes and rabies poles are not allowed.

The rodeo concludes with the fourth and final challenge, the surgical prep competition. Both skill and speed are called for here as the event is strictly a race between the contestant and the clock. An anesthetized patient will have to be shaved and prepped for a routine spay. The clipper provided has three teeth missing. Judging is based on speed and thoroughness. However, points are lost for each nipple that is accidentally removed.

So, get your staff together and assess your talents. We're looking forward to some friendly inter-hospital competition. And, if the proposed events don't suit you, don't worry. Several other events are already being considered for inclusion in future rodeos. For example, there is the dreaded obstacle course. The object will be to carry a 70-pound anesthetized dog back to his kennel. The obstacles encountered along the way will not be that difficult. However, when arriving at the ward, there will be six people visiting the dog in the neighboring kennel. Points are lost if the dog soils the contestant or the floors during the walk. Soiling of ward visitors, although not necessarily desirable, does tend to amuse the judges.

Another possible future competition would be veterinarian handwriting analysis, an event that may attract some of our less athletic technicians. Contestants would have to decipher a note which was written on a paper towel and then left in the treatment room by a veterinarian who has since left for the day. According to several members of my staff who claim to speak from experience, this event would be almost impossible. Personally, I think they tend to exaggerate. Just last week, they brought one of my notes back to me claiming that no one could understand it. Not only was I able to tell them exactly what it meant but, I was able to figure it out in less than an hour!

November 1997

Chapter 1: Flights of Fancy

Dream day is just that— a dream

Never in the history of our profession has there been a day like last Thursday.

It all started with a visit from the Harmony family. I entered the exam room just in time to see absolutely nothing happening. The kids were not swinging on the end of the exam table or looking in the drawers, and no one was playing with the scale.

Little did I know that even stranger events were about to follow. When the dog looked at me and growled, nobody laughed. Instead, Mr. Harmony got up out of the chair, gave the dog's leash a strong corrective yank, and said, "I'll hold him for you, Doc. We don't put up with behavior like that at our house."

Naturally, I was shocked. The perfect office call seemed to be unfolding before my eyes. Mrs. Harmony put in her two cents worth.

"Doctor, someone told us that when a dog behaves that way, it means that he was abused when he was young. Did you ever hear such nonsense? I personally think he's just plain nasty."

I found myself wishing for a tape recorder. Surely, no one would believe this had happened unless I could offer proof.

Things became even more bizarre when I asked if the dog had been eating. I got only one answer from all four people in the room. This trend continued with each question that I asked. Where were the dueling histories that families usually give? Where were the disagreements over even the most trivial items such as: How old is he and what is his name?

Even more extraordinary, they had no trouble finding the lump that they brought the dog in for and, after identifying it, they got out of my way.

"Your fingers are much more experienced than ours, Doctor," Mr. Harmony said. "I'll just hold his head and keep him still for you."

I was trembling with excitement. By the time the office call ended, I was ready to take a break and reflect on the amazing events that I had just witnessed. Luckily, there would now be a hole in the schedule. This was because my next appointment was with Alice Tardy. In 20 years as my client, she has never been on time. Little did I know, as I walked toward the waiting room, that I was about to receive another shock. Oh, my gosh! Could it be? There was Alice showing up five minutes early for her appointment!

Now I had seen everything. Or, at least I thought I had. The biggest shock of the day was yet to come. The mailman brought it. The return address read: Mrs.

Where did I go wrong?

> *Little did I know that even stranger events were about to follow.*

Thumpmortis. I recognized the name as belonging to my clinic's biggest deadbeat. She had sent in a check. Of course, she had said that the check was "in the mail." But, to my amazement, the check actually *was* in the mail!

You could have knocked me over with a feather. The events of the day were not to be believed. Perhaps something had happened to alter the natural order of the universe as we know it. Or, maybe I was somehow transported through a time warp to another planet in a parallel universe, a planet where things are the opposite of the earth where I usually practice our profession.

Just for fun, I picked up my otoscope and spoke into the lens.

"Beam me up, Scotty." Nothing happened.

Mr. Cadabra came in right after lunchtime because his dog, Abra, was due for routine vaccines. When I asked him to put Abra on the table, he began asking the dog to jump up.

He smacked the table top.

"Up boy! Jump up, Abra!"

The dog actually did it! Now I was wishing for a tape recorder and a camera as well. How many things can go right in one day? What could explain this wierd series of events?

Thursdays are usually strange, but not this strange. Moments later, I had my explanation. It came to me as the alarm clock went off and I woke up. It was only Thursday morning. The perfect day had not yet occurred. Somehow, I doubted that it would.

October 1997

OSHA inspector takes top prize in daytime comedy awards

And now, the moment you have all been waiting for: presentation of the award for the Best Performance By An Actor in a Daytime Comedy Series. Before announcing the nominees, however, I must help you set the scene.

First of all, imagine yourself in formal attire seated in a huge auditorium full of similar would-be dignitaries. Before you lies an elaborately decorated stage, the center of which is occupied by a tasteful glass podium. We are ready to begin.

A distinguished-looking gentleman steps up to the microphone. It is me. (Played by Leslie Nielsen). He speaks.

"For Best Performance in an Ongoing Daytime Comedy, the nominees are: The Client, The OSHA Inspector and the Veterinarian.

Now, if you'll direct your eyes to the giant—but imaginary—television screen above the stage, you will be treated to an excerpt from each nominated performance.

The screen lights up with two words: The Client.

Soon, we see a video of Josh Quipster (played by Dan Rather), talking to the receptionist as he leaves the veterinarian's office.

"You say that will be $52?" he asks. Then turning to his dog: "OK, Fluffy, you heard the lady. Pay the bill."

There is a pause while he laughs at his own joke before continuing.

"Say, can I put this on my medical insurance?" he asks. Finally, he delivers the zinger we all expect to hear, "Can I deduct this on my income tax?"

If a horse was as lame as this guy's attempts at humor, it would have to be put down.

The screen moves on to the next candidate, The OSHA Inspector. Our subject, Dick Tater (played by Jack Nicholson), is explaining some rules to a veterinarian.

"It's very important to never recap your needles, except, of course, sometimes when you don't have to or shouldn't. As a veterinarian, you must realize that this depends on what we at OSHA refer to as "the whim factor." That means, that it all depends on which one of us you talk to.

You also need a library of Material Safety Data Sheets on all chemicals used in your practice, even though the same things can be bought by anyone right down the street at K-mart. And don't forget who you are dealing with. Remember, it was

FINES-R-US, as we like to be called, that had sawdust declared a dangerous chemical."

This man is funny without even trying. Nobody is laughing.

The screen moves on to our hero, The Veterinarian. It's Dr. Slapstick (played by Jerry Seinfeld). A man and woman (both played by Dennis Rodman) enter his office along with their two children (played by Beavis and Butthead).

The laughs begin immediately. When their cat refuses to come out of the carrier, all four go into hysterics. As the cat growls and tries to bite the doctor, the family is doubled up with laughter. Beavis practically swallows his tongue. Fearing that the family might pass out from laughing so hard, our hero holds off on his best trick. Then, after sensing that they have taken in enough oxygen to survive another laughing binge, he reaches for a rectal thermometer. The kid's eyes go wide. The room is filled with anticipation. Insertion of the thermometer brings the entire family to its knees.

> *...the family is doubled up with laughter. Beavis practically swallows his tongue.*

Not wishing to be responsible for causing permanent brain damage to these clients, our hero takes the cat to another room. He wonders, though, if any new brain damage would be noticeable.

We return to our main stage. It's me (Leslie Nielsen) again.

"May I have the envelope, please?"

I look at the name of the winner, and make my announcement.

"Ladies and gentlemen, this year's award goes to... The OSHA Inspector!"

(Actually, he wasn't the real winner—he doesn't deserve to win and his name was not the one in the envelope. But I'm not going to be the one to tell him.)

July 1996

'Wrong Way' Obenski's brain declined for advancement of science

Did you know that, in 1927, Harry M. Warner, the president of Warner Brothers Pictures, declared that talking movies would never catch on. In fact, he has been quoted as asking, somewhat bluntly, "Who the hell wants to hear actors talk?"

I found out about this when I visited with him last week at his current residence—the fictitious Institute for Post-Mortem Brain Preservation. I was touring the institute by special invitation.

It all started back in April when the director of the facility, Dr. Figment, stopped by my office and let me in on one of the world's best-kept secrets. It seems that, during the mid-1800s, his great-great-grandfather, Eureka Figment, discovered a way to extract the brain during an autopsy and keep it alive in a nutrient solution. His next breakthrough was even more astounding. He was able to hook up some electrodes to the neural tissue and harvest fresh ideas from the still productive cerebrum.

Naturally, I was honored to be chosen as one of the few individual to know about the institute and jumped at the chance to take a tour. That's how I met Harry M. "Screw-up" Warner.

The rest of the inmate population was just as impressive. Each resided in a bubbling glass cauldron sitting atop a stainless-steel pedestal.

Just down the hall from Mr. Warner, I met the former CEO of the IBM Corporation, Thomas J. "Blooper" Watson. While still alive back in 1943, he stated, "I think there is a world market for about five computers." Interestingly enough, he made that statement the same day he took his dog, Bytes, to the veterinarian. When the pooch attempted to perforate the doctor, Mr. Watson made veterinary history. He is credited as being the very first veterinary client to theorize, "I think someone abused him when he was young and that's why he gets so nasty." Believe it or not, history was made again on that same visit to the animal hospital. It was another first when, upon observing the panting pooch pulling at the leash, Mr. Watson deduced that the dog was thirsty, and asked the receptionist for a bowl of water.

I explained to Dr. Figment that the most earth-shattering event that will ever occur in a veterinary office would be if some dog would actually drink the water!

He explained to me that the Watson brain had been a disappointment. The only idea actually harvested from it since admission to the institute was several decades back when it came up with the idea for the Nehru jacket.

As we walked from jar to jar, Dr. Figment explained to me that the preservation process is very sensitive.

"The brain must be harvested rapidly," he explained. "The entire process must be completed before any decomposition has had a chance to take place."

The next brain I met turned out to be a fountain of post-mortem ideas. It was the famous newspaper editor, Horace "Oops" Greeley. On August 14, 1864, he flatly observed, "Mr. Lincoln is already beaten. He cannot be re-elected."

Dr. Figment thought that I'd be particularly interested in this specimen because he produces ideas almost every day, including many related to my profession. "The Greeley brain has been with us the longest and is a fountain of fresh thought," he explained. "It gave us the ideas for such things as supermarket vaccination clinics, the Edsel, pet superstores, swine flu vaccine, OSHA, and of course, the Clinton National Health Care Plan, to name a few."

I detected a pattern, but before I could say anything, I was distracted by the contents of the next cauldron. It was empty. However, it explained the reason for my invitation to tour the institute. Across the pedestal there was a banner that read, "Future Home of Dr. Michael 'Wrong Way' Obenski."

The bad news came a few days later in the form of a letter from Dr. Figment.

It said, "We are sorry to inform you that, upon further review, your brain will not be acceptable for our purposes. When you go, your brain will just have to decompose like most other people's. In fact, after meeting with you and reading your magazine column, we feel that the decomposition process must be pretty far along already."

Come to think of it, upon further review, I'll be in better company.

June 1996

Prune Juice left in dust as DVM hero rides into the sunset on white bronco

Get your imaginary television screens ready, because I'm going to tell you about the proposed adventures of Matt Dillon, DVM.

In our opening scene, Dr. Dillon, small town marshal and practicing veterinarian, is sitting in the waiting room of his combination jailhouse and animal hospital, waiting for either an office call or a crime to occur. Faithful sidekick, deputy and veterinary technician Chester Good bursts into the room.

"Marshal Dillon, Marshal Dillon, there's been a murder over at the Juice ranch. Two people were found dead."

Our hero runs out the front door and jumps on his horse. It's one of those Hollywood horses—you never have to feed it or saddle it. It just stands at the front door all tacked up and ready to go.

Upon viewing the murder scene, Marshal Dillon immediately suspects that Prune Juice, former rodeo champ, is a primary suspect. He heads over to the bunk house to confront the man. Unfortunately, "P.J."—as his fans call him—doesn't want to talk. Instead, he announces his intention to ride around town for awhile on his white bronco.

P.J. is huge and athletic compared to our hero, who would be no match for him in a fight. As if that weren't enough, P.J. brandishes a gun. The sight of the weapon is enough provocation for the marshall. A six-shooter leaps to his right hand. BLAM!… Mr. Juice is history.

Chester is upset by the action. "You can't do that, Marshal. We have to get 26 episodes out of this murder. Now there won't be books written from prison, court-room circus antics, or even endless talk shows on the subject."

"Tough luck, Chester," Dillon replies. "I go by the old adage: 'God created all men, but Sam Colt made all men equal.' Mr. Juice just got equalized. That's all."

Just then, 12 angry men rode up. They were all sizes, colors and ethnic backgrounds. They were the would-be team of defense lawyers, and needless to say, they were miffed at our hero. BLAM! X 12… Problem solved.

"That's just the tip of the iceberg, Marshall," Chester said. "Look over

> *Call me a hopeless romantic, but I love a happy ending.*

yonder. There's an army coming. Looks like reporters, and there must be a thousand of them. BLAM! X 103... another obstacle overcome.

Dillon looks pensively at his revolver. "Don't you just love these Hollywood guns, Chester? You never have to reload until there's a pause in action."

The entire Juice case is solved by the time our show gets to the first commercial. It is one of those clever ads that make it hard to tell where the show stops and the commercial begins. The scene is back at the animal hospital. The fellas are discussing dinner plans when a strange noise is heard coming from the next room. Suddenly, the door bursts open and a rabbit with a base drum walks across the screen.

An announcer is heard to say: "The Energizer, it keeps on going and going and..."—BLAM!... America stands and cheers while Chester runs for a cooking pot and his favorite rabbit skinning knife.

Later in the afternoon, during Dr. Dillon's nap, Chester announces that an OSHA representative has arrived to inspect the hospital.

You guessed it—BLAM!... The nap was only temporarily interrupted. Leaving out the unimportant parts of the plots, here are some examples of future episodes:

- Mrs. Jones threatens legal action over her cat's treatment... BLAM!
- An I.R.S. agent comes to visit the doctor... BLAM!
- A pet superstore decides to open up in town... BLAM!

You get the idea. Call me a hopeless romantic, but I love a happy ending.

April 1995

Chapter 2:
Fables and Friends

'Old Fogysaurus' rears ugly head

At first, the task seemed simple. All I had to do was to give the pooch an injection, dispense a few pills and send him home.

I headed for the pharmacy. Unfortunately, that's when the trouble started.

"Let's see now," I said to myself as I read the label directions out loud. "Give 2.27 to 6.83 grains per kilogram of body weight."

I had to stop and think. Multiple questions began to swim in my head.

"How many grams are in a grain? How do you convert pounds to kilograms? Is that Fahrenheit or centigrade? Why can't I put metal in the microwave oven? Why don't they write the bottle label in English?

It seems to me that this all should have been taken care of in 1776. This is the America of pounds and inches. The medication in the bottle is made by a company located right here in the good old U.S.A. They sold the drug to me. Why don't they just tell me how much to give the dog? Is it a secret?

According to my calculations, the dog needed an intra-muscular injection of 4,200 cc. That seemed a little high to me. (The medication comes in a 10 cc bottle.) Perhaps the label was wrong? I did the calculations again. I started by attempting to convert the dog's weight to kilograms. I discovered that it couldn't be done.

Not being one to give up easily, I decided to skip that step and move on to the next. All I had to do was to convert "grains per 10 ml" to milligrams per cc." As coincidence would have it, I discovered that this calculation was also impossible.

Then, in a flash, I had a revelation. It struck me out of the blue. How could I have been so foolish? All I had to do to solve the problem was to switch medications. It wouldn't matter what antibiotic I chose, just as long as the directions were printed in milliliters per pound. Within minutes, the dog was happily wagging his tail and drooling all over the car seats as his family drove him home.

Feeling that I deserved a reward for my ingenuity in solving the medication problem, I decided to have a jelly donut. While doing so, I called my friend, Arnie, to discuss my displeasure with the drug company's label. He was not sympathetic.

"For God's sake, Mike," he said. "Get with the program. That's the way things are written nowadays. If you weren't so cheap, you'd buy a good calculator for your pharmacy area and you wouldn't have these problems."

I told him that a calculator wouldn't help. Wasn't he listening when I explained that the calculations were impossible?

"Mike," he said. "You are a dinosaur; an Old-Fogysaurus. You should consider getting some younger veterinarians with more modern ideas to join your practice before your last remaining neuron gives out. "I suppose that's not a bad idea," I told him. "Perhaps I should try to interview a few younger guys."

"Don't you know anything, Mike?" he asked. "Did you sleep through the last two decades? Do you even realize the '60s are over? When you interview veterinarians, they are mostly girls, not guys, and you can't call them girls because that's politically incorrect. They are women."

The conversation with Arnie ruined my jelly donut experience. However, I had to admit that there was a ring of truth to his assessment of me. Sometimes I may be a little out of touch with the current trends. Still, America should think in terms of pounds and inches, not milithings and kilothings, and I have half a mind to write President Nixon and tell him so.

February 2002

Veterinary terminology: Sometimes the meaning can go awry

Misinterpretation of 'botzofer,' 'foreign bodies' can sully communication

The lettering on the door said Department of Anesthesiology, Hal O'Thane, DVM. Duey Hafta didn't even bother to read it. He had been knocking on every door in the veterinary school trying to find a botzofer. His patience had worn thin by this point. He felt as though he had asked a million people so far, and none of them seemed to know where the botzofer was or, for that matter, what it was.

Dr. O'Thane didn't know for sure, either, but he had a pretty good idea. You see, Mr. Hafta was a veterinary student with a reputation for shirking responsibility. He was famous for whining over every little assignment. So, it stood to reason that someone was playing a joke on him. This wouldn't sit well with the dean of the school. The university had outlawed any form of hazing back in 1978. This botzofer thing bore a striking similarity to a snipe hunt or a quest for a left-handed smoke shifter.

Dr. O'Thane took Duey over to Dean Highcollar's office where he was asked to explain what was going on. The situation, as it turns out, was not very complicated. Dr. Hoofpincer, one of the clinicians in the equine medicine department, had simply told Duey to get the botzofer. Not being willing to admit that he was unfamiliar with the term, Duey set off on his futile quest.

Soon, the three of them headed for the equine clinic, each with a different motivation. Duey was going under

orders. He didn't really want to be present when the situation hit the fan. Dr. O'Thane tagged along simply out of curiosity. Dean Highcollar, on the other hand, was a man on a mission. He would straighten out Dr. Hoofpincer in no uncertain terms. The message would be clear. Childish buffoonery such as this would not be tolerated in his school.

The dean was all set to shoot from the hip when they arrived, but Dr. Hoofpincer beat him to the draw. "Duey, where the heck have you been?" she asked. "This mare has been tied up here in the treatment room for more than an hour. Didn't I tell you to get the botts off her?"

Dr. O'Thane laughed like a hyena.

Duey was confused, and the dean was speechless. A few years after the incident, I met Dr. Hoofpincer in Arizona, and she told me the story. It serves as a good illustration of veterinary terminology gone awry.

Allow me another example. Mrs. Obtuse had taken her dog, Corncob, to see my friend Arnie. The pooch had been vomiting for two days and was getting weak. When told that there was a palpable abdominal foreign body, she balked at the diagnosis. "Don't be ridiculous, doctor," she protested. "There is no way he could have a foreign body; he has never even been out of the country."

These incidents come to mind because of a phone call I got last month from an old friend of mine. It seems that he was treating a poodle for a routine hot spot on its back end when the owners questioned him about the origin of the disease. He began by mentioning that fleas could be at fault. This, of course, set the owners off on a long tirade of "fleanial". They mentioned that it would be impossible for the dog to have fleas because they have a fence around their yard.

Undaunted, our colleague continued to list other causes. Things went smoothly until he mentioned that the problems could be caused by trouble with the anal sacs.

The dog's owners clearly became angered and literally stormed out of the office.

What did he say to cause such a reaction? The situation did not become clear until two days later when a letter arrived from the disgruntled clients. They requested copies of their dog's record so that they could go to another veterinarian. It seems that they could not trust anyone who would suspect that their dog had "anal ..."

(Now, just in case you haven't guessed that second word, it's three letters long and rhymes with "tex", but since this is a professional publication, we should probably just leave it at that.)

September 2005

Real science, real jargon

Some veterinary client syndromes in desperate need of classification

Vera Doubtful did not want to believe that her cat was sick.

"Hydrant just can't be sick, Doctor." She said, "I've had him for 18 years, and he hasn't been sick a day in his life. You must be wrong. Maybe you got his blood tests mixed up with someone else's. Things like that do happen, you know."

A glance at the medical record told me that there had been quite a number of medical problems over the last few years, all of which Mrs. Doubtful chose to ignore.

Like many of my clients, she seems to feel that refusal to acknowledge a problem will cause it to go away.

"I don't care what the laboratory results say," she continued, "his kidneys are fine. Why, he passes more water now than ever before."

Before I could continue my gentle, but firm, rebuttal, the office visit was interrupted by a phone call from my friend, Arnie. "Sorry to bother you in the middle of office hours, Mike," he said. "But, I have an important question for you. Do you think that we are real scientists?"

I responded that I had always considered myself to be a scientific thinker. Arnie, however, was quick to disagree. "We can't be, Mike, because we never change the names of anything. Real scientists are always changing nomenclature. In the 30 plus years that we have been in practice, the names of disease syndromes, viruses, bacteria and even drug companies have changed many times. You and I never change anything. I think it's time for us to shake up the world of veterinary jargon."

Foolishly, I asked for an example. "Funny you should ask, Mike, because I have few in mind. This morning, my receptionist put a guy in the exam room with his dog. Naturally, he didn't stay

> It's time for us to shake up the world.

there. He wandered out into the hall blocking traffic and looking impatient waiting for his turn. That's the typical client behavior that you always called the free-roaming hall stander. From now on, I think it should be called the Julius Caesar syndrome because the guy is Roman the hall. Get it, Mike? Roman the hall?

You see, real scientists name syndromes after famous people. Let me give you another example. When I told that same guy it was time to examine the dog, he started smacking the tabletop and yelling for the dog to jump up by himself. He was what you always called a last minute dog trainer. From now on, we're going to call this Pavlov's syndrome, because he was Russian to train the dog. Get it, Mike? Russian to train the dog?"

"I get the picture, Arnie," I said. "But the idea is ridiculous. Besides, you are turning into a real Hammurabi. That's the king of Babylon. Babble on, that is. Get it, Arnie?"

"No Mike, I'm being a real Hemingway here. Ernest, that is. Let me explain more. I saw a dog last week that was hit by a car. The femur was fractured. We'll call that the Napoleon syndrome because there was a Bonaparte. Naturally, I ordered a couple of Clark Kents. That's what we're going to call X-rays now. Well, the case turned out to be a real Goodyear, because we were all tired by the end of it. By the time surgery was over, the bill was a real Galileo, meaning the sum was astronomical. When the owner saw it, he got the Hindenburg syndrome. He was really burned up. I could go on and on, Mike, but it's getting close to lunch time, and I'm getting a case of the Attilas. You know, Attila the hungry.

Armed with a head full of Arnie's silly ideas, I headed back to the exam room to continue my discussion with Mrs. Doubtful. I explained that Hydrant's kidneys had the JFK syndrome. They were shot. This caused Van Cliburn symptoms. He was the pianist cat you could ever imagine. My explanations fell on deaf ears. Vera Doubtful refused to accept the reality of the situation. She was a staunch Cleopatra, queen of denial.

August 2005

Fake stethescopes are more than a novelty

The best inventions help practitioners better communicate with their clients

In 1929, while working in his laboratory at the University of London, Sir Alexander Fleming discovered a strange green substance growing rapidly on several culture plates. It didn't take him long to realize that he had stumbled upon a discovery that would change history. He had invented the Chia Pet.

Although his future fame and fortune were now sealed, he experimented with other uses for the greenish mold. Unsure as to whether or not he had also invented Rogaine, he tried rubbing some on the balding head of Petulance Brawn, the ladies field hockey coach. This did not go over well, to say the least. Perhaps he should have asked for Mrs. Brawn's permission first.

Later, after he regained consciousness, he was given the Nobel Prize for the discovery of penicillin, the achievement for which he is best known to this day. For some reason, his name never seems to be associated with his other now famous discoveries, including the whoopee cushion and fake dog poop, just to name a couple.

Condemned to repeat it?

Why am I giving you a history lesson? Well, as you might recall, I pointed out in last month's column that Thomas Edison invented the voting machine. (Note: If you spend your time reading this column every month, you really ought to get a life.) Anyway, I just thought it might be time to give credit to some other brilliant inventors.

Take, for example, Mr. Eureka. His dog, Feerbyter, likes to cower under the exam room chair. His head reaches out just far enough to vi-

> In this particular case, I got a complete history after just three repeated attempts to listen to the chest.

ciously bite anyone foolish enough to get close. He employs the strategy of a cornered snapping turtle. Using the chair as his shell, he snaps and retreats.

Pretending like a turtle?

The last time they were in to see me, Feerbyter was right in the middle of his turtle imitation when Mr. Eureka was stricken with a brilliant idea. "You know, Doc," he said. "Feerbyter doesn't want to come out from under that chair. I'll bet he feels safer under there than he does when he's up on the table. (Gee, do you think so?) Why don't you have a chair fastened on top of each exam table? Then dogs and cats could hide under a chair while they're up there." (Now, why didn't I think of that?)

After giving the idea an appropriate amount of thought, I decided to leave the furniture the way it was. Having a chair on the table would change everything. Instead of having the dog lunge at my knees, I could have him lunging at my face.

The very next office call was Mrs. Softalk. Apparently her cat "wasn't himself" that day, and she wanted me to check him out. It took me five minutes just to get that much information from her. She didn't say much, and when she did it was in a soft almost inaudible voice.

I put the stethescope in my ears, and as soon as I did, I could see her lips moving. Hoping to get a morsel of history, I stopped what I was doing and asked her to repeat what she had said. She told me that the critter had vomited once.

Once again, I began to listen, and once again she was talking while I couldn't hear her. You get the idea. Some clients only talk while the stethoscope is in use. When they see you using it, they are stimulated to talk. The rest of the time, you feel like taking their pulse to see if they are still alive. In this particular case, I got a complete history after just three repeated attempts to listen to the chest.

The reason I was able to accomplish this so quickly was that I used an invention that my friend and colleague Arnie had come up with. When Mrs. Softalk started babbling for the third time, I was using a special fake stethoscope that he had developed. It has holes in the tubes. This allows me to pretend to listen to an animal, stimulate the client to begin chattering, and actually hear what he or she is saying at the same time.

Is it any wonder that I consider Arnie the greatest inventor of all time?

November 2004

Dr. Hardway no match for rugrats
Obnoxious, ferret-faced brats No. 1 reason old doc checked into Cold Embers

Last week, sensing that spring was in the air, I realized that it was time for my annual visit to our old friend and colleague, Dr. Leonard D. Hardway. As you may recall, Leonard is a stressed out veterinarian who now resides at The Cold Ember Home for Burned Out Veterinarians, located in Rope's End.

When I arrived at the home, I noticed a rather distinguished-looking older gentleman approaching the reception desk. It was me.

"Checking in?" the young lady behind the desk asked.

"No, not yet anyway," I replied and told her that I was just there to visit Dr. Hardway. She directed me to his room.

Leonard was thrilled to see me.

"You know, Mike," he said, "I look forward to your annual visits. Tell me, have you come to your senses yet and retired from practice?"

As I do every year, I was forced to disappoint him. Veterinary practice was much too frustrating for him, but I still manage to weather its storms.

"What do you want to talk about his year?" I asked him.

"I've been thinking about it," he said. "And I'd like to talk about kids."

I started to tell him how my children were doing, but he stopped me.

"Not those kids," he said. "I don't want to talk about our kids. I want to talk about the obnoxious ferret-faced rugrats that come to the office with practically every sick dog or cat. If I had to make a list of the things that drove me out of veterinary practice, they would be number one."

I knew exactly what behaviors were bothering him, but I asked for an example just so he could vent.

"OK, how about this?" he asked. "You walk into the exam room and one of the little urchins is swinging from the end of the exam table. Another is looking in all the drawers. And, worst of all, the stupid parents are just standing there letting

them do it. Can you beat that?"

"Sure I can," I said. "It's even worse when the parents expect a 60-pound kid to hold an 80-pound dog while they sit back and watch."

Now that we had gotten the ball rolling, the conversation took off. Leonard and I began traiding examples of veterinary office child behavior.

There is a reason why Leonard lives at the Cold Ember Home. Behaviors which most of us find, at most, slightly annoying, drove Leonard up the wall. He told me how he hated it when families brought in some nondescript mutt and the kids, based on what they saw in some dog book, insisted it was something like a purebred Latvian Fluglehound. Or how he would seethe whenever he asked how old a dog was and the children would respond, "In dog years or people years?"

"I used to get really frustrated when people didn't pay attention to what I was telling them," he said. "After a thorough examination and diagnosis, I would try to explain my findings, but they would be too busy lifting their 4-year-old onto the exam table like it was a ride at Disneyland. Or, we would all have to stop everything and listen to some 9-year-old give us his

> I knew exactly what behaviors were bothering him.

diagnosis based on what he read in the World Book Encyclopedia."

"That doesn't happen anymore," I said. "They all have computers now. They don't read. They just download."

"Just answer one question for me, Mike," he said. "Every time an office call ended and more than one kid was present, there was always the big fight over which one gets to hold the leash or carry the cat carrier. Every time I witnessed that argument, the same question would pop into my head. Maybe you can answer it. Since they insisted in bringing their kids along when they came to my office, why the hell didn't they take their dog along when they went to see their pediatrician?"

I had no answer.

May 2004

Answer: All of the above
'Fungi' Arnie wears Dr. O out with corny puns and one-liners; does this story ever end...?

Telephone calls from my friend, Arnie, fall into a category I term E-calls.

They are informative and yet, at the same time, you would have to label them frustrating. And, although amusing, they have a way of being too time-consuming. Therefore, I refer to them as E-calls because they are "all of the above."

Our most recent conversation fit that pattern well.

"I just called to share some more of the veterinary office terminology that we've been formulating at my clinic," he said.

I knew that I was in for another dose of Arnie's bad puns and corny one-liners. However, realizing that there was no way to stop him, I let him go on.

"My last office call was very interesting," he said. "This lady brought her cat in to see me because it was a pony. You know, a little hoarse. Get it Mike? A little hoarse? (*horse*)?

"I get it, Arnie," I told him. "Go ahead with your silly story."

"Well, anyway," he continued, "there wasn't much wrong with the cat, but the lady was a regular Humpty Dumpty. You know, ready to fall to pieces. And, she wanted me to run all sort of tests on the cat. I wasn't too thrilled with the idea because the last time he was here, this cat was a real Roman. That is, he Claudius (*clawed us*) all up. Are you with me so far, Mike?"

"I follow you, Arnie. When you call, I'm an elephant, all ears that is. But I have to tell you, one call from you and I get the

Ben and Jerry syndrome. I scream (*ice cream*) if you get what I mean. After all, your puns are real Oscar Meyers. That is to say, they are the wurst (*worst*.)

"Thanks for the encouragement," he said undaunted. "I just make these things up for the fun of it. It has never been my intention to be like Rommel and

Chapter 2: Fables and Friends

> "The reason they call me mushroom is because I'm a fungi (*fun guy*.)"

get lots of tanks (*thanks*). But let me go on with the story. I ran a bunch of tests, but couldn't find out why the cat was listless. When I explained it to the lady, she told me that he had been this way all of his life and it was normal for him. He had never been a Gutenburg, a moveable type, that is.

"Does this story have an ending?" I asked. "Because you're getting to be more and more of a chauffeur. You're driving me crazy!"

"Relax, I'm just getting to the good part. After asking me to run all those tests, it turns out that she doesn't have any money. The bill is a hundred and ninety dollars and she hands me a Pavarotti, a tenor (*tenner*). But, I didn't let it bother me. Nobody is going to call me Ernest and Julio. I don't wine (*whine*) when things don't go my way. After all, that's why they call me mushroom."

"I get this one, Arnie," I said. "I'll bet they call you mushroom because you seem to be in the dark most of the time."

"Wrong, Mike. Care to take another guess?" he asked.

"Sure," I replied. "I don't know why I didn't think of this first. Mushroom would be a good name for you since you thrive on manure."

"Wrong again," he said. "The reason they call me mushroom is because I'm a fungi (*fun guy*)."

June 2003

Rebates: Dumb, dumb and dumber

Clients' 'reasonable' requests for prorated bill stymies Dr. O

I was just finishing my supper, when the call came in on the home phone. It was Mr. Izzy A. Payne calling about his dog, Yessiree Bob. "I'm sorry to call you at home, doctor," he said. "I wanted to report that Bob is doing great since his surgery. You and those other doctors sure did a wonderful job."

Naturally, I was elated to hear the news. However, it was the type of report that I enjoy much more when it comes written on a thank-you note attached to a bottle of 30-year-old scotch.

"Anyway, doctor," he continued. "The reason that I'm calling is that we have a problem. Between your bills, the internist, ultrasounds, surgeons fees and chemotherapy, we've spent over $3,000. So, money is a little tight."

I knew that the expenses incurred at my clinic were minimal, and that they were paid long ago, so I asked the reason for his call.

"Well," he answered. "We have six of those pills left. Can you take them from us and give us a rebate? We got them online at petpillpushers.com. I'm sure you could use the pills for some other dog, and we could use the $12."

Let's be reasonable

It was a very reasonable request. Oh no! Wait! That was his opinion. I thought it was just plain stupid. I turned him down, but I was so polite that he didn't even realize that I was calling him an idiot.

His call was still on my mind when Wanda Rebate called the next day. She was hopping mad and did not hesitate to give it to me with both barrels.

"Doctor, I'm very upset with your clinic. I had my son bring our cat there yesterday because it was injured, and you wound up having to put it to sleep. I can understand that it was nec-

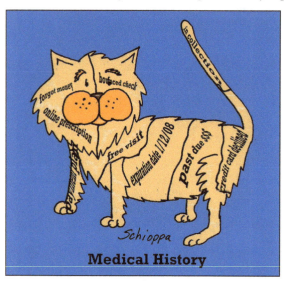

> I was so polite that he didn't even realize that I was calling him an idiot.

essary, but I can't believe that you had the nerve to charge us for the visit. You may not remember, but, the same cat was in there for his annual vaccinations just four months ago. Those shots are very expensive and are supposed to last one whole year. If my cat only lived for one third of the year, you owe me two-thirds of my money back. The very least you could have done would have been to deduct that amount from yesterday's fee."

I explained that her request would not be granted and why. She, of course, was not happy with my explanation and, though I was extremely polite, I lost her as a client.

It was no great loss. Nonetheless, that conversation kept replaying in my head for the rest of the day. It made me feel bad. Her request was inane. Her assumptions were asinine. Maybe I should have told her so. Perhaps my policy of always being nice to everyone, whether they deserve it or not, is due for an adjustment.

I should have said something like: "Are you nuts? If you think I'm going to give you a refund for eight months' worth of unused antibodies, you haven't got both oars in the water."

I'd have lost the client anyway, but, perhaps I'd have gained the self-esteem of having stood up for myself and having said what was on my mind instead of what was polite.

I vowed to give some thought to speaking my mind once in a while. After all, you're never too old to change. Maybe you can teach an old dog (that's me) new tricks. For example: When I'm told that the check is in the mail, I might reply: "Of course it is. Now tell me the one about Goldilocks."

When the teenage daughter is sent in with $20 to pick up a dog whose bill is $200, I could ask: "Which 10 percent of the dog would you like to take home?"

Serving as evidence that such a change might not be bad, is my colleague Dr. Ken Tankerous. He seems to enjoy telling off clients and he always seems to feel good about himself.

I spoke to Ken last week and explained that I might change my ways. "Good for you, Mike," he said. "Personally, I just could never bring myself to cater to people's whims. Clients aggravate me and I let them know it. I don't see how you always manage to be so nice to people even when they don't deserve it. Sure, I've lost countless clients to guys like you. Sure, your practice has grown while mine barely survives. But, I like to get my own way and the costs are worth it to me."

His remarks made me realize something.

I am too old to change.

February 2003

'Love Training:' This book report long overdue

Suckers for new fad training books are born every minute

I watched them for five minutes.

Mrs. Crowbait looked at the horse, and as might be expected, the horse looked at her. Neither of them moved.

"Is anything wrong?" I asked.

"Oh no," she said. "I was just lunging him. We'll be done soon."

Not seeing any lunge line or whip, I foolishly asked how she was going to exercise the horse.

"Aren't you familiar with love-lunging?" she asked. "I read about it in that new book, 'Love Training' by Kenny T. Walker. His research has proven that horses respond to affection. If you kiss a horse on the nose, pet him, and talk baby talk to him long enough, he will eventually do anything you want. There is never any need to use force. It's an exciting new concept."

Likening Mr. Walker to the northern end of southbound horse, I explained that his training method was nonsense and that his book was predicated on the theory that there is a sucker born every minute. She was not happy with my opinion of her new-found guru.

The incident reminded me of a time two years ago when Mrs. Fruitcake brought her cat, Peepers, in to see me.

"Something's terribly wrong, doctor," she said. "Peepers won't respond to the winkies. Winkies are supposed to be very important to a cat, but he just ignores them. I read all about it in my new book, 'Think Like Your Cat,' by Clair Voyant."

It turned out that a winkie is a kind of squinty-blinky motion that you make with your eyes. Your cat is then obligated to return the gesture. Supposedly, it represents some sort of cosmic mental link between cats and humans. In scientific terms, this is known as crapola.

I explained that this was Clair Voyant's third book of

stupid ideas, and that each was based on the premise that someone would be dumb enough to spend $12.95 for it. Mrs. Fruitcake did not appreciate my book review. "I suppose you won't like this book either," she said as she handed me a copy of 'Treating Pet Ailments with Herbs and Spices.'

"Who wrote this one?" I asked. "Colonel Sanders?"

She stormed out of the office.

These incidents were on my mind as I was having lunch with my friend, Arnie, last week. However, when I brought up the subject of nonsense in pet care literature, he gave it to me with both barrels.

"You are a fine one to talk, Mike," he said. "Do you know how many magazine articles you've written? I'll tell you, 278. I know because I've read every one of them. Not only that, but I keep a written list of everything worthwhile that you ever wrote. Do you know where I keep the list? On a small card in my wallet, that's where."

"You surprise me, Arnie," I said. "I had no idea that you could read, let alone write. Or did you have your mommy make the list for you?"

"Don't try to change the subject," he said. "Your writing makes Clair Voyant look like Einstein."

"Some people like what I write, Arnie," I told him in my own defense. "Try having your grandchildren explain the big words to you. Maybe that will help."

"That does it," he said. "I'm calling Mrs. Spectacled."

> She was not happy with my opinion of her new-found guru.

I asked him not to, but I knew that he would. The call came in two hours later. "Mikey? Is that you Mikey?" she asked.

It was Bea Spectacled, my seventh grade English teacher. "Arnie tells me that you have been writing magazine articles. I've heard it all now. You could never even diagram a sentence. Those people at that magazine must be crazy. And, one more thing, I never did get your book report on 'The Scarlet Letter.' That's going to remain incomplete on your seventh grade record for the rest of your life, young man."

A few minutes later, Arnie called, laughing like a hyena.

"Did she talk you into giving up writing?" he asked.

"Absolutely not," I told him. "In fact, it looks like I'll be writing more this month. Apparently, I owe her a book report."

"That's right," he said. "She told me about 'The Scarlet Letter.'"

"Well, I'm sending it in," I said. "But this time, I choose the title, like it or not, she's getting a book report on 'Love-Training' by Kenny T. Walker."

January 2003

'Ninth pin' ruins otherwise good day

Have you ever noticed the similarity between hiring an employee and purchasing a new shirt?

The shirt looks good in the store. You take it home, remove it from the wrapper and proceed to find and remove each of the eight pins that hold it to the cardboard. However, when you try it on, you find the ninth pin. Or should I say it finds you.

The job applicant may have a great resume and answer each of your questions as if they could read your mind. You may think that you left no stone unturned. Then, their second day on the job, you find out they are leaving town in six months, are on probation for embezzlement and don't know the alphabet.

The only veterinarian I know who has never run into such a problem is my friend, Arnie. As I have written many times, Arnie is the greatest source of wit and wisdom that veterinary medicine has ever known. He can find the ninth pin in any job candidate. So, when he invited me to join him as he interviewed for a new technician, I jumped at the chance.

The first applicant was Rosy Outlook. Arnie, knowing that the secret to a suc-

> You may think that you left no stone unturned.

cessful interview lies in doing more listening and less talking, asked Rosy about her previous job.

"It was great," she said. "We all got along so well that the days seemed short. There was a spirit of teamwork that I just loved. We all had official job descriptions, but no one let a task go undone just because it was someone else's responsibility. Sometimes we would go out together after work just to laugh at the things that happened during the day; you know, things that clients do, like insisting on giving their dog's age in dog years or asking for a bowl of water in the exam room because they think their dog is thirsty. One time we had a client complain about the fleas on her dog. She claimed that they must have come from his visit to the clinic eight months earlier. You know why? Because she was sure that her dog couldn't get fleas at home since there was a fence around her yard. Our hospital had a Bone Head Hall of Fame and she won a place of honor there. I was sorry that my husband's employer moved us to Pennsylvania. If I get a job here, do you think I'll find the co-workers to be as nice as the ones I left?"

Arnie assured her that she would find his staff to be just as pleasant.

Our next candidate, Alice Grousing, had a very different previous job experience.

"I hated my last job," she said. "The clients were idiots. There must have been something in the water in that town. A person would come in because there was a lump on their cat and then, when they got to the hospital, they couldn't find it. Or, they would tell you that their stupid mutt was a purebred just because it resembled a picture in the dog book. I remember one moron who didn't want anyone to hold his nasty cat while I took a blood sample. He wanted to do bird calls to distract the cat while I risked my fingers on his stupid animal. I could've punched the guy. The people I worked with weren't much better. I used to count the number of times that I answered the phone. Sometimes it was more than other people and I'd just let it ring until someone else got it. If I wasn't careful, I'd have wound up doing more than my share. They were the kind of people who had more to say behind your back than they did to your face. It was a relief when the boss told me that he wouldn't be needing me anymore. If I get a job here, I hope I'll find the people a lot better to work with than the ones I left."

Arnie gave her the disappointing news. She would find his staff to be just as bad. I told you he was a wise man.

October 2002

Dr. Hardway can only plead 'temporary insanity'

Last month, I had the opportunity to visit our old friend, Leonard D. Hardway.

You may remember, if you have habitually wasted your time reading my column over the years, that Leonard is a resident of the Cold Ember Home for Burned Out Veterinarians, a well-padded retirement facility located in beautiful Ropes End, Wis.

In previous interviews, Dr. Hardway has been able to document for us many of the pitfalls of veterinary practice. I hoped, as we began this most recent interview, that he would have more bits of wisdom to share with us.

Dr. O: I'm sorry to keep dredging up painful memories for you, Leonard. I know that every bit of knowledge you share with us was gained through personal mistakes and painful lessons. Rest assured that those of us who are still in the barrel appreciate any insights that you can share with us.

Dr. Hardway: No problem, Mike. Veterinary practice can be one of life's greener pastures. Maybe, with my help, those who follow in my footsteps won't have to soil their shoes in the same places I did.

Dr. O: So, you really stepped in it a few times. Is that what you're trying to say, Leonard?

Dr. Hardway: You'd better believe it. For example, there was the time I told Mrs. Milewide that her dog was too fat. She went off like Mount St. Helens. That's when it dawned on me that you should never tell a fat person their dog is too skinny or a stupid person that their dog is stupid. The list goes on and on.

Dr. O: You told us about the Milewide incident in a previous interview.

Dr. Hardway: Yes, but I forgot to tell you about a similar and equally important pitfall. We all know that many people look like their pet and vice versa. One of the worst errors you can make is to

point it out to them. I once remarked on the resemblance between Lotta Chins and her Bulldog, Jowls. As if that wasn't foolish enough, I did it while she was carrying a weapon. You should have seen the bruise I got when she threw her frozen Snickers bar at me.

Dr. O: You walked right into that one, Leonard. I have to tell you, in all honesty, that few of our readers would be dumb enough to pull a stunt like that. How about sharing something a little less obvious.

Dr. Hardway: All right, Mr. Know-It-All, how about this. Never come right out and ask what kind of dog you are looking at. All dog owners are convinced that they have a purebred dog. They have very little faith in a veterinarian who doesn't even recognize a purebred Spit-a-poo or St. Bernoodle when he sees one.

Dr. O: I've got to agree with you there. You can never be sure if the pooch being presented is a representative of some new exotic breed or a conglomeration resulting from Fido jumping the fence.

Dr. Hardway: Here is another rule you can live by. Never stand at the front desk or in the waiting room. People coming in to pick up pills, drop off a stool sample or for any one of a hundred other reasons, will get hold of you and, you'll never get loose. They will have questions which you have already answered several times, stories about the dog they had as a child, and suggestions concerning better ways to run your practice.

Dr. O: Words of wisdom indeed, Leonard. Tell me, what is the biggest mistake that you ever made?

Dr. Hardway: It's a toss-up Mike. First of all, I lived at the hospital. That was pretty foolish. People would barge right in with emergencies at any hour. But, the worst single incident I can remember occurred when Otto Funds showed up for an emergency night call. The man had owed me money for months. The collection agency had been unable to contact him. He apologized profusely and offered to give me a check for the previous balance as well as the current charges. There was just one problem. He didn't have enough gas to get home. I let him write the check for five dollars extra and gave him some cash to get gas.

Dr. O: Let me guess. The check bounced, and you never saw him again.

Dr. Hardway: That's right. When I found out what happened, I was so mad I could have killed the guy. No jury would have convicted me either. I'd have pleaded temporary insanity.

Dr. O: Leonard, you lived at the hospital. You loaned money to a known deadbeat. What do you mean "temporary"?

November 2000

Long IRS fingers reach Arnie

If last month was particularly hard on you and your practice, please don't place all the blame on poor Bill. April's misfortunes are not his fault, at least not entirely.

You see, Bill was only 8 years old at the end of the war. Growing up he witnessed the economic devastation that crippled post-war America and vowed to do something about it. It would have been nice if he could have accomplished his goals without involving veterinarians, but it didn't work out that way.

In 1913 his plans came together. Alphonso and Louise Taft's little boy, who, by the way, weighed more than 300 pounds and was the largest man ever to serve as our president, saw the 16th amendment added to our constitution. As if that weren't enough, the Underwood-Simmons Tariff Act passed the same year. And so, a new joy was added to the American lifestyle: income tax.

Now, to those of you who just yelled, "Oops! I forgot all about that," I'd like to recommend that you drop this magazine and get to work on your tax return. The rest of you may want to read on because Arnie and I have discovered some interesting facts concerning our taxes and the agency responsible for collecting them.

You may remember that, during 1997, there were congressional hearings concerning the IRS. We were promised a kinder, gentler Internal Revenue Service in 1998. Well, I don't know about you, but they weren't any kinder or gentler to me.

Arnie and I decided to launch our own investigation. We had questions about the true nature of the IRS. Is the emphasis on fairness or just on producing additional tax revenue by any means?

Are the agents ordinary citizens doing an unpopular job, or are they blood-sucking fiends who channel their vindictive tendencies through legal channels? Do they go after everyone with equal zeal, or do they place special emphasis on veterinarians?

In order to find out, we let it be known throughout the Allentown underground that we were looking for a disgruntled agent, one who would be willing to spill the beans on the IRS. Within three days, we were contacted by Rose Trudy Ranks. She had been with the IRS for 20 years. Starting as a secretary, she worked her way up to being an auditor. At that point, it became obvious that she lacked the necessary killer instinct and they let her go. Rose was bitter about being fired.

"The other agents used to make fun of me because I was reluctant to 'go for the throat,'" she said. "They called me a coward and even had a nickname for me. You want to know what it was?"

"I already know," said Arnie. "I'll bet they called you the Yellow Rose of Taxes."

"Yes! But how did you know?"

"Simple deduction."

"They hate that word down at the IRS."

"Nonetheless, I figured out your nickname as soon as I realized that we are, at this very moment, appearing in one of Obenski's columns. I knew that it would be just like him to write something corny."

"How do you stand him?"

I was forced to interrupt their inane conversation and remind Rose that she promised to put us in touch with a man who could answer our questions. She provided a name and, within minutes, we were on our way to his office at the local IRS headquarters.

The room was impressive. We met a small man sitting behind a large desk. There was a plaque on the wall which read, very appropriately, "The Buck Stops Here." There was a large picture of President William Howard Taft on the wall. Considering their push toward a new image, I was expecting a picture of Barney the Dinosaur.

We explained our questions.

"So you think there might still be some devious people in our organization?" he asked. "I'll see what I can do about getting you some information about our new attitude toward taxpayers. Of course, we can't talk freely here, but I'll see to it that you get my message."

Moments later, while walking back to the car, the same man approached us. Apparently, he had something more to say, something that couldn't be said in his office. He patted Arnie on the back, said something about getting us the message, and walked away.

Arnie seemed happy all of a sudden. "I think we got what we came for," he said. "That IRS guy just slipped something into my pocket. It's probably our answers."

He reached into his pocket and pulled out a small note. It read, "Inspected by No. 6."

"Arnie, you bozo! That note was in there since you bought those pants!" I said. "Didn't he leave any other message for us?"

"I think he did, Mike. My wallet's gone."

May 1998

'Abe's Practical Practice Scripts' destined for bestseller list

Abe Raisive is a friend and colleague. Unfortunately, Abe is also one of the most tactless people I've ever met. In fact, he is downright caustic.

This would explain the stunted growth of his practice.

As his receptionist escorted me to his office, he motioned for me to sit down and went on with his telephone conversation.

"Yes, this is Abe. I'm glad you called. I've been meaning to talk to one of you fellas. I have all but given up skydiving since my heart condition worsened. Now, I spend most of my spare time volunteering with the local fire company. They really need me since there are only two of us on the bomb squad. I definitely could use more ... Hello? Hello?"

"How about that?" he said. "The guy hung up on me."

I was thoroughly confused. "What was that all about?" I asked. "When it comes to airplanes, you are afraid to get on one, let alone jump out of one. You are not on any bomb squad and everybody knows that you don't even have a heart."

"You're absolutely right," he said. "What you just witnessed was my new way of getting rid of a life insurance salesman. It's all part of my latest project. I call it 'Abe's Practical Practice Scripts.' Let me explain. I used to have one comment for every situation. Know what it was? 'Kiss my butt!' For example, if a client asked for a multiple pet discount, I would say, 'Kiss my butt!' Employee asks for a raise? 'Kiss my butt!' Can I stay after hours? 'Kiss my butt!' See the pattern?

"Now, I'm thinking that my favorite phrase might not be much of a practice builder so, I've decided to turn over a new leaf. By writing down a script in advance, I can handle any situation tactfully. Besides, I'm gonna make a fortune selling these clever phrases to other veterinarians."

Foolishly, I asked for an example.

"All right," he said. "Let's suppose that you are in the examination room with a family of clients and their dog when, all of a sudden, they decide that it would be a good idea to have someone bring the parched pooch a bowl of water. Instead of sending for the water, you employ Practice Script No. 12. Here's how it works. Open the exam room door and yell, 'Waitress!'

One of your employees comes to the room carrying a note pad and asks if you would be interested in a small, medium or large. You point out that the large, although it cost more, is more economical and that, for a small additional fee, straws will be provided so that the entire family can share. By this point, nine out of 10 people will tell you to forget the whole thing."

I told him I was not impressed.

"You're probably just jealous because you didn't think of this idea yourself," he said. "When these scripts are all put into one book, veterinarians like you are going to be standing in line to get a copy."

Just then, his secretary interrupted us with another phone call and I was treated to a third lame example.

"Hello, Abe speaking ... Why that's amazing! You say that my money might triple or even quadruple if I invest with you?

> *"...You are not on any bomb squad and everybody knows that you don't even have a heart."*

Sign me up! One thing, though, I'm a little short on cash right now. Can you loan me a few thousand? Just until it triples, then I'll pay you back with interest. Hello? Hello?"

"How do you like that?" he asked with a grin. "That guy hung up on me, too. That's another one of my scripts that works great."

I decided that it was time to call the question.

"Is this script thing of yours the reason you asked me to stop by today?" I asked.

"It sure is," he said. "I thought maybe you could mention it in that silly magazine column of yours. That might help it to sell."

"Abe," I said, "This is the dumbest idea you ever brought me."

"Mike," he said, "Kiss my butt!"

August 1997

Fail-safe client bait delivers jolt

Are you old enough to remember a toy called The Pluto Platter? Financially, it became one of the most successful toys of all time.

You probably have had one or more and don't even know it. Why? Because you got yours after they changed the name to Frisbee. Its' popularity followed closely on the heels of another great success story, The Hula Hoop.

However, while you were busy wiggling and tossing, I had better things to do. I had an Echo Box. You may never have seen one, and believe me, it's your loss.

Mine came from a mail-order catalog. It was on the same page with the hand buzzers and whoopee cushions. It looked like a small radio. There was a cloth-covered opening for the speaker and, just beneath that, a solitary button. The directions read: "The Echo Box allows you to hear your own voice. Shout into the speaker, then quickly press the button. You will hear yourself yell."

Remember, this was the '50s. The box seemed truly amazing! It used no batteries or any other source of power, for that matter. And, it had only one moving part. The secret of the device was concealed in the button, which had a small hole in the center. When pressed, the button moved downward revealing a needle that was concealed there. The box's victim was automatically harpooned. As promised, the user immediately heard his own voice as he blurted out some four-letter word. For our purposes, in this article, we will assume it was "ouch!"

There was no need to go looking for victims. All I had to do was to leave the box where people would see it and wait. Moments later, I would hear, "Hello!... Ouch!"

I seriously doubt that you or I will ever see another Echo Box. On the other hand, my friend, Abe, recently invented something similar.

Now, if your practice has been in the doldrums this summer and you have had time to waste reading my column, then you have already been introduced to my friend, Abe. On the other hand, if you were too busy to read the last two month's episodes, or if your personal standards are too high to allow you to flush away precious time reading my column, then you are probably not reading this now. Anyway, those of you who are not reading this may go about doing whatever it is you do while I explain Abe's latest idea to my loyal readers.

Based on the rather obvious principle that the greatest frustrations in veterinary practice come from the inconsiderate antics of certain clients, Abe has invented a new line of veterinary hospital instrumentation. Each piece of equipment is designed to allow you, the frustrated veterinarian, to follow the age-old rule, "Don't get mad, get even."

Chapter 2: Fables and Friends

Much like the Echo Box, Abe's equipment uses people's natural curiosity to get them in trouble. For example, there is Abe's Self-Destructing Ophthalmoscope. It can be yours for $29.99. You simply leave the desired client in the same room with it. As soon as they pick it up and start to fiddle with it, the whole thing falls apart. There are impressive looking little springs, lenses and wires. Simultaneously, a little flag unfolds. It says, "You break it, you bought it. $190."

For those interested in a more high-tech instrument, there is Abe's Electronic Client Confuser. You can get yours for just $779. Adorned with a variety of fake dials and lights, it makes an impressive addition to any exam room. The mechanism is made up of two distinct parts. First, there is a simple mechanical timer. It makes a clicking noise which acts as bait to attract the client. Secondly, there is an electric fence charger attached to the dials. Contact with the dials will provide quite a jolt of negative reinforcement.

Abe's main obstacle in designing his new line of Echo Box-type instruments was to find a way to be sure that enough clients would swallow the bait. The solution was simple. Each item will bear a prominent label reading, "Please do not touch."

September 1997

Chapter 3:
Doctor O's Diary

Medical genius or ice cream delivery driver; too close to call for some clients

It happened in a little-known place called the Elwood Ivins Steel Tube Mill in Horsham, Pa. The year was 1968.

I was feeding the end of a large pipe into a mechanical glutton called the rotating swage hammer when the tail of my shirt got caught in the mechanism. Fortunately, I escaped a few seconds before the machine was able to start chewing me into half-inch pieces. My shirt was not as lucky. It succumbed to the fate that the device had intended for me. After that, I made it a point to keep my shirt tail tucked in at all times.

My point? It's simple. The clothes we wear can get us into sticky situations. Take, for example, the case of Dr. Flashing. She wrote to me recently to relate an embarrassing experience that occurred in her practice. When it happened, she was still a fairly recent graduate. Being a woman, she felt it appropriate to dress in skirts, feeling that they gave her a positive professional image. With the addition of white shoes at one end and a stethoscope draped around her neck at the other, she was the picture of clinical confidence. Then one day, the Gander family came in with their new puppy, Curtain.

When she bent down to pick up the little pooch, the earpiece of her stethoscope hooked the bottom hem of her skirt. Placing the patient on the table, she didn't know that the curtain had risen in more ways than one. In fact, it wasn't until she reached for the stethoscope that she realized why the Gander children were giggling. Her skirt was well above her waist. (Yes, the slip was hooked, too.)

Needless to say, a smooth recovery was almost impossible. Mr. Gander's face was crimson, and the children never did stop laughing. Dr.

Flashing wears slacks now.

A similar, yet opposite, incident was related to me by a colleague, Dr. Kammi Flagje, a large animal practitioner from Wisconsin. She was new on the job and was going to Mr. Brandish's dairy farm for the first time. It was a bitter-cold winter day. Bundled up as she was in boots, coveralls, hat scarf and gloves, Mr. Brandish apparently did not realize that she was a woman. That would explain why, when she looked up from her examination of the cow, she was greeted with the scene of Mr. Brandish relieving himself into the gutter behind the stanchions. She felt it best to pay close attention to her patient until sufficient time had elapsed to ensure that Mr. Brandish had finished experiencing the draftiness of the barn.

In both of the examples, a colleague got into an embarrassing situation due to the clothes they were wearing. However, my friend, Dr. Target, wasn't even wearing the outfit that got him in trouble. It all started while he was vaccinating Mr. Quickly's Tom Cat, Spurt.

Not having the fastest of reflexes, Dr. Target got dosed with a good quantity of ripe Tom Cat urine (something we have all experienced). The trouble didn't come until three days later when he went to pick up the ill-fated outfit at the dry cleaners. The manager wanted to talk to him. In front of several other customers, he was told that they had to change all of their cleaning solutions because of him. Apparently, the entire store smelled like a Tom Cat the day they tried to clean those clothes. Furthermore, he was told that he would not be welcomed back if he ever brought in a similar problem. Naturally, after having been spoken to like that, he never went back anyway.

As a final example, I'd like to tell you something that happened to me during my senior year in veterinary school. (This was four years after my disagreement with the swage hammer.) On my way home from the teaching hospital, I stopped at the market to pick up some groceries. My clinical attire, including white pants and white lab coat made me feel that I was set apart from the crowd. Surely, I looked the role of a future medical genius. That bubble burst when I saw a lady point right at me, and say to her friend, "Let's be sure to buy ice cream today. It must be fresh because the delivery man is still here."

May 2006

Bankers test relationship between me, myself and Michael

Automated processes, forms might not garner the data you seek

I feel as if I've known Michael all my life. In fact, even in my earliest recollections of childhood, he is there. To this day, we are constant companions, see eye to eye on most things, and even work together at my clinic.

That's because we are the same person.

I know this is true because we have the same Social Security number.

Recently, however, our friendship was tested when some bankers asked me to rat on my friend. It seems that Michael, the self-employed employee, (that's me) had applied for a new home mortgage. The bankers, in their infinite wisdom, required that character reference forms and verification of employment forms be filled out by his self-employed employer (that's me too).

Having known myself for so many years, I thought that answering few questions would be easy. I was wrong.

Paragraph No. 1 boldly stated that the employer, who's name and address were shown in section four, was not under any circumstances, to share the contents of the forms with the employee, who's name and address were listed in section six. It didn't take long to figure out that this rule would be hard to follow since the names and addresses were the same.

At the bottom of the page

> He let me know, in no uncertain terms, that the bank always knows what it's doing.

there was a toll-free number to be called in case there were any questions. Frankly, I thought that sending me the forms was a silly mistake, so I called the number fully expecting the bankers to laugh along with me at their faux pas. I was wrong again. My call was answered by one of those computerized voice-mail systems. It kept giving me options and telling me what buttons to push on my phone depending on which one I chose.

The machine was obviously determined to deprive me of any opportunity to speak with a real human being. However, I was equally determined to work my way through the maze until I could do just that. The battle between man and machine lasted almost 40 minutes. When it was over, my call was taken by an abrasive fellow named Carl Borundum. His personality was not as nice as the computer's. He let me know, in no uncertain terms, that the bank always knows what it's doing. Furthermore, that the form was written in plain English with simple directions and the processing of the applicant's mortgage would not continue until it was completed.

I decided to fill out the form. So, in blatant defiance of the rules, I began reading and answering the questions in full view of the employee (that's me again).

Naturally, I considered giving them a barrage of sarcastic answers, but it is never wise to use sarcasm on people who are destined to go through life with no sense of humor. The best course of action seemed to be straight honest answers.

First, they wanted to know how long I had known the person listed in section six. I simply filled in my age. Then, there was a series of questions concerning character issues such as honesty, reliability and morality. I gave myself a glowing report.

Proceeding down the page, the questions got harder to answer. How long was I planning to keep the applicant employed in his current position with my company? I couldn't put down "forever." So, I wrote that he had a job with me until he voluntarily chose to retire. They asked if the person was a relative. I had to put down "yes". This, of course, meant that I had to answer the next question. What is the exact relationship (i.e. uncle, cousin, child, etc.)? I wrote "self".

Near the bottom of the page, there was a space for comments. I wrote that the applicant and I were one and the same person, and that if there were any questions concerning this matter, to call me at my office. I don't think they'll call though. If they did, how would they know which one of us to ask for?

May 2005

Good old days getting a little blurry

EKGs, potbellies, acid reflux replace kegs, growing pot, acid rock as time marches on

He was only about 18 inches tall and seemed completely motionless. I wanted to get up close and take his picture, but I was afraid to approach him. Then, one of his eyes flicked open. I jumped 30 feet. The crocodile was only 12 feet long.

Knowing what I would do if I woke up from a nap and found myself lying next to a jelly donut, I decided to take the prudent course of action and run like hell.

You see, we don't have crocodiles in Allentown, Pa. Up until this incident, the closest I had ever gotten to one was when I was watching that crocodile guy on the Animal Planet channel. He seems to have a knack for handling the beasts. However, I prefer my own system, the "run like hell" system. It worked great.

This all occurred just a few weeks ago in Costa Rica, a beautiful, unspoiled country located a long way from Allentown. Oh, sure, there is abundant wildlife, rainforests, volcanoes and ecosystems. However, what I meant by unspoiled is that you can light up a cigar anywhere without inciting the formation of a lynch mob. (Note: Don't bother to contact me with information concerning cigars and my health. I don't need a warning from you. I'm married.)

My wife and I were in Costa Rica for the annual Pennsylvania Veterinary Medical Association Winter Meeting, a week of continuing education lectures, scheduled with plenty of spare time for other vacation activities.

(Note to the State Board of Veterinary Medical Examiners: I attended every single lecture and I have a certificate to prove it.)

Old dogs, new tricks............

> Pretty soon, the conversation got just plain silly.

Many of the people in attendance were old friends and classmates. There was a lot of catching up to do. Sometimes, we would take sightseeing trips together, go out for dinner or just meet for drinks at the bar.

(Note to the Internal Revenue Service: every single charge on my credit card was incurred during business discussions with colleagues.)

On one occasion, a bunch of us old fogies rented a van and went out for the evening. It was a harrowing trip. Costa Rica is mountainous. The roads are narrow, twisty and dangerous. The Costa Rican highway commission (motto: "What's a guardrail?") does not actually exist.

Nonetheless, we arrived safely at our destination, had a few drinks and started to reflect on how we've changed over the years.

Pretty soon, the conversation got just plain silly.

Slim got the ball rolling.

"Remember 1972 when we graduated?" he asked. "I had long hair down to my shoulders. Look at me now! I've gone from long hair to longing for hair."

Stew went next. In college we called him "The Guzzler."

"We're all getting pretty old," he said. "In 1972 it was KEG. Now it's EKG."

"I've got one," said Dan. "Back then, I was into acid rock. Now it's acid reflux."

Stew wanted to go again.

"How about this one?" he asked. "When we graduated, the big thing was the Rolling Stones. Now I'm worried about kidney stones."

It was my turn.

"Remember when we were always looking for new, hip joints to go to? Now half of us need new hip joints."

Stew was back on his feet.

"In college, I was into growing pot. Now, the only thing I'm growing is a potbelly."

Finally, Gerry chimed in. He had been quiet for the entire evening and, in fact, had been under the weather for most of the trip.

"In 1972," he said. "I was hoping for a BMW. Now, I'm just hoping for a BM."

The other patrons in the restaurant probably wondered why those "old men" seemed hysterical. They might not have been familiar with the old saying, "You laugh best when you can laugh at yourself."

April 2004

Pet psychics bridge gap in medical knowledge

Claire Voyant, Charlotte Tan called in to divine true cause of Hale and Hearty's chronic maladies

It was a landmark phone call.

Mrs. Itis, is concerned about the health of her aging cats, needed to talk to the doctor "right away."

It seemed that they might have been eating poorly, acting sluggish or possibly losing weight. This, in and of itself, was nothing new. Imogene Itis calls almost every day. Over the years her cats have had examinations, X-rays, blood tests and referrals to specialists. No one has ever gotten to the bottom of the problems because there is nothing wrong with the cats. In fact, any problem that does exist with these kitties, is to be found only within the vacuous space between the ears of their owner.

Though similar to previous calls, this one would turn out to be very different. There were two reasons for this. First of all, it represented a milestone. You see, she has called about a zillion times each year for about a zillion years. So, using higher mathematics, anyone can see that this was her one bazillionth phone call. I have no doubt that, once they hear about me hitting the one bazillion mark, the McDonalds hamburger counters will be looking up with envy.

Secondly, I knew that the conversation would be taking a whole new course when she asked about a different type of specialist.

"Doctor, do you think I could use some mental help?"

Having decided to avoid the first answer that came to mind, I wasn't sure what to say. Her questions continued before I had a chance to say anything at all.

"Do you know Charlotte Tan, the pet psychic?" she asked.

I told her that we have more than a kajillion records

> No psychic has called yet, but my hopes are high.

in our files and that I wasn't sure offhand.

"No, no, you don't understand what I mean," she said. "How about Claire Voyant? Surely you've heard of her?"

I may be slow, but by this stage of the conversation, I was catching on. She was mentioning people famous for their mental powers, those who could supposedly read minds, solve mysteries or communicate telepathically with animals. Personally, I have no faith in these individuals at all. I formed this opinion one day in 1998. As luck would have it, while attending a play on Broadway, I noticed that the "Amazing Claire Voyant" was seated just four rows in front of me. I ignored the stage and spent three hours staring at the back of her head trying to send a message of greeting. What a snob! She never even turned around to say hello. I guess superior mental powers don't necessarily come with good manners. (Although, I must admit, that she may have had a bazillion other messages coming in at the time and couldn't possibly acknowledge them all.)

The conversation with Mrs. Itis now took the expected course.

"Couldn't we get one of them to tell us what's wrong with my cats?" she asked. "I've heard they can diagnose disease. They would know what's wrong with Hale and Hearty."

She was serious and I wasn't about to laugh at her, at least not until I hung up the phone.

"Do you know how to get in touch with them?" I asked foolishly.

"You don't call them. They call you," she said. "Don't you know anything, Doctor?"

I had to admit that this was to be my first experience with consulting a mentalist. (Though I did consider it once while trying to balance a checkbook.)

Mrs. Itis proceeded to give me directions.

"You have to think about me and my cats," she said. "If you and I both think about the cats and what's wrong with them, Claire Voyant or Charlotte Tan will get the message and call us.

I just know it will work, doctor. Promise me you won't just forget about this phone call as soon as you hang up."

"No chance of that," I assured her. In fact, I promised to mention the call to several of my friends.

No psychic has called yet, but my hopes are high. In fact, I'm making a list of things I want to ask. Because, if someone calls who has all the answers, I have about a kaptillion questions.

December 2003

Aren't we lucky we don't have to deal with people?

Dee Crepit's powers of observation still border on non-existent

I could hardly believe my eyes, but there he was.

Wearing the somewhat traditional Day-Glo orange colors of a hunter, some clown was crawling along the paddock fence not 15 feet from my Appaloosa gelding.

It was a year ago on the first Monday after Thanksgiving, a date that is significant for two reasons. First, it is the opening day of deer season in Pennsylvania.

Second, the leaves are off the trees by late November, so I could clearly see this jerk through the wooded area that stood between us.

I don't allow hunting on my property, and even if I did, you'd have to be an idiot to hunt so close to horses. So, I launched a verbal salvo of the variety that you might expect Sergeant Snorkel to deliver in the direction of Beetle Bailey.

I questioned everything from this guy's intelligence to his ancestry.

Then, the unexpected happened. He turned and bolted straight toward me. He maintained a low posture almost like crawling, but moved faster than I thought a human could go. Not knowing who he was or what his intentions were, I got a little scared. The feeling turned to just plain embarrassment however, when I realized that the "hunter" I had been yelling at was the neighbor's Golden Retriever, Bowie. Like many rural pets, the pooch always wears an orange vest when he goes out during hunting season.

I had read the situation

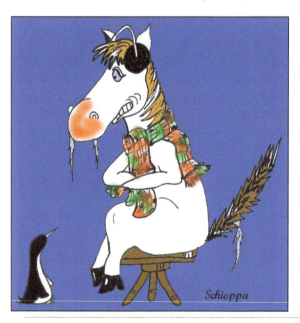

incorrectly, something that I am apt to do on occasion. Some of my clients, however, seem to have sharpened their powers of faulty observation to a level far beyond anything I have achieved.

Take for example, Dee Crepit, who runs a local business named, appropriately enough, Dee Crepit Pets and Supplies. Her powers of observation border on non-existent. She comes to see me about twice a year with a sick kitten that she is trying to sell. It may be 6 months old, weigh 1 pound, have four teeth and border on unconsciousness. Still, she will say: "This kitten was perfectly fine yesterday. It was eating and active, and growing nicely. Today, when I came into the store, it looked like this all of a sudden." Anyone could see, looking at such a patient, that it took weeks or months to arrive at the current pitiful condition. Yet, she claims otherwise. Each time I see her, I marvel that anyone could be so obtuse.

A colleague who practices in northern Michigan once recounted a similar incident. On a bitter day in 1967, he had been called upon to examine a horse that was down. The owners lived in a small rented farm house on the outskirts of town. A dozen or so of them shared, in commune fashion as was not uncommon in the '60s, everything from beds to toothbrushes. As near as our colleague could figure, they pretty much spent their days sitting by the fire, smoking pot and contemplating whatever it was they chose to contemplate.

Twice daily, one of them would bundle up and brave the elements in order to give a shot of penicillin to the horse that lay in his stall covered with blankets.

The examination of the patient was very brief. The veterinarian discovered, as soon as he began to insert a thermometer, that the horse was frozen solid. The news was taken hard by the inhabitants of the house. They all agreed that he had been a wonderful pet for the short time they had him and that he would be missed. However, as they came to stand around the body and eulogize their lost friend, it became apparent that no one had ever actually seen the horse moving during the two weeks they had lived in the house. Apparently, he was already frozen when they moved in.

This incident and the case of Dee Crepit are isolated occurrences involving just one client each. There is, however, one example of faulty observation that seems to be common to a very large percentage of our clients. For that matter, even our acquaintances and relatives often seem prone to sharing in the common mistake. They see our practices. They observe our lifestyle, and still they say, completely erroneously, "You're lucky to be a veterinarian, because you don't have to deal with people."

November 2003

Bad college habits catch up with you after all

From predicting winter weather to curing worms, theorists are out there

I was just finishing up the office call with his dog, when Mr. Isobar asked me an important question.

"Do you think today counts, Doc? It's kind of foggy outside, but it isn't real bad."

As often happens during conversations with my clients, I had no idea what he was talking about. He must have figured that out from the look on my face, because he went on to explain.

"They say that the number of foggy

days in August will always be the same as the number of snowstorms in the coming winter," he said. "The trouble is, Doc, I can't decide whether today should count or not."

I suggested that the day might represent a rather small future snowstorm and that seemed to make him happy.

Just a few hours later, I heard a similar theory from Mr. Barley down at the Farmway Store. We were loading horse feed onto my truck when he predicted a harsh winter.

"The husks are tight on the sweet corn this year, Doc," he said. "That's gonna mean a rough winter with plenty of snowstorms for sure."

I asked if he didn't subscribe to the foggy-days-in-August theory.

"Oh, that's just an old wive's tale," he said. "The only things you can count on are the stripes on the fuzzy caterpillar, and the husks on the sweet corn."

I drove away feeling a little disappointed in myself for having been unfamiliar with these gems of forecasting knowledge. These are the things I should have known because I took a course in meteorology as an undergraduate at Penn State. Unfortunately, the only thing I remember from that course is that State College, Pa. harbored a unique combination of air temperature, wind speed

...I was able to cover for my lack of knowledge...

and classroom locations which, when taken as a whole, made me feel that it was inconvenient to attend the class on a regular basis.

I realized now that there have been many times when my lack of knowledge could be traced directly to my poor study habits in college and veterinary school.

For example, I was attending a Grange meeting with a friend of mine recently when someone expressed concern about a few cases of botulism that had been reported in the horses in our area. One of the fellas present, who was particularly knowledgeable about such things, explained to the group that botulism occurs when you don't comb the bots off your horse. The horse licks at those, swallows the bots and gets botulism.

I didn't know that! I thought botulism was some kind of food poisoning. They must have covered that in my third year medicine class the day I decided to go fishing.

Then there was the time Mr. Yokel came to see me because his dog had worms.

"Old Blue has got the worms, Doc." He said. "Something must be wrong because I dosed him good with gunpowder just like my granpappy always told me to do, but the worms are still there. I called one danged fool veterinarian who told me granpappy's treatment was wrong. It was some young guy. Probably doesn't know his stuff."

At that point, I didn't want to admit that I hadn't heard of the gunpowder treatment. They probably went over that in parasitology class the day some of my classmates and I drove to Delaware to check out that topless bar. At any rate, I was able to cover for my lack of knowledge by pointing out that Mr. Yokel had used smokeless powder, whereas in my granpappy's day, they used black powder. He was happy with the explanation.

When Mrs. Pigment came to my office with her new puppy, Hybrid, my lazy habits of the past haunted me once again.

"What kind of dog is he, Doctor?" she asked. "I know he's a purebred. You can tell by those black areas in his mouth."

You can? That must have been covered in genetics class the day I went to that football game. Besides, this dog didn't even seem to represent one species, let alone a particular breed. I told her I wasn't sure if the black gum theory always held true. Her confidence in me was seriously shaken.

Well, I've learned my lesson. The next time I go on one of those continuing education trips, I'm going to actually attend some of the lectures, not all of them mind you. There's no reason to become a fanatic.

August 2003

Daisy pulls quick one on Mike

Caution! You may be one of the 12 veterinarians who are going to be highly annoyed by the material in this column.

If so, you may be very disappointed with me. However, I cannot explain why right now. First, I have to tell you what happened to Dr. Eachofus.

Dr. Eachofus was explaining to Mrs. Deeword the cause of her dog's problem. Ordinarily, she was a pleasant and cooperative client, but as she listened to Dr. Eachofus, her attitude changed dramatically.

You see, when he explained that the dog's pain came from a problem with the "anal sacs," she thought he said "anal sex." Naturally, she became even more appalled as he explained that many dogs need regular attention in this area and that it was something she could learn to do at home.

As she visibly turned seven shades of purple, our hero could see that the office call wasn't going well. Thinking that she was squeamish about the thought of attending to this messy business at home, he suggested that a groomer would be glad to do it once a month or so.

She went ballistic. Grabbing her little Yorkie from the table and vowing never to return, she stormed off in search of a second opinion. The good doctor didn't understand what had gone wrong until her nasty letter arrived four days later.

And now, 12 of you are probably annoyed with me. You may think that I stole your story. But, I didn't. You see, in one form or another, you and 11 of your colleagues submitted that story to the Mike Obenski Writing Contest. It's a good story. In fact, I've written about it before, so please forgive me for using it now.

How did I get into this mess? It all started in December when

> ..."never trust anyone who can diagram a sentence."

the editor of this magazine, Daisy Deadline, called me with an idea. (Note: Curious readers can uncover the true identity of the editor by glancing at page 5 and reading her real name which is printed next to the word "Editor." (Go ahead. I'll wait ….)

Anyway, Maureen, oops!!!! I mean Daisy suggested that we hold a writing contest. We would ask veterinarians to submit an interesting story, award prizes for the best ones and print the winning entries in future issues. She was sure that such a contest would go over big with our readers. I was against it. I told her we would be lucky to get four entries and three of those wouldn't be any good. Besides, I have found through experience that Daisy's expectations are often unrealistic. For example, she expects my column to be submitted on time, *even during football season!*

Now, you may have heard the old adage, the boss may not always be right, but she's always the boss. Well, in this case, she was right. After announcing the contest in January, scores of entries began rolling in. Most of them were good, except for the ones from my friend, Arnie.

Best of all, Daisy hinted that the contest might somehow provide me with a little time off. That sounded good to me! Somehow I was going to get a vacation out of this deal.

By the end of February, several Federal Express boxes of entries had been forwarded to my office. Reading them was a joy. However, picking a winner was very difficult. Nonetheless, I eventually narrowed the field to just a few and finally chose my favorite. The winner was notified last month and will be published in our next issue.

By the way, I never did get that vacation. Apparently, Daisy played me for a sucker. It only proves the value of a rule I have stuck by ever since junior high school, "never trust anyone who can diagram a sentence."

Note to Mike from Maureen, er, from Daisy: I was right about another thing, too. You're always wondering 'who reads this drivel' referring to your column. Well, from the kudos you received with some of the entries I'm surprised your head still fits through your exam room door! What's the saying, "often imitated, never equaled?" …. Hats off to (as one entrant put it) "the master."

May 2002

Arnie tries contest 'end run'

I could hardly believe my eyes. My boss, Dr. Oldguy, was throwing away pieces of mail without even opening them.

He just looked at the envelopes, saved some and dropped others right into the trash. At the time, it seemed like a risky and somehow rude practice to me. Now, 30 years later, I find myself doing that same thing practically every day.

Then, back on Feb. 6, the unbelievable happened. Every piece of mail that came in that day was worthy of attention. One letter of particular interest bore the incredible news that I may already have won $10 million! It was from Megasell Magazine Company. All I had to do to find out was to place some stickers in the appropriate places on the entry blank. Naturally, I ordered a bunch of magazines, also. Heck, I can afford it now that my $10 million is practically on the way!

I even considered retiring immediately, but my wife thinks I should keep working until the check actually arrives.

The same day, the mail also contained a free sample of a new miracle room deodorant, a dried up roundworm that Mrs. Scooper found in her cat's litter pan, and a check for $1 from the Rebate Pet Tag Company.

However, all of the things I've mentioned so far pale in comparison to one very important letter. It was the first entry in the Mike Obenski Writing Contest and was submitted by Dr. Einra of Allentown, Pa. I could tell instantly that it was a feeble attempt by my friend, Arnie, to disguise his name. The story he submitted went something like this:

Some clients invited Dr. Einra to go along on a little camping trip that they were planning for last August. Unfortunately, the three-day excursion, which was to include quite a bit of hiking, fell on one of the hottest days the Allentown area has had in years.

The wisest of the hikers were careful to keep their backpacks as light as possible and to bring plenty of water. Naturally, they were surprised to see one of Dr. Einra's clients show up dragging, of all things, a car door. When questioned about it, he informed the other hikers that he had purchased it at the junkyard for this camping trip.

"Why would anyone want to drag a 70-pound car door on a hike?" they all wanted to know.

"It's simple," he said. "If we get too hot, we can roll down the window."

I called Arnie to let him know that I recognized his work and that he was disqualified because the contest is for true stories, not old jokes.

"I suppose then," he said, "that you don't want me to send in the story about the veterinarian who fell into a lens grinder. I understand he made a spectacle of himself."

"That's right," I told him. "Besides, that joke is older than you are."

Sensing that the conversation was getting me nowhere, I decided to go for his throat.

"Arnie," I said. "I almost forgot to tell you that I got a phone message for you today. It was from your proctologist. He had some good news. It seems that he found your head."

"That's quite a coincidence, Mike," he said. "Because I got a phone message for you today, also. It was from Hollywood. They were thinking of making your life into a TV show, but they couldn't figure out which actor would play you, Beavis or Butthead."

"Well, if they ever need an actor to play you, Arnie, they'll have to teach Mr. Ed to always face away from the camera."

And so the conversation went on, getting nowhere, as our conversations usually do. Arnie, I'm sure, will have more contributions for us in the next few months. I hope yours are better than his.

April 2002

Granny's cookies as 'natural' as Arnie's stories

I have an important confession to make.

So, stand by for that while I tell you about an incident that occurred last week.

It was Saturday morning. All three otoscopes were dead. So, we sent the most expendable person to the store for batteries. It was me.

I was waiting in the checkout line when I saw them, Granny's Old-Fashioned Cookies. The box said they were just like the kind my dear old grandmother used to make. I snatched three boxes.

Just looking at them reminded me of childhood visits to Granny's house. It wasn't the cookies that brought on a wave of nostalgia, it was the list of ingredients. I read it and was immediately transported back to 1953. I could almost hear the dear lady calling to me from her kitchen, the sound of her voice mixed with the heavenly aromas of her oven at work.

"Mikey, could you run to the store for me? I'm right in the middle of baking the cookies, and I ran out of potassium sorbate."

In a flash, I was off to the corner store.

My grandmother yelled out of the window, "Better get some FD&C Yellow No. 6, also."

The corner store was run by Polly Valent. Her store was so full of wholesome natural foods that it smelled almost as good as Granny's house. There was an open barrel of malto-dextrin, and sometimes free samples of sodium hexametaphosphate.

No sooner had I gotten back from the store, than another shortage was discovered.

"Mikey, could you run over to Mrs. Davenport's house and ask to borrow a cup of calcium propionate?"

Once again, I was gone in a flash. I loved to drop in on Mrs. Dupont because she was an avid baker also, and if my timing was right, she would let me lick out the bowl of diglycerides.

Shocked into reality

All of a sudden, I was shocked back to 2002. It happened when I tasted the cookies. They weren't anything like the cookies of 49 years ago. In fact, to tell you the truth, my grandmother wouldn't know a diglyceride if it ran up and bit her. You see, I made up most of what you just read. The only true parts are that I do eat cookies, and I did have a grandmother.

Furthermore, that is the confession that you have been waiting to hear. For the first time in 25 years of writing this column, I made up a story. Granted, my column is usually nothing but a bunch of silly nonsense, but it has always been true silly nonsense.

Why would I perpetuate such a hoax? Could it be brain damage from the ingredients in last week's nauseating cookies? Not at all. It's just that we have now reached the conclusion of the Mike Obenski Writing Contest. There were scores of great entries, and only a few bad ones. The bad ones all have two things in common. They are obviously made up stories, and they all came from my friend Arnie.

New challenges

Just for fun, I thought I'd try my hand at making one up. Frankly, it wasn't any better than his last attempt that went something like this:

A veterinarian was working in a pasture by the side of the road. He was alone, and had his hands full trying to deliver a calf without assistance. A traveler who was passing by offered to lend him a hand, and the veterinarian gratefully accepted. It took over an hour of hard work, but the two were rewarded by the sight of a healthy baby, wobbling on a set of brand new legs and getting to know mommy for the first time. While the men were cleaning themselves up, the veterinarian offered to pay the traveler for his assistance.

"No thanks, Doc," the man said. "It was an interesting experience for me, and one that I'll never forget. Just tell me one thing, though. How fast was that little fella going when he ran into the back of that cow?"

After reading it, I called Arnie to let him know that this latest entry, just like the previous seven, failed to qualify for the contest, not only because it was obviously a made-up story, but also because it is an old joke that every veterinarian has heard a hundred times.

"You should be ashamed of yourself," I told him. "There were almost 200 hundred stories submitted to the contest, and they all had one thing in common. They were all better than yours. You'll see what I mean as you read the winning entries over the next few months. I do have some good news for you though, Arnie. It seems that you have qualified for a special prize.

I've decided to reward the person who sent in the most entries, and you win hands-down in that category. So, I'm sending over two and a half boxes of cookies."

June 2002

Where did I go wrong?

Good fences make good neighbors

By Terry Grandt, DVM
CONTRIBUTING AUTHOR

To many people, a large animal is a Golden Retriever. To me, it's a dairy cow.

I certainly like dogs and cats and our own pets have been important members of our household. It's just that my experience as a veterinarian has been primarily with dairy cattle. As an employee in a mixed animal practice in rural Wisconsin in the late 1970s, I had to take my turn at spending one afternoon a week treating small animals.

Most of the time I spent in the clinic I wished I was back out with the cows, but I did my best to understand what the client wanted and to treat the animal accordingly.

One such afternoon I had one of those "they'll never believe this," episodes that I found hard to believe myself.

Mr. Goodneighbor brought his young female Beagle, Cleopatra, in for an examination. We had not seen the dog before, but her rabies tag was current and she seemed to be in good health. I asked if she had been having any problems lately or if there were any changes in her behavior.

"No," he said.

I asked if she had been eating and drinking normally.

"Yes," was his reply.

I asked him exactly why he had brought her in for an exam, but his answer was vague. He said he wanted her to have a routine exam just to make sure she was OK.

I proceeded to take her temperature, check her heart, lungs, eyes, ears, nose and throat. I told him that his dog was fine. As far as I was concerned the exam was over and I made my move toward the door. Mr. Goodneighbor stayed right where he was. Evidently, I hadn't done what he wanted me to do.

He said that Cleo had just been in heat for the first time. I saw that her vulva was slightly swollen and agreed with him that she had recently been in heat. She looked fine now. Once again I was ready to end the exam, but he still wasn't finished.

He told me his neighbor had a male dog that he didn't like and that the dog came in and out of his yard and he didn't like that either. In fact, a few days ago the male dog had come into his yard and mated with Cleo and that really made him mad. Evidently this fellow never heard the saying that good fences make good neighbors. I suggested that any time

Chapter 3: Doctor O's Diary

his female dog was in heat, to be careful when she was let out to avoid unwanted mating. I also told him he should consider having his dog spayed.

Not listening to a word I said, he continued by telling me that the two dogs had gotten stuck together and they wouldn't come apart. Cleo was struggling and yelping and he was determined to separate them.

First, he tried throwing water on them but they stayed stuck. I could have told him that wouldn't work, but I just listened and nodded. Then he tried pulling them apart and that didn't work either. I told him that dogs do get stuck together in this situation and that the best thing to do is leave them alone until they separate themselves. But he wasn't willing to wait for that to happen.

When he was trying to pull the two dogs apart for the second time, the male dog bit him. (I imagined that he'd bite, too, if he was in that situation.) By then, he was so angry that he went into his house, brought out his gun and shot and killed the male dog! I couldn't believe what I was hearing! And yet, I did believe him because he was absolutely serious in the telling of his tale, and I don't think anyone could make up such a bizarre story! I couldn't imagine anyone doing such a thing! I couldn't imagine what happened when his neighbor found out!

By this time, I really wished I was outside with the cows or anywhere else for that matter. However, Cleo was in good shape and it remained a mystery to me what he still wanted me to do to the dog.

Much to my relief, his lengthy story was coming to a conclusion. Even after he shot the male, the two dogs remained stuck together. Cleo continued to struggle and yelp. He still couldn't get them apart. So he went back into his house, brought out a knife and cut off the dead dog's male member. But he never saw the part he cut off fall out of his dog. He thought that if he brought his dog in for an exam, I would routinely check inside her and let him know if I found anything. Finally, I knew the reason for the exam!

Within a minute I was able to assure him that there was no male member inside his female. Once he found out what he wanted to know, Mr. Goodneighbor and Cleo left promptly. An exam that should have taken five minutes took 35 minutes and seemed like an hour. At least his was the last appointment for the day. I wasn't up for any more surprises.

We never heard from Mr. Goodneighbor again. Considering what happened, I would imagine he moved to a place far away. Somewhere with a good fence. Nowhere near the place where I was happily tending the dairy cows.

Dr. Grandt grew up in rural Farmington, Ill. He received his DVM degree in 1973 from the University of Illinois. He has worked as a mixed and small animal practitioner during his career. He currently works part time seeing beef cattle and some small animals in a Farmington practice. He says his two sons must know something he didn't—neither one became a veterinarian!

June 2002

The Terminator

Ham-fisted motorcycle thug has soft spot and big wad of cash for Doc

By Mark E. Peters, DVM, PC
CONTRIBUTING AUTHOR

It was in the summer of 1984, about a year after I'd opened my solo small animal practice, that it began.

On a fine June afternoon, my front door was wrenched violently open and in strode a fellow with a very bloody Pit Bull Terrier in his arms.

When I say "fellow," I want you to picture the bad guy in the movie, "*Raising Arizona*—a huge, long-haired, bearded, black-leather-clad, fingerless-glove-wearing, metal-studded, um … fellow. He was followed closely by five or six companions of more or less the same description.

"Hey, Doc," he growled. "Ah need yuh ta tek cara *mah dawg!*"

Unsettling as this situation was, especially having erupted so suddenly, I summoned my best calm and professional demeanor (which I'd been practicing a lot lately) and said, "Fine, sir, bring him into my examination room."

In truth, just then, I didn't feel like I had much choice. Into my exam room he came, bloody dog and all, crowded closely by his minions. My exam room isn't very big, and I soon felt that it had been invaded by a herd of curious, if somewhat menacing, buffalo.

'Gee, Doc, I dunno'

The dog in question, whose name I don't recall, had suffered a large number of lacerations, macerations and puncture wounds—the origins of which were baffling and mysterious to his presenters upon questioning.

In spite of his injuries, the dog was amazingly stable and unconcerned, though all of you who have worked with the breed know you practically have to shoot them to kill them.

In any event, I anesthetized the brute, dealt with his punctures and lacerations, placed a few drains, gave him a big shot of antibiotic and in a day or two, sent him home with his scary owner.

Hoping to discourage further visits, I charged what I thought was an inordinate amount. I think it was more than 300 bucks. He paid it happily, drawing a hairy paw from a pocket and peeling the cash off of a thick roll. He was wearing a sort of horrible gap-toothed grin and I construed this as gratitude. This was reinforced by a number of bone-jarring thumps on the back, administered upon his departure.

In the beginning

Before I go any further, I think a bit of background is in order.

I was born and raised in Council Bluffs, Iowa, but was new back in town after a seven-year stint in undergrad and veterinary school at Iowa State. It was widely rumored, I came to find out, that a certain part of town, roughly "down by the river," was home to lawless and immoral behavior of all kinds—gambling, drug-dealing, dog fighting, girls you wouldn't take home to meet your mother and who knows what else. Of all such, I was happily ignorant, content mostly with trying to avoid foreclosure on my small enterprise.

Back to our story

Getting back to the hairy cabal described earlier, it seems they took a shine to me and a pattern developed that continued throughout that summer. The "Terminator" or one of his henchmen would barge in about once a week with a chewed up, to one degree or another, dog. I even devised my own evaluation system grading them on a kind of triage basis, Mangle 1 through Mangle 5, the last being, obviously, the worst. We got used to it. I'd say to my vet techs, "OK girls, henchman in Exam 1, Mangle 2, you know the drill. Stat!"

To those readers, presumably colleagues, who are intently frowning at this moment, let me say that I had, from the outset, an ethical problem regarding this matter.

The dogs were obviously injured from fighting, but I was fresh out of school, unsure of which authority I should contact, and whether if I did so, it would violate doctor/client/patient confidentiality. I sought out an older practitioner in the community whom I'd always respected. I sat in his office and explained the situation, of which he was mostly already aware.

He looked wearily over the top of his glasses and said, "Hells a matter with you son? You'd best just stick to veterinary medicine; keep you in one piece."

So that's what I did. They brought 'em to the clinic in whatever grade of Mangle, I patched 'em up and they paid handsomely in cash.

Until the last one.

Late that summer, a #4 Mangle was brought in, not by the Terminator, but by one of his associates who seemed to be in a big hurry. I performed my usual ministrations, and the same henchman picked up the dog the following day. Oddly for them, he said he had no money just then and "The Boss" would be in to settle up the next day.

Well, the next day came and nobody showed up. There were rumors of a big police bust "down by the river" with lots of arrests and all those implicated headed to The Big House for a long state-funded vacation. After that, it got pretty quiet.

The reunion

Three years later, in the summer of 1987, I went, late on a Saturday afternoon, to a small butcher shop in the neighborhood to purchase a steak to grill that evening. As I exited, the steak in hand, and started to get into my car, a very ominous looking car pulled in tightly behind me, blocking me in with no conceivable route of escape. It was a very grubby white Cadillac lowrider, about a '63, and it was absolutely bristling with big, hairy motorcycle guys. There were at least a dozen of them jammed in there, yelling and throwing stuff and chugging beers. In the rear view, I see the driver heave his considerable bulk from the seat, and after a cursory weave to get his bearings, make a beeline for me.

Gigantic nightmare

He was just huge, truly the stuff of nightmares, and as he bore down on me, I began to panic. The driver's window was open and for some reason, perhaps violent trembling on my part, it wouldn't roll up. Ham-sized fists grabbed the top of the driver's side door and this apparition stuck his whole head through the window. We were about an inch apart and his breath smelled like stale beer, tobacco and something dead.

In a flash, I recognized him! It was the Terminator! His bloodshot eyes got all narrow and as he poked me in the chest he growled, "Wal, if it ain't the Doc! I b'leve I got a *bone* to pick with *you, Mister!*"

At this point, I just wanted somebody to shoot me and get it over with, but then the Terminator extracted his head, took a step back and so help me, started to giggle!

"Hee, hee! *Skeered* ya didn't I, Doc! Truth is, haw, haw, I b'leve ah owe yuh some *money,* and you ain't even had the decency to send me a *!!##%$! bill!*"

'You OK, Doc'

Immensely pleased with himself, he pulled out the usual roll of cash, whipped off some hundred dollar bills and dropped them in my lap. He cuffed me then, playfully, on the head like a momma bear would her cub. As he lurched away, he stopped and turned. Waggling a hairy finger at me, he said, "By Gaw, Doc, *you OK!*"

Shortly, the lowrider pulled away in a kind of flurry, empty beer cans flying in every direction and all the boys giving me a vigorous thumbs up shouting, "*Hell, yes, Doc! You all right!*"

I haven't seen 'em since. Truth be known, I kinda miss 'em.

I was born and raised, happily in Council Bluffs, Iowa. I entered Iowa State University in the fall of 1975 and graduated from veterinary school there in 1982. I worked for a year in a multi-veterinarian practice in Lincoln, Neb., then opened my own practice in Council Bluffs in the summer of 1983. My wife, Diane, and I live on 57 acres in the Loess Hills, north of Council Bluffs with three dogs, lots of wildlife and a pet raccoon named Tinkerbelle. Don't ask.

July 2002

Client translation an acquired skill

I waited politely while the two young men seated next to me finished their conversation.

I wanted to join in, but I couldn't. That is because they were speaking in Lithuanian. Or at least that's what I thought at first. Within a few minutes, though, I decided that it must be Japanese. Then, a strange thing happened. I thought I heard a word of English. It was the word "up." I decided to listen more carefully. Within a few minutes, I distinctly heard the word, "down." Perhaps they *were* speaking English. That would make sense since the two men were two of my own children and I was pretty sure that neither one of them could speak a foreign language.

You see, my two sons are pilots. Whenever they get together they speak in some sort of aeronautic techno-language that no one else understands. So the rest of the family went ahead and enjoyed New Year's Day while the pilots babbled on.

I was a little disappointed with myself, though. I should have understood more of their conversation. After all, I spend most of my day translating pet owner language into plain English. This requires decoding innuendoes, deciphering euphemisms and reading between the lines. So, for the benefit of those of you who just graduated from veterinary school (or are just about to), let me give some examples.

Clara Fye called me last week to share some important facts concerning her dog's history.

"Doctor, my husband was in to see you yesterday with our dog. Do you remember?"

Of course I remembered. It took me 15 minutes to explain why the pooch needed ear surgery. It should have taken two minutes, but Mr. Fye is not the sharpest knife in the drawer. (If this guy was any more stupid, he would have to be watered twice a week.)

She continued, "Well, doctor, I don't know if my husband

mentioned it to you, but he's not really our dog. He's a stray."
Translation: "We have no intention of spending any money on this dog."
Let's look at another example. This time, the phone call was from Hugh Mustadunit, another of my clients whose IQ never quite measures up to room temperature.
(Somewhere there is a village that this guy is depriving of an idiot.)
"I think my cat must have picked up a sickness when he was at your office. He has been vomiting for three days."
I glanced at the medical record. He brought the cat in for a toenail clip three months ago. At the time, he couldn't understand why he was charged for something that he could have done at home. (It probably takes this guy an hour and a half to watch *60 Minutes*).
"Since he got sick at your hospital, don't you think that you should take care of his problem for me?"
Translation: "I have no intention of spending any money on this cat."
Just in case you haven't picked up on the trend yet, let's move on to a third example. Several times a year, I get a call from Althea Never. It usually goes something like this: "My dog is limping, has a cough and that rash is no better. Could you tell me how to treat him at home? I have a lot of experience with animals and I could administer any type of treatment that you would prescribe. (She has delusions of adequacy.) I would bring him in, but he gets too upset when he comes to your office."
Translation: "I have no intention of spending any money on this dog."
Hopefully, your translation skills are improving as we go along here. However, for those of you who need a few more examples, let's look at two more.
Client: "We would hate to put him through X-rays and tests when you can't tell us the diagnosis first. Isn't it true that sometimes tests come out normal? Besides, we don't want him to suffer."
Translation: "We have no intention of spending any money on this dog."
Client: "I am so glad that I found you. Our last vet didn't really care about animals. All he cared about was getting paid. He always wanted to know when he was going to get his money. We are bringing all of our animals here from now on."
Translation: "We are deadbeats." (I threw in a different one at the end just to confuse you.)
Hopefully, these few examples have helped improve your translation skills. Don't be discouraged if it seems confusing. It just takes practice. Most strange languages can be mastered with time and patience. In fact, some day, I may even be able to communicate with my sons in their own language.
Unfortunately, my daughter is a different story. I will never understand what she is talking about. She is in the computer business.

January 2001

Chapter 3: Doctor O's Diary

Ahoy mateys! 'Thar he blows!

After all these years in practice, you can still find me at my office 51 weeks out of the year.

My reason for this is quite simple. Someday, when I strangle one of my annoying clients, I'll be able to plead insanity.

Last week, however, was the annual exception. Following an exhaustive search, you would have found me relaxing on the beach of a little island somewhere in the Caribbean. Relaxing, that is, until I noticed something on the lounge chair next to mine. It was a pile of books. There were classic titles such as 'Chat With Your Cat' by Felicity Clueless, 'Interpreting Your Dog's Dreams' by A. Lotta Hocum and 'Be Your Own Veterinarian' by Fuller B. Lony.

Obviously the chair next to mine was soon to be occupied by someone who would have a million questions. But wait! Luck was with me. They would have no way of knowing that I am a veterinarian.

I figured that I could just play dumb (no big trick for me).

I decided to simply keep my profession a secret for the rest of the week. My relaxed attitude returned and I took a stroll down to the water's edge. That's when I saw it lying on the beach. It was too big to be a man and too small to be a whale. Curiosity caused me to approach for a closer look. Oh no! It was Dick Moby, the world's largest veterinary client! This was not the first time I had run into him while on vacation. Still, all was not lost. Hoping that I had not been spotted, I turned and strolled away. Unfortunately, I didn't get far.

"Hello! Doctor Obenski! Is that you? What a stroke of luck running into you!" (Stroke of luck for him. Just a stroke for me!) "Wait until my wife finds out you are here! She'll be thrilled!"

My hopes for a relaxing vacation began to dim. No wait! It wasn't just my hopes. The day itself was getting dim. Something was blocking the light. I didn't have to look. I new what was blocking out the sun. It was Dick's wife, Eclipse Moby. This woman throws a large shadow. In fact, she bears a striking resemblance to Mount Rushmore (The George Washington portion, in particular.)

The mountain spoke.

"It sure is a treat running into you, Doctor. I brought along some great books about animals. Maybe you'd like to borrow one."

(It was 90 degrees that day. Why would I need paper to start a fire?)

I tried to maintain a low profile for the rest of the day. My luck only lasted a few hours, though. I ran into the Mobys over by the ice cream bar. For some reason, they seemed to have decided that they should be my best friends for the rest of the week.

"Doctor, have you seen the fitness center they have here? It has all the latest equipment. Wouldn't this be a good time to start getting in shape?"

I informed them that I was on vacation to relax and that exercise resembles work.

"How about that salad bar, Doctor? It will be easy to eat healthy here."

(They were missing the point of my vacation. I was only interested in the three major food groups—fatty food, salty food and alcohol.)

"Are you going to attend the 6 a.m. aerobics classes?"

(These people were not getting the message.)

"How about joining us for a drink at the bar later?"

(Now they were talking.)

We arranged to meet for a drink later that same evening. Then, they hit me with the good news.

"We met several other couples here who love animals. We'll get them to join us. Just wait until they hear we have a vet to talk about animals with us!"

I considered slashing my wrists, but that would have annoyed my wife. Besides, I didn't want to do anything that might cause me to miss the midnight buffet.

And so, later that evening, my wife and I met with the Mobys and two other couples. The first was Mr. and Mrs. Finchnoggin. They were anxious to tell me about their dog, Whizzer. It seemed the pooch was drinking over a gallon of water a day, and was urinating uncontrollably. Mr. Finchnoggin theorized that the dog's dry food was too salty. I informed him that his theory, much like his dog, didn't hold water, and that he had better have his vet check into the matter.

The other couple, Mr. and Mrs. Loonytune, were anxious to identify themselves as "pet psychics." They explained that they could always tell what a dog or cat was thinking (It's a good thing they couldn't tell what I was thinking!)

We parted from our new group of friends vowing to keep an eye out for each other for the rest of the week (my reasons were different from theirs.)

Luckily, we didn't bump into each other much during the rest of the vacation. It was almost as if I was avoiding them.

And now, back in my office, it's already time to plan next year's vacation. After running into the Mobys two years in a row, I'm hoping for a change of luck. In fact, I plan to inquire as to when the space shuttle will begin taking vacationing passengers. I know the Mobys couldn't get on such a flight. If either of them were on board, the thing would never get off the ground.

March 2000

Howdy, Jake and Binky? Nah, more like Larry, Curly and Mo

Beauty is in the eye of the beholder, and so is paradise. The vision I saw before me represented both. There was a beautiful mountain stream running through miles of unspoiled woods. Behind me, glistening in the morning sun, was my 1993 Harley-Davidson Electra Glide. It rested and cooled by the side of a country road as I cast my fishing line into the water. A few feet below the surface, the trout were waiting in line for a chance at my hook. It would have been perfect except for one thing. I wasn't there.

The daydream quickly faded as I was jolted back to reality. Mrs. Fable was just finishing a fascinating story about her dog, Lumpy. I can't tell you what the story was about because I wasn't paying attention. You see, so many office calls begin with a clever pet story that I have started tuning them out.

People don't seem to realize what it takes to make an animal story interesting. Stories concerning the inane antics of their pet are about as interesting to me as the latest word on their kid's report card. A truly fascinating animal story needs one key element that people always seem to overlook. It has to be about one of my own pets.

Howdy is a 2-year-old Golden Retriever. Not realizing that he was supposed to stop growing at some reasonable size, he continued until he now resembles a furry walrus. Howdy is also a genius. If only he would use his intellectual powers for good and not evil, the world could be a better place.

Can't find your car keys? Don't bother to look for them. Just ask Howdy where they are. He'll find them for you. After all, he's the one who hid them in the first place. And, provided that you come across with a tasty bribe, he'll be glad to return them.

One day in March, I was treated to a demonstration of his unique ingenuity. It all started when I brought home a Frisbee for the dogs to play with. My youngest son spent an entire afternoon throwing the disc and waiting for the pooch to get tired

Where did I go wrong?

of retrieving the thing. It didn't happen. Howdy's considerable bulk rocketed after the soaring wafer about a zillion times. He had found a game even more fun than hiding car keys. Retrieving a Frisbee instantly became his favorite activity. It certainly seemed like a wholesome, fun, harmless dog activity to me. I was wrong. The next morning I found three hub caps on my front porch. So far, I have not been able to find out where he got them even though I notified every neighbor within a mile of my house.

Howdy's trickery becomes even more successful when he enlists an accomplice. Unfortunately, he has two.

Binky, a 2-year-old kitten, is Howdy's best friend. Binky thinks he's a dog. Since he was a day-old orphan, he was raised by the large, clumsy Golden. The only mommy to have licked him clean, the only furry body that he cuddled up to, the only role model that he ever had, was Howdy. His canine mentor has taught him to knock food down from high shelves and cabinets so the dog can continue to grow wider day by day.

Jake, an Appaloosa gelding, is Howdy's other buddy. Jake thinks he's a dog, too. Somehow, Howdy taught him to play tag, fetch a stick and, unfortunately, to open gates. Once the horse learned to let himself out, he took off whenever he wanted. I outsmarted him by rattling a container of sweet feed every time he escaped. That would bring him running back for the treat. He has since proceeded to outsmart me by letting himself out every time he wants a snack.

These three "partners in crime" are always hanging out together and being the ringleader of a "gang" is something Howdy really seems to enjoy. He easily taught the cat to steal car keys from the top shelf and deliver them to his big, spitty dog mouth. Furthermore he seems to enjoy playing tag with his horse friend just as much as he enjoys a game of Frisbee with people.

I just hope he doesn't teach the whole gang how to steal hub caps.

June 1997

Nowhere to run, nowhere to hide

I have a great deal of difficulty delivering bad news.

Even after 25 years in practice, I get very nervous when I have to tell people that their greatest fears are about to be realized. Nonetheless, it is one of the duties of my profession. So, one morning last week, I faced Mrs. Fobia and gave it to her straight. The news hit her like a ton of bricks.

"Oh, no! I was afraid that this might happen some day, Doctor," she said. "Do you really have to take a vacation? Isn't there some way we can avoid it?"

She ran through the usual list of questions.

"What if one of my precious babies gets sick while you're gone?"

"Is there a number where I can reach you if I have a question?"

"What will I do if I need your help?"

I looked her in the eye and gave my standard answer.

"If you have a problem while I'm gone, just handle it the same way you would if I was dead."

Unfortunately, she was not the only client to panic over my vacation. Mrs. Moonbeam was agitated because the only time she could come for an appointment was on a day right in the middle of my trip. She had never seen me before, but her numerologist told her that she had to see a vet whose name started with an O.

Mr. Button was upset because I am the only veterinarian who will handle his nasty cat, Panic. Wouldn't you know it, the cat's vaccinations were due the week I was going to be away?

It turned out that most of my pre-vacation week was spent trying to calm the mass hysteria. Clearing my schedule for a vacation seemed comparable to escaping from Alcatraz.

Come to think of it, the prison escape would only involve breaking through some impenetrable walls, subduing several armed opponents with my bare hands, and swimming a few miles through shark-infested waters. *Big deal!* It would be a small task compared to getting my clients to take 'no' for an answer.

Eventually though, perseverance paid off, and, this week, I write to you from aboard a ship somewhere in the Caribbean. The cruise started out just fine. For two days, I didn't answer one question about urine on the rug

Where did I go wrong?

or itchy ears. Furthermore, I wasn't forced to listen politely to one cute pet story. Then, yesterday, it happened. I was on the Promenade Deck when I heard it. "Yoo-hoo, Doctor Obenski! Is that you?"

I turned and saw him coming toward me. It was Dick Mobey, the world's largest veterinary client. Surprisingly, the ship, which only weighs 150 million pounds, was not tilted in his direction. I concluded his wife must have been on the other side, thereby balancing the load.

I wished for a harpoon, but, it was too late. Before I could stop him, he spilled the beans about my being a veterinarian. My troubles began immediately. A lady who was seated in a nearby lounge chair dropped her romance novel and confronted me on the spot.

"You're a veterinarian? How fascinating. Do you know Betty White?"

After that, word spread throughout the ship that there was a veterinarian on board. Everywhere I go, there are questions to be answered such as:

"How come there aren't more animal shows on television?" "Do Polar Bears catch cold?" "How much do you charge for a spay?"

And I swear, I'm not making this up, "If Kermit isn't a real frog, how do they make him talk?"

This morning, a group of excited passengers called me over to the side of the ship. It seems they had made an exciting discovery. There was a dead fish floating in the water. The same question for the vet was on everyone's lips.

"What did he die from?"

It was time to lay it on thick.

"Looks like an obvious case of pectoral non-stabilium," I said. "It's a rare disease that fishermen refer to as fin-wobble. The fish got muscle spasms in his front fins so that he could only swim up and not down. That caused his head and gills to stick up. So, he drowned in the air the way people could drown in water."

They fell for it hook, line and sinker.

It was fun fooling them, but, if I ever get another vacation, I am going to try harder to protect my anonymity. When people know I'm a veterinarian, they feel compelled to share every personal detail about their pets. Next time, I'm going to tell people that I'm with the IRS.

June 1997

Nourishment-challenged clients pose portly problems

As you may recall from last month's adventure, our hero, (that's me) was trapped on a cruise ship in the middle of the Caribbean with Dick Mobey, the world's largest veterinary client.

I had taken a vacation to get away from it all. Unfortunately, some of it came with me. But, the dark cloud of answering pet questions and listening to animal stories turned out to have a silver lining. Mr. Mobey had been on many cruises and was able to give me a few tips on taking advantage of the many on-board opportunities. He made up a schedule of the available dining times and pointed out that it was possible to eat 11 meals a day without even counting room service which was free and available around the clock.

One look at Dick and you knew that he was serious. In fact, from the first time I met him, I could tell he was a big eater. It was 1992. He had come to me for a second opinion after apparently telling his previous veterinarian several things, including where he could go, what other species might share his family tree, and in which anatomic orifice he could store his medical records.

You see, my predecessor had the nerve to tell Mr. Mobey that his dog, Portly, was too fat. I couldn't disagree. You don't see a lot of 70-pound Beagles. Still, the situation called for tact. This man had barely squeezed through the doorway and he literally filled the exam room all by himself. I knew that if I made him hopping mad, my clinic could suffer structural damage.

Honesty would clearly not be the best policy. I decided to fall back upon my favorite and most fool-proof client handling technique.

Simply stated, the procedure is: You can catch more flies with honey than you can with vinegar, but you can catch the most flies with a shovel full of manure. I laid it on thick.

We set up a plan to alter Portly's lifestyle and diet for a variety of reasons. The word "fat" was never mentioned.

You see, when it comes to the weight of their pets, our clients can be very sensitive. You cannot tell a fat person that their dog is too fat, nor can you tell a thin person that their dog is too thin. Take, for example, Ann O'Rexic. She is convinced her cat, Spindle, is too fat. Ann is about 5'9" and weighs, I would guess, about 90 pounds. She always wears high-heeled shoes and has her hair done up in a bun. She looks like a pencil. Spindle is perfectly normal.

"What are we going to do, Doctor," she laments. "Spindle is getting so porky. Isn't he going to be prone to heart problems or diabetes or something if we don't keep his weight down? He just keeps getting heavier and heavier."

I glanced at the record. The cat hadn't gained an ounce in four years. I tried to explain to her that the world is comprised of a mixture of Kramdens and Nortons. Furthermore, I told her that Spindle already leans toward Nortonism and is not in need of change. She was too young to understand my example. So, I helped her establish a diet plan for improved health. The phrase "weight loss" was never mentioned, at least, not by me.

As for myself, even though no one would categorize me as the athletic type, I can rise to a physical challenge when I have to. So, armed with Dick's schedule of available dining times, I started at 6 a.m. one day and faced the 11 meal challenge. It was a piece of cake! (No pun intended).

Not only was I able to enjoy 11 meals that day, but I found that seven meals a day provided a nice, comfortable full feeling for the next three days in a row.

I can hardly wait to book my next cruise. For pure relaxation there seems to be nothing like it. There was one drawback, though. Apparently something in that fresh ocean breeze and tropical climate caused all the clothing I had brought along to shrink (... and I still haven't figured out why the clothes I left at home shrunk, too...)

April 1997

Drugs on rugs? $2,000 for a ticket to a football game? Who's dumber?

I could hardly believe what I was seeing.

Looking very much like the lynch mob in an old Western movie, there was a crowd of people headed straight for me.

The expression on each and every one of their faces gave the impression that they were friendly, but desperate. Apparently, I was the object of their pursuit.

A somewhat large gentleman got to me first. The others followed in a trail behind him that stretched half-way across the airport.

"I need your ticket," he announced. "I'll give you $800 for it right now."

A woman behind him was shouting, "Nine hundred, $900!"

Never have I felt so wanted. For a moment, I almost considered taking one of their offers. After all, I had only paid $175 for my ticket in the first place. But then, my trip would have had no purpose.

You see, I was arriving in town for the Super Bowl. And, what these people wanted was my ticket to the game.

Traditionally, the Super Bowl gets almost as much publicity as the O.J. Simpson trial. There are pre-game shows about the players, the players' wives, the weather, the blimp and even the grass on the field. There is a much-touted halftime show, and there are Super Bowl parties all over America. All of this surrounds what always turns out to be a dull and disappointing football game. It was this dull game that my wife and I had come to town to see.

Everywhere we went, we were accosted by a similar mob of ticket seekers. As game day approached, ticket offers neared $2,000! In the hotel lobby or at the shopping mall, total strangers would strike up conversations. Sometimes they would work their way up to the big questions with small talk such as:

"Hi! Are you in town for the

game? Where are you from? What line of work are you in there?"

Eventually, though, they all got to the point.

"Wanna sell your ticket?"

However, the fascinating part of these conversations always came before the ticket offer. It would happen when the person found out that I was a veterinarian. Comments would follow such as:

"Oh, you're a veterinarian. You're lucky. You don't have to deal with people." Or, "I always thought that would be a fascinating line of work for me. Do you have to go to school to do that?"

I actually had one guy say, "Wow, you're a veterinarian. How did you ever learn to give up eating meat?"

Some people had technical questions for me.

For example, one lady who was anxious to draw on my professional expertise said, "I'm glad I ran into you today. If you are an animal doctor, perhaps you could settle an argument for me. What kind of frogs do they use when they make pickled frog's legs?"

However, the all-time knucklehead award goes to a lady from New Jersey who had an important question about Rogaine®.

"Well, doctor, perhaps you could explain something to me," she said. "You know that stuff they sell to rub on your head to get the hair growing? Well, my dog keeps making digging motions on the living room rug, like he's trying to bury a bone or something. Now the rug has a bare spot. Do you think that stuff would help? Will it work on rugs?"

I didn't know what to say. It may well have been the dumbest question I had every heard!

"Give it a try," I said. "As far as I know, it couldn't hurt."

Later, on the flight home, I met some people who took as much as $2,000 for their ticket and then watched the game from their hotel room. I wondered who was dumber, someone who expects a drug to work on a rug or someone who offers to pay $2,000 to see a football game.

I decided that the dumbest were people like me, who got offered $2,000 and didn't take it.

February 1997

Old dogs can teach new tricks

When I first met him, Dr. Oldog had been in practice for more than 40 years. He had seen it all. He had done it all.

I was a third-year veterinary student. So, naturally, I knew it all.

Along with a colleague, Dr. Newtrix, I lived in Dr. Oldog's hospital. In exchange for room and board, we helped out at night and on weekends.

It was 1970. In those days, syringes were made of glass, pills were allowed to have more than one ingredient, and veterinary clients were, well, come to think, of it, they were the same wacky bunch that they are today.

The practice was called The Ardmore Animal Hospital, and had been in the same building since the 1930s. It was a magnificent facility and the equipment was state of the art. We had an X-ray machine that Dr. Oldog never used, an inhalation anesthesia machine which was stored in the basement and an in-house laboratory where we kept the lawn mower during the winter months.

Dr. Newtrix, who was also a third-year student, was as appalled as I was at some of the things we saw Dr. Oldog do. My God! He would perform surgery without a cap and gown or even gloves for that matter. We knew from vet school that you couldn't spay a cat without dressing up until you resembled an astronaut. And so, we waited and waited for the inevitable postoperative infections that would follow these surgeries. For some reason, they never came.

The man would use medicine that had been outdated for days or even weeks.

Dr. Oldog would often make a diagnosis right in the office; just on the basis of a physical exam and the history, he would treat a case without taking blood, sending it to the lab and making the same diagnosis three days later. We waited and waited for these cases to blow up in his face. For some reason, they never did.

The man would use medicine that had been outdated for days or even weeks. This seemed like a dangerous practice to us. After all, who knows what sinister

Where did I go wrong?

chemical reactions begin to occur on the day the label tells them to start. We waited and waited for a horrible reaction to occur from one of these danger doses. For some reason, it never happened.

Sometimes, the old fool would even tackle an orthopedic case by splinting or pinning a leg that clearly would have been handled better by an orthopedic surgeon over at the university. We waited and waited for one of his cases to fail to heal properly. For some reason, they always did well.

And so, I learned a great many things during my years there. Not the least of which was that Dr. Oldog didn't need me at all. I was just one of a long line of veterinary students who lived in that hospital over the many decades of its operation and benefited from the charitable nature of a kindly veterinarian from a previous era. I foolishly thought that he stood in the way of progress when, in actuality, he was unselfishly lending a helping hand to the next generation.

I've often thought about going back to visit the hospital where I learned so much 25 years ago. Even though Dr. Oldog has passed away, a walk through the old building would bring back a flood of memories. For some reason, though, I have never gotten around to it. Then, last month, opportunity knocked. My daughter moved to Ardmore, Pa. I found myself within a mile of my professional birthplace.

We all piled into my truck and headed over to visit the place where "daddy" lived while he was in veterinary school.

It was gone.

The site is now occupied by a new building. The place which allowed me to come of age in my beloved profession is now a place where kids can earn minimum wage flipping hamburgers.

Well, that's progress.

January 1997

First interactive column has Dr. O looking for the blue cup

I'd like to take you back to when I was 8-years-old, even if I have to drag you kicking and screaming.

Our family car was a snazzy Studabaker, my favorite T.V. show was the Honeymooners and my most prized possession was a phonograph record entitled, "Bozo Under the Sea." This little 78 rpm beauty told a story about Bozo the Clown, (often thought to be the common ancestory of most veterinary clients), and was accompanied by a book of illustrations that allowed you to look at the pictures as you listened to the story.

Now, pay attention, here comes the interesting part. As I accompanied Bozo on his deep sea diving adventure, the record made an occasional "beep" sound so that I would know when to turn the page.

What an idea! The Bozo people had created an interactive children's record. This seems like an idea worth stealing.

So, let's return to the present where, unless you come to your senses immediately, you are about to read my first interactive magazine column. Here's how it works. Every time you come to the symbol (**), insert the phrase, "Into the blue cup."

And now, on with our story entitled, "Bozo Finds the Equipment."

In my office, the oldest piece of equipment (other than myself) is the blue plastic cup which sits on the shelf next to the treatment room sink. It has been with me since 1976, at which time it cost 15 cents. (That's $19.95 by today's standards). Other pieces of equipment wear out, employees come and go, but the blue cup is always there.

Furthermore, if one follows a simple "rinse it out and use it again" philosophy, the life span of the blue cup should be infinite.

Over the span of 20 years, countless free catch urine samples have gone (**). Numerous disgusting necropsy specimens have been dropped (**). Almost daily, abcesses have been drained (**).

Many times, when needed to measure detergent, bleach, disinfectant or even cat litter, it would go (**).

Dead mouse in the basement?

No problem, Drop it (**) and take it to the dumpster.

Then there was the time Mr. Blowhard came in with his cat, Mr. Puffy, and the blue cup was able to provide me with a good laugh. There was quite an abcess on the cat's side and it was really ripe.

Every time you come to the symbol (**), insert the phrase, "Into the blue cup."

"You know, Doc, I go huntin' and fishin' all the time. I ain't afraid of a little mess," Mr. B announced. "Go ahead and drain that infection. It won't bother me." We knew, of course, that such big talk is often followed by the client fainting a moment later. So, as always, we shielded our work from the owner's eyes by standing in his line of sight. It didn't work. Two minutes later, he hit the floor like a 200-pound sack of manure. What was his mistake? He looked (**).

So, taking all of the above into consideration, you can understand why I was upset last week when I noticed that this valued plastic friend was missing. I had gone to the treatment room for a drink of water when I happened to glance at the shelf and take notice of its absence. Naturally, all less important hospital functions would have to stop until this valuable chalice was returned.

I called for all available staff members to assist in an immediate search of the building. The search didn't take long. One of them spotted it instantly. Unfortunately, when they pointed it out, I was not as pleased at its recovery as I thought I'd be. It had been in an obvious location all the time. In fact, it was literally right under my nose. Oh, my gosh! Could it be? I had absentmindedly been using it to get my drink of water. I was so disgusted I almost vomited (**).

Novmeber 1996

Reckless ways catch up with Dr. O

My mother never reads this magazine. As a result, I am about to let you in on a secret that has been bottled up inside me for more than 40 years.

I didn't wash the apple.

That's right! Many times throughout the 1950s my Mom would ask something like, "Mike, did you wash that apple before you started eating it?"

Invariably, my answer was, "Sure, Mom."

The truth be known, I don't think I ever washed a piece of fruit in my life. Furthermore, I believe that the dangers associated with unwashed fruit have been greatly exaggerated. Never once have I seen a newspaper article about someone committing suicide by gulping down an unbathed apple. Nor have I heard of a despondent postal worker showing up at the post office and wiping out six co-workers with a fruit basket of unscrubbed goodies.

I believe it is facts such as these that led me to pursue a life of recklessness.

By the time I was 10 years old, having defied death through many apple incidents, I took the next logical step. It was during the summer of 1957, on a day that I'll never forget. My family was on a picnic at the county park when I decided to take the ultimate risk. I went swimming only 50 minutes after having a hot dog. Contrary to what I had been taught all my life, I didn't get cramps and drown. This incident served to encourage my reckless ways.

As I reached my 20s, the risks got larger.

One time, I removed the tag from a new mattress; you know, the one that says, "Do not remove, under penalty of law." For about a month after that, I slept with one eye open. But the Tag Police never showed up.

A decade later, we got our first microwave oven. Naturally, I had to try putting a piece of metal in it. Once again, I lived to tell the story.

Unfortunately, having tempted fate so many times, I may have become overconfident. Because last week, I went too far and found myself standing toe-to-toe with The Grim Reaper.

It all began when I saw a familiar little red car pull into our parking lot. The thing had a list to the left like a cat with an ear infection. With a groan, the driver, Lotta Tonnage, stepped from the car. With a similar groan, the little vehicle straightened up.

She lifted what looked like a heavy bag of laundry from the back seat. I recognized it immediately as her dog, Mega, the 70-pound Beagle. All I had to do was treat a little rash and send the portly pooch home. There was no reason to place myself in danger, but I couldn't help it. With reckless disregard for my own safety, I said what needed saying:

"Mrs. Tonnage, Mega is way too fat."

Mount Lotta erupted. She screamed about my insensitivity toward weight-challenged individuals. She stomped up and down the hallway while the rafters of my little hospital trembled. My life flashed before my eyes when she charged straight at me like a locomotive about to hit a squirrel. Moments before impact, however, she stopped, scooped up her "little" dog and piloted her considerable girth toward the front door. About an hour later, my heart rate dropped to normal. The entire incident reminded me of a similar stupid mistake that I made several years ago.

Ann O'Rexic was in to see me with Slimba the Afghan Hound. She was slim, somewhat attractive, and had long blond hair—a description that applied equally to both her and the dog. She looked somewhat familiar. I knew that she had been in before. Furthermore, she seemed to be a pleasant lady.

Unfortunately, I didn't realize that she was just bringing Slimba in for her parents. Nor did I remember that her dog, Pugsly, was a Bulldog. So I really stepped in it when I took a chance that she wouldn't be insulted and mentioned that she and her dog looked a lot alike.

She gave me a look that I'm sure snakes give just before striking. Then, in a flash, she was out the door never to return.

Have I learned my lesson? I guess so. I'll be more careful about what I say to people in the office; however, I'm still not washing fruit. That is, if you'll promise me one thing. Don't tell my Mom.

May 1996

Watch out for abductions when looking for that 'extraterrestrial' vehicle

I was born at a very early age. Perhaps that's why I don't remember many details about my first few years here on planet Earth.

In the many decades since then, however, I've noticed that most things don't seem to follow any pattern of logic. Therefore, I am suspicious—suspicious that this is not really my home planet.

Perhaps I actually come from a place where more things make sense than they do here.

Just when I think I've got these wacky earthlings figured out, some new and unexplainable occurrence will send my alien brain back to square one. That's what happened last week when, after half a century here on the third rock from the sun, I drove my 10-year-old Jeep into a parking space and happened to look into the window of a Ford truck that was parked next to me.

Oh, sure, it looked like an ordinary truck on the outside, but what I saw through the window sent my mind reeling. It was the price sticker, and it said, $32,587.

I took a few minutes to catch my breath. As I did so, a salesman, Hugh Deservit, came running over.

"She's quite a beauty isn't she, sir," he said. "Want to take her for a spin?"

I couldn't answer at first. I was too busy concentrating on what I had just seen. The way I saw it, there were several possibilities. Perhaps it was a misprint. Or, maybe it was a practical joke of some sort. Least logical of all would be that they expected someone to fork over an arm and a leg just to be the proud owner of a truck that gets 12 miles to the gallon. If that were the case, it certainly wasn't going to be me, I'll tell you that. After all, I paid less than half of that for my Jeep.

(Before you die from suspense, let me reveal that the third possibility did, in fact, turn out to be true.)

Where did I go wrong?

At Hugh's insistence, I settled down in the heated, leather, six-way power, electric lumbar support, driver's seat. The cockpit had more controls than the starship Enterprise.

An on-board computer monitored all the vehicle operating systems.

I asked if the computer could do my income taxes.

Hugh wasn't sure. He added that he would have to look it up in the owner's manual.

The audio system (formerly known as the radio) had eight speakers. (That is seven more than necessary.) Hugh proudly pointed out that it played both CDs and cassettes. This didn't do me any good. I haven't purchased my first CD yet, and Hugh didn't seem to think I could get a new truck with an 8-track tape player.

(For those of you who are too young to remember disco, let me stop here and explain that an 8-track was a type of audio tape. It was a lot like Colin Powell, very popular but not for very long.)

We took it out for a spin.

"She has great pick-up," Hugh said. "Give it some gas and feel that acceleration."

He was right. This truck really took off.

I pushed my foot to the floor. The tachometer shot up. The speedometer shot up. The price of Exxon stock shot up.

As I watched the gas gauge plummet, I recalled something I have heard Arnie say many times. "If you can afford a Cadillac, you can't complain about the price of gas."

I guess the same rule could apply to this truck.

"Don't worry about gas mileage," Hugh said. "This baby has a 44-gallon tank." Then he got down to business. "All the trucks on our lot have similar features to this one. Let's go back and pick out a color you like."

As we pulled back into the dealership, I looked down the line of trucks. I have to admit, they were an impressive bunch. Still, it was no contest. There was one that looked nicer to me than all the others.

It was my old Jeep.

January 1996

Chapter 4:
Dumb

'Dim Bulb' competition heats up

Every now and then, one of my clients comes up with a good idea. (Believe me, it doesn't happen often.)

I was reminded of this recently, when a colleague from Michigan wrote to tell me about Mr. Feeblethought and his cat, Seesaw. It seems that, during an office call, the cat kept jumping off the exam table and hiding under the chair in the corner of the room (imagine that!) Instead of holding onto his cat, the man seemed to be daydreaming. He was lost in thought. Just as the doctor was about to hold a mirror under his nose to see if he was still among the living, the man came up with a brainstorm, one that could change the way in which we all run our practices.

"I have an idea, Doc," he said. "Why don't you mount a chair on top of the exam table? The cats would stay up there without being held." (Now, why didn't I think of that?)

My colleague from Michigan assured me that the man was deadpan serious. It is, of course, not unusual for our clients to share practice tips designed to make our hospitals run more efficiently. It goes without saying, though, that their train of thought is usually derailed.

In my practice, I can always tell when a client is about to share an idea. I can actually see the imaginary light bulb appear over their head, just like in a cartoon. The bulb is almost always burned out. This is because of the inevitable short circuit which is so prevalent in pet-owner thinking.

For these reasons, my staff and I occasionally honor a client with the Dim Bulb Award. Presented *in absentia*, of course, it honors those whose ideas are truly ludicrous.

Mr. Warbler represents a recent example. His cat, Dracula, is one of our worst patients. Just touching the beast requires half my staff, two pairs of gloves and a restraint pole. Naturally, Mr. Warbler doesn't believe in declawing, but comes in every three weeks for a toenail trim. Each visit leaves the exam room redecorated with materials that fly from every bodily orifice (of the cat).

Last month, things were going to be different. Why? Because Mr. Warbler had an idea.

"Doctor," he said, "My wife and I put our wits together and came up with a plan." (For those of you keeping score, that would make one whole wit between the two of them.) "Dracula loves to listen to bird calls. Don't scare him with those people of yours with the gloves. Just trim his nails while I distract him with his favorite, the call of the loon." (I was hearing the call of the loon already.)

Being somewhat fond of all 10 fingers, (we've grown attached over the years), I decided to stick with our old system. He went home disappointed with my reluctance to try new ideas. Little did he know that he was a shoe-in for the coveted Dim Bulb Award. He didn't get it, though. He was edged out by a last-minute entry. It was Iva Hunch with her dog, Glutton.

"Hello, doctor," she said when she called. "You don't know me. I moved here recently from New York. My dog isn't feeling well. I called a vet closer to my house, Dr. Juan Armup, but he wouldn't see us. He said it was a large animal practice. I told him that Glutton is a large dog, but that didn't seem to make any difference. I'm never going to him again." (Again? I knew I had a winner on the phone.)

She wanted to know if she should rush right in because Glutton had been licking on a spot near his elbow for the last two-and-a-half years. Two hours later, she was in my office. As soon as I met her, it was obvious she was not the sharpest knife in the drawer.

The dog had a simple infection that would require a few pills. I explained the diagnosis and treatment while she seemed to be listening (a foolish assumption on my part).

"I'm sorry, doctor," she said. "Could you repeat that? I wasn't listening. My mind was elsewhere." (Good luck finding it).

It was during explanation number two that the burned out bulb appeared above her head.

"You know, I have never been able to give Glutton a pill," she said. "Do you think they can be mixed with milk? I would crush the pill, mix it with the milk and give it to him that way. Would that be OK?"

I told her that the plan could work if I chose an antibiotic that didn't taste bad and that would not be harmed by mixing with milk.

"You'll have to come up with a better plan than that," she said. "Glutton won't take it. He hates milk."

Naturally, she won the award for last month. I called my friend, Arnie, to tell him about the light bulbs, the awards and the winners.

"You're making this whole thing up," was his accusation. "It seems to me that all of this stuff is just a filament of your imagination."

December 1999

Telephone a mixed blessing

I've said it before and I'll say it again. He was the greatest practical joker that ever lived. With just a few pieces of wire and a homemade battery, he has managed to cause more confusion than even the most sophisticated of computer viruses. I am referring, of course, to that madcap funster, Alexander Graham Bell.

His inspiration came in the early 1870s. America was healing from the Civil War. The Indian Wars were raging in the west, and Alex Bell's dog, Watson, was 12 years old. (That's right. In spite of what you may have heard to the contrary, Watson was the Bell family pooch.)

Watson's veterinarian, Dr. Chortle, was a close friend of Alex's. Between the two of them, they came up with some of the world's most classic gags. It is a little-known fact that Dr. Chortle invented the whoopee cushion and the dribble glass. Not to be outdone, Alex designed the first handshake buzzer and the original prototype for an ice cube with a fly in it.

Both men enjoyed the joke invention rivalry, which they shared until the day Dr. Chortle unveiled his masterpiece, fake dog poop. Alex was overcome with jealousy. Their friendly relationship turned sour. In order to get even with his former friend, as well as all the rest of the world's veterinarians, Alex invented the telephone. Never again would a veterinarian have an uninterrupted day to sit around inventing jokes. The telephone would see to that.

Now, over a century later, his plan is still working beautifully. Just yesterday, he got me three times. The first was when Mrs. Muffle called about her Dachshund, Hunch. I couldn't understand a word she said. Her voice was so soft that it was barely more than a whisper. Luckily, our office telephone has a volume control so I was able to turn her up.

"Hello, Doctor, she said. "This is Mrs. Muffle. Can you hear me OK? I have to whisper so Hunch doesn't hear me. If he knows I'm calling the vet, he'll pee on the rug."

She had a long list of questions, which consumed 12 minutes that I really couldn't spare. Humoring her, I suggested that she call from a pay phone next time. That would ensure security from an eavesdropping pup.

My next call was from Mr. Decibel. If he was a factory, he would be cited for noise pollution. His voice is louder than a rock concert. He probably doesn't need a phone for conversations of less than two miles distance, but he uses one anyway. I put the phone to my ear without realizing that the volume was still turned up from Mrs. Muffle's call. I was knocked senseless. My hearing took two hours to return fully. Alex Bell undoubtedly chuckled in his grave.

After recuperating, I was given a message to call Mr. Macho about his dog, Pansy. But when I called the Macho home number, I was surprised to hear a man answer, "Kelly's Bar. May I help you?" I explained that I wanted the Macho house and must have dialed the wrong number.

"Oh, no, you got the right place," he said. "Macho spends a lot of time here so he used the call forwarding on his home phone to get his calls transferred to us. I'll get him for you."

A moment later, I heard the same voice yell, "Hey, Macho! You got a dog named Pansy? Your vet's on the phone."

I could hear the bar patrons burst into laughter. Comments such as, "Pansy? What's the matter, Macho, was the name Buttercup already taken?" and "What happened, did the dog wee wee on one of your lace doilies?"

When he got to the phone, his voice was a little louder than necessary.

"Thanks for calling, Doctor. We've been concerned about Panther, you know, our Pit Bull. He's been getting very aggressive lately."

I knew that the call was supposed to be about Pansy, the puffy Poodle.

Apparently, Mr. Macho was trying to save face with his friends by pretending to own Panther, the pugnacious Pit Bull. I played along. It was fun, but it wasted more time and therefore, Alex got me again.

Because of instances such as these, I have always viewed the telephone as a mixed blessing. It is a necessary evil and, as I have said, the greatest practical joke of all time. There is no use complaining, however, because I suppose it is here to stay. By the way, this column is rated **PG**. If I gave you my opinion of people who put me on hold while they answer their call waiting I would have to rate it an **R**.

September 2001

'Blue pill' cures variety of ills

Mr. Change shuffled into the clinic and deposited his carcass in the nearest chair. His movements were like those of a person, still half asleep, groping their way to the bathroom in the middle of the night.

In the past, each time he drove his wife to the clinic with one of their dogs or cats, he would flop into a chair and appear to sleep sitting up. This visit was no different. There was one time when he made it all the way to the exam room before shifting into neutral, but usually he just got as far as the closest chair to the door.

In the 16 years that the Changes had been clients, no one on the hospital staff had ever seen him make anything that could be described as a fast move. The receptionists would joke that someone ought to hold a mirror under the man's nose to see if he was still alive.

His wife, Wanda Change, usually arrived five minutes ahead of her husband. She accomplished this by sprinting from the car to the clinic door while her husband meandered at a snail's pace. She tended to move quickly, speak quickly and always be full of energy. In short, she was the opposite of her husband.

On this particular occasion, Strudel, the Dachshund, was very ill. One glance at the dog and Dr. Goodvet could tell from the difficulty breathing and the fluid retention that serious heart disease was present. Through his stethoscope, he heard strange sounds which he recognized immediately. They were the same sounds his 1954 Nash was making just before it died on the highway. In both cases, the diagnosis amounted to "bad valves." The Nash had been towed away and disposed of. Strudel would be luckier. He would get a miracle treatment known as the "blue pill."

What was in the blue pill? The answer is simple: "heart medicine." You see, it was 1964 and the Food and Drug Administration either didn't know or didn't care how many medications you crammed into one pill. And so, Strudel would be taking a variety of drugs, hormones, vitamins and what-have-you, all wrapped up in a neat blue sphere.

I feel compelled to tell you the story of the blue pill because I have been under fire lately. Several colleagues have said that I am making up the stories I report to you. They say the veterinary office incidents that I describe are too outlandish to have actually happened.

And so, I have something to say to those of you who don't believe that these incidents occurred exactly as I have reported them:

"Congratulations on your recent graduation from veterinary school!"

And now, whether you choose to believe it or not, I will subject you to the saga of the blue pills as told to me by Dr. Goodvet himself.

It seems that he no longer remembers exactly what was in those pills, but they seemed to help some heart conditions a great deal. In the case of Strudel, that was surprising because the dog seemed to be at death's door when treatment was begun. Nonetheless, Wanda Change kept coming back for refills of the prescription for almost a year. Each time, she reported favorable results.

On more than one occasion, it was suggested that the dog be re-examined, but Mrs. Change never got around to scheduling the appointment. Eventually, when she was told that there could be no more refills without an examination, she was forced to confess. "To tell you the truth, Doctor, Strudel died a few weeks after he started the pills. I wasn't surprised. I know he was very sick. But you know what? He developed a funny habit while he was on those pills. That silly old dog kept grabbing people's legs and even tried to hug the cat, if you know what I mean. I've been dissolving a blue pill in my husband's coffee every day since then."

November 2001

It's déjà moo all over again

Mr. Bullfeather was beside himself with concern over his cat, Raisin.

"Poor old Raisin is mighty sick this time, Doc," he said. "It's been going on for a couple of weeks now. I tried these pills, but they didn't do a bit of good."

He handed me the vial. The label was from my hospital, but it was handwritten. That meant it was dispensed before we computerized. Those pills were more than six years old. Wait a minute! The label had our old address. They were more than 22 years old! The writing was faded. I had no idea what the pills were.

"You know how I feel about my animals, Doc," he continued. "I treat them as if they were my children. Is there anything we can do for poor old Raisin?"

The cat was at death's door. He was dehydrated, hypothermic and barely conscious. I recommended a course of tests and treatment. His next words were no surprise: "I'm not one who believes in spending a lot of money on animals. Can't you just give me some better pills or something?"

It was all I could do to convince him to let me try some conservative treatment. He would not allow tests, but we would see if fluids, warmth, vitamins and other nursing care would bring the poor feline around within a day or two. He would authorize no more than $100.

Early the next morning, he was on the phone with some important questions. "Isn't there anything that can be done in a case like this? If there is any treatment, I'd sure like to know about it. Mind you, I'm not saying that I'd go for it, but I'd still like to know."

Of course, he continued to refuse any proper testing, but was sure to mention that he treats his animals as if they were his children.

A few hours later, a call came in from the daughter of the owner's aunt's boyfriend. "Hello, doctor?" she began. "This is Annie Helminth. I used to work for a veterinarian, so I know a lot about animals. I'm surprised that you can't figure out what's wrong with Mr. Bullfeather's cat. I was thinking that it might be worms. Did you think of that? You know there is a test called fecal sample that you could check."

(Wow! I'll have to write that down.)

"I sure hope you can help him," she continued. "You know, his pets are very important to him. He treats them as if they were his children."

By the second day, there was little or no improvement in Raisin's condition, and Mr. B decided to take him home. It seemed much more logical to let the cat spend his last hours at home rather than put him through the expense of euthanasia. But there were a few last-minute questions.

"Did you ever figure out exactly what is wrong with him, Doc?

I explained that dehydration was the main symptom, but that only led to more questions.

"What causes dehydration?"

My best guess was kidney failure, but he was quick to set me straight. "It can't be that, Doc. No matter how sick he was, he kept on peeing, even when he stopped drinking water."

At any rate, he promised me that if Raisin started to suffer, he would bring him back for euthanasia.

"I only want the best for Raisin, Doc," he gulped. "You know how I feel about my animals. I treat them as if they were my own children."

It was a case of déjà moo; I had heard that bull before.

July 2006

Secret second opinions sought in Mr. Nomad's clandestine city tour

I found Mrs. Clueless anxiously awaiting my return to the exam room as I entered with the bad news.

It seemed that her cat, Boulder, had a large bladder stone and would require surgery to have it removed.

"You know, doctor," she said. "I have a medical background and some knowledge of radiography. Would you mind showing me the X-ray?"

I placed Boulder's film on the viewer and waited a minute while she studied the image. Her next words were exactly what I had expected.

"What am I looking at, doctor?"

I gave her a quick tour of the X-ray, going out of my way to name most of the important structures and points of reference.

"Thank you, doctor," she said. "You know, I have a working knowledge of anatomy. So, I understand perfectly what you are showing me. Are those the stones?"

With her finger, she was pointing to the lumbar vertebrae.

"No, that's the back bone." I said, and traced for her the outline of the calculus in the urinary bladder.

She felt that the stone looked pretty small and questioned whether a little thing like that could actually be making the cat sick. (It was likely the largest stone I had ever seen in a cat. In fact, during surgery I would have to remember to be careful not to drop it on my foot.)

Between a rock and a hard place

Well, I gave my recommendations. Boulder would definitely need bladder surgery, followed by analysis of the stone to determine what

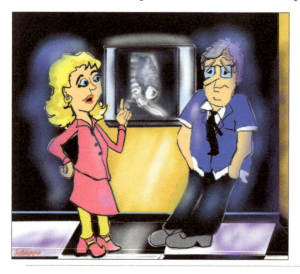

had caused it to form in the first place.

"You know, doctor," she said. "I know a little about physiognomy, and I already know what caused the stone. So there won't be any reason to have it analyzed. You see, I've been using that clumping cat litter, and I'll bet he got some inside and it clumped into that stone in his bladder. Don't you think we should try giving him an enema to get it out of there?" (Wrong again.)

I explained the surgical procedure. Due to her "working knowledge" of surgery, she claimed to understand me perfectly. The truth is, however, that the cat probably understood better than his owner did. Surgery was scheduled for the next day.

Mrs. Clueless was my last appointment that day. So, as she was leaving the office, my thoughts turned to visions of my dinner waiting at home. Unfortunately, there was a hitch in the gitalong.

The great horse jumper

It seems that Mr. Nomad was rushing over with his dog, Pencil.

The pooch had not eaten in three weeks, and now it was an "emergency." We would have to squeeze him in before we left.

The dog looked terrible. He was literally skin and bones. In fact, he bore an uncanny resemblance to a bag of wrenches. The only facts that Mr. Nomad could give me were that Pencil had not eaten in three weeks and was getting terribly weak and thin. There was no other history.

I recommended some blood tests that would be necessary combined with fluid therapy and nourishment to keep the pooch going while we figured out how to make him well.

"They already did that at the last vet," he said. "Why don't you call them and get the test results?"

(You guessed it. This was one of those secret second opinion cases. I hate those.)

His explanation continued, "My regular vet wasn't available two weeks ago when this started, so I took him to a place near my house. They ran tests, but it didn't help. Then, the next week, my regular vet did the same thing. I don't see any reason to run the same tests again."

(Now it was a third opinion case. Mr. Nomad was jumping from horse to horse in the middle of the stream.)

I devised a plan. Since this guy was always looking for new opinions, I would stabilize the dog and send him to see some specialists. I was half tempted though to send him to a real expert, Mrs. Clueless.

June 2006

Where did I go wrong?

Bad things come in threes

These pet owners seemed to suffer from 'the exact same thing'

Mr. and Mrs. Lunkhead showed up at my office one day last month. It was their first visit. It didn't take me long to hope it would also be their last. Their cat, Goner, looked about half dead.

"He's been like this for about a week, Doc," Mr. Lunkhead said. "He just lays there and doesn't move. How do you think this happened?"

I explained that Goner was near death. His vital signs were so bad that it might be impossible to get him healthy enough to even make a definitive diagnosis. That caused Mr. Lunkhead to share some important observations that he had made.

"You know, Doctor, our dog died from the exact same thing. He sat motionless for about a week before he died too. What do you think it is?"

(It sounded like two similar cases of owner neglect to me.)

I asked if the dog or the cat had shown any symptoms.

"No, they both just lost weight for a few months, stopped eating and eventually died." He added, "I sure hope you can get to the bottom of this. Haven't you ever seen anything like this before?"

When I told him that I had, I knew what his next questions would be.

"What was it Doc? Whatever you saw before was probably the same thing that killed my dog. I sure hope you can save Goner. He has the exact same thing." (His logic seemed quite reasonable. No, wait! That was his opinion.)

Of course, when we discussed what it might take to save the cat, the Lunkheads decided that they didn't want to put their "best friend" through all that trouble and expense. (They were real humanitarians.)

But in the end, it turned out that they were right. Goner and their dog did share the exact same medical condition. In fact, they shared several. Both had kicked the bucket, bit the dust and bought the farm.

Following euthanasia, they vowed never to get another pet, saying that "It is too bad when you lose them." I wanted to thank them on behalf of the entire animal kingdom.

Of course, they wanted to know if Goner's body could be donated to a university for research to help treat other animals who get the exact same thing. I told them that I didn't think so.

Just as they left, a call came in from Mrs. Ditto.

"I have good news doctor," she said. "I figured out what's wrong with Sniffy. My neighbor's cat had the exact same thing. (Here we go again.) He was drinking a lot of water and losing weight. It turned out that he had diabetes. Doesn't that sound like what Sniffy has?

I didn't see any similarity at all. Her cat had a sinus condition secondary to being hit by a car three years ago. There were no other symptoms. I was forced to tell her that her theory, much like the neighbor's cat, did not hold water.

Knowing that bad things seem to come in threes, I half expected it when Abe Toose walked in the door minutes later. He wanted to let me know that those prescription foods that we sell are a rip off. He found the exact same thing at the supermarket for a lot less money. "I read the ingredients on the back of the can, and the supermarket foods have a lot of the same ingredients as that expensive stuff you sell," he said.

I never argue. I simply explained that there were important differences. Unbelievably, he saw things my way and vowed to keep his cat on the proper food. His decision made me feel good. I felt secure in the knowledge that, by doing so, he would avoid experiencing the exact same thing as the Lunkheads.

March 2006

A toast to Chablis

Even in death, the Nutsabouts' bond might be a little too tight

One day last month, I was cruising along a winding, two-lane country road when I noticed a man jogging up the street in the opposite direction. A moment later, I saw a lady walking briskly along a crossroad. She was wearing earphones and apparently listening to her favorite music as she waddled her way to fitness. Within the next few minutes, I counted six more people running, walking or exercising outdoors. This adds up to a strange set of circumstances for a wintry Sunday afternoon in eastern Pennsylvania. I wasn't surprised though. You see, it was Jan. 1, New Year's Day, and all those people had undoubtedly resolved to slim down and get fit during 2006.

After a brisk workout, they probably planned a healthy dinner on the order of yogurt and a salad. I knew that within a week, 90 percent of them would be back to sleeping late, drinking beer and dining on stuffed pig's stomach. It happens every year.

(Cultural note: Here in Pennsylvania Dutch country, stuffed pig's stomach is a popular delicacy. In answer to the obvious question: No, I have never tried it.)

At any rate, I was on my way to the office to see an emergency. It was Mr. And Mrs. Nutsabout and their cat, Chablis. They weren't able to give me any details over the phone other than that it was a "dire emergency" that required immediate attention.

Upon arrival, the diagnosis was easy. The cat had been dead for some time. The problem was breaking the news to the owners that the fat feline had gone from corpulent to corpse-ulent. In other words, he was no longer at death's door. He had in fact, gone through and slammed it shut from the other side. Knowing Chablis, he probably sprayed urine all over it as well.

Tactfully, I informed them

that the cat had been smitten with a somewhat serious case of death.

"We know that, Doctor," they said. "He died yesterday. We needed to see you today to get some pictures. We don't have any photos of his visits to your office. So, we thought you could pretend to examine him as if he were still alive while we take a few candid snapshots."

A few minutes later, Mr. Nutsabout went to their car and got his video camera. "We need some action shots, Doc," he said. "See if you can make him look lively while you handle him."

This was a tall order considering that Chablis was as stiff as a Bordeaux. I did my best though, and soon they were on their way home to bury their friend in the back yard.

Many of our clients are like the Nutsabouts to some degree. We are often asked to retrieve a lock of hair from a deceased pet or to make copies of medical records as a keepsake. Such things seem to me to be a part of the normal grieving process. Some people, however, go way overboard.

Take, for example, Mr. Blubber. His cat, Longone, died more than three years ago. He still calls us twice a month to reminisce. Occasionally, he stops in and asks to see the exam room where he used to bring Longone in the "good old days." We enjoy his visits. (He brings doughnuts.) However, considering that Longone has been part of the soil enrichment program at the Golden Hydrant Pet Cemetery for several years, I find his behavior a little strange.

But none of my clients hold a candle to Mr. and Mrs. Tribute. They win the Super Glue Award for the most unbreakable human-animal bond. Their veterinarian contacted me recently to tell me about them.

It seems that when their dog passed away, they wanted to do something to remember him. They asked our colleague if he could keep the body for six days until the custom-made casket would be ready, and possibly longer if preparation of the grave site was not completed.

"We're going to have a simple grave prepared, Doctor," Mrs. Tribute eulogized. "There won't be any big stone or anything, but it may take a few extra days for the gas company to run the underground pipe to the eternal flame that we are putting in."

February 2006

Cats age, but owners seldom mature

Declaw denial leaves the peanut gallery disenfranchised and displaced

It was last Thursday. The next surgery on my list was a nice old cat named Hooks. He was scheduled to be declawed. Unfortunately, there was a problem (a hitch in the gitalong). Hooks was 14 years old, and his pre-operative blood tests showed that his kidneys weren't doing too well. I gave his owners a call. The surgery would need to be canceled.

Mr. Topblower did not take the news well. He could have asked me about the cat's prognosis. He could have asked me about treatment options. However, he had a much more important question. "How much did that bit of news cost me?"

I explained that a few blood tests cost a lot less than a surgery that might have left us with a dead patient. He could not follow my logic.

"Now look," he said. "I'm not accustomed to spending money for nothing. We took our cat there for surgery, and he better get it!"

I told him to come and take Hooks home.

Within 10 minutes, his fiancee, Anna Mossity, was on the phone. "What is this nonsense about Hooks not getting his surgery?" she said. "We've been good customers here for 15 years. I can't believe we're being treated like this. We shopped around to every veterinarian in the phone book, and your price was the cheapest. Then when I got there, I was told that I had to get those unnecessary tests. Now you declaw that cat right now!"

I told her to come and take Hooks home.

She sent her friend, Lee Vinnahuff, to pick up the cat. She had a few words for me as well: "What is wrong with you people? My friend Anna said you are against declawing. If you don't believe in that surgery, why did you let them schedule it in the first place?"

> She sent her friend, Lee Vinnahuff, to pick up the cat. She had a few words for me as well ...

I never had time to answer her question because Mrs. Meddle was in the waiting room and jumped in the conversation uninvited. Appointing herself chief negotiator between me and Miss Vinnahuff, she began to spout unwanted advice on a multitude of subjects. I chose to ignore her because Mrs. Meddle is known to be a gross ignoramus (that's 144 times worse than a regular ignoramus).

I told them that Hooks should go home.

Once the cat was out of the building, I thought my problems were over (wrong).

Within half an hour, Fancy Davenport was on the phone. She gave it to me with both barrels. "You may cost me a sale," she said. "Mr. Topblower is threatening to cancel his order for a new couch unless you declaw his cat. Do you have any idea what furniture costs these days? This is going to be a hefty commission. Surely, as a fellow businessperson you can understand that we can both make a lot more money if you would just do your job and stop being so fussy."

I told her that I sent Hooks home already.

The saga continued the next morning. Mr. Topblower called to let me know that he was no fool and that he had stopped payment on his check from the previous day.

"I am not paying one penny for those unnecessary tests," he said. "Why, the last time we had Hooks in there to see you, you said he seemed perfectly healthy."

That was true; it is also true that Bill Clinton was president.

A little before noon, a phone call that I fully expected came in. It was Downtheroad Animal Hospital calling for blood test results. It seems that Hooks was there for surgery, and the owners said that he didn't need tests because they were just done yesterday. I gave them the results. I also advised them to send Hooks home.

Later that afternoon, I had a meeting with Will Blankslate. Will is a bright young man who wanted to talk to me about a career in veterinary medicine. Will had a great misconception about our profession: "I'd really like to have a job like yours," he said. "It would be great not to have to deal with people." (He might be in for a surprise.)

November 2005

Stereo's incessant chatter leaves out small diagnostic detail: What's wrong?

Worried owners sometimes need a little coaxing to get to the root problem

Mr. and Mrs. Stereo began to chatter the minute I entered the exam room. Neither one seemed to notice that the other one was also talking. Fortunately, due to my decades of veterinary office experience, I was able to listen to both simultaneously.

She was singing the praises of their dog. "Puddles is the best dog we ever had, Doctor. When I get home from work, he always runs to the door to greet me. He is very active and just loves people. Why, he has hardly ever been sick a day in his life."

Mr. Stereo had plenty to say as well. "This little guy has never had an accident in the house in all the time we've owned him. He gets along great with our other dogs, too. They all spend a lot of time together, and nothing is wrong with any of the others."

This one-sided conversation was what I refer to as a reverse history. This happens when people become so eager to educate you as to what is normal, that they forget to tell you what is wrong.

At this point, I was left with two choices. I could read between the lines and assume that the dog was inactive and had pooped on the floor, or I could try to elicit more useful information in an attempt to find out why they had come to see me. Foolishly, I chose the latter.

> This one-sided conversation was what I refer to as a reverse history.

"I don't know if you'll remember this, Doctor, but Puddles was here about a year ago when he had that problem." They announced.

I assured them that I did remember. (I was faking it.) Glancing at the pooch's record, I saw that there had been an anal gland abscess at the time. (Now we were getting somewhere.)

"That got better within a week and has been great ever since, Doc. You sure did a good job on that, whatever it was." They informed me. (Back to square one.)

I decided to try the direct approach. "What seems to be the trouble today?"

There was a long pause. Finally, Mr. Stereo took the reins.

"We have never been in this situation before," he said. "We don't know how to handle it. When we called, your nurse suggested that we bring him in so that you could check him out. We just don't understand it; he's always been so good."

(Eureka! My receptionist would know why they were here.)

I excused myself and ran out to the front desk to find out why they made the appointment.

Guess what? It turned out the dog was acting lethargic and had pooped on the floor. (I should have gone with my original instinct.)

I headed back to the exam room. It was time to examine the dog. Unfortunately, the reverse history continued.

"Don't worry about that growling, Doctor. He doesn't bite." (We've all heard that one before.)

After the dog's first attempt to amputate my hand, I called in help, diagnosed, treated and had them on their way home in just a few minutes.

As they were leaving, I heard Mrs. Stereo talking to my receptionist.

"You know, we usually like to pay our bills right on time ... " (Uh, oh!)

February 2005

Where did I go wrong?

Mrs. Bedlam's offspring know how to keep office visit calm

Restraint can be the best strategy for maintaining client relationships

I was still out in the parking lot of my clinic when I heard the noise. It was a sort of loud, rhythmic thumping, and it seemed to be coming from inside the building. As I walked in, I couldn't help but wonder what sort of problem would generate such noise.

Could it be a malfunctioning piece of equipment? Even worse, was one of my staff members using a hammer on that piece of equipment?

Fortunately, it turned out to be none of those things. Unfortunately, it was just as bad. It was my first afternoon appointment, Mrs. Bedlam and her two obnoxious kids. (I don't know their names, but my staff refers to the little rugrats as Loud and Louder.)

The scene in the exam room was strange. There was a large cardboard box on the table. One of the kids was hitting the side of the box with a large stick. The other kid was yelling typical kid phrases, such as:

"It's my turn."

"I want to hit it for a while."

"Mom, make him let me do it now."

Looking into the box, I saw a terrified little puppy. He couldn't have been more than 6 weeks old. I ordered an end to the box beating and asked for an explanation.

Blair Bedlam was quick to answer.

"You know, Doctor, I read somewhere that tapping on the side of the box will calm a puppy. To them, it sounds like their mother's heartbeat." (Was his mother a kettle drum?)

> "Hit that box with a stick one more time, and I'll pee in your shoes when we get home."

As soon as she finished her statement, the pounding started again, thus prompting me to take possession of the stick. Then, in an unbelievable display of willpower, I refrained from hitting anybody over the head with it.

I picked up the petrified pooch to look him over, and he began to yell at me in a shrill voice.

"Put me down! I like it in my box. If you give me a needle, I'm going to bite you."

You guessed it. One of the kids was speaking for the dog. (It was so cute.) As I proceeded with the exam, all three of them blurted out inane comments on behalf of my patient. (Note: What the dog should have said was "Hit that box with a stick one more time, and I'll pee in your shoes when we get home.")

The rest of the office call went smoothly because, first of all, I chose to ignore anything they were saying, and more importantly, I continued my policy of not hitting anyone with the stick.

As I would with any new pet owner, I gave them some instructions concerning the proper care of their new puppy. In this case, I included very specific directions concerning the proper way to tap on the side of the box. My advice went something like this: "Don't do that!"

Just to be sure, I kept the stick.

They proceeded from the exam room to the checkout desk as the usual child-to-child argument ensued.

"I want to carry him."

"You had a turn already."

"Mom, make him let me have a turn."

I turned to my technician and asked for one little favor. Wisely, she refused. "No, Doc," she said, "I will not hand you the stick."

December 2004

'A veterinarian afraid of a little kitty?'

Heavy armament needed to fend off this 24-pound bundle of meanness

A large wooden cat carrier perched atop my exam table was boldly emblazoned with the name Sweetie. Hissing and growling noises emanated from somewhere deep within the recesses of this obviously homemade box.

Mrs. Hollonoggin was quick to explain. "Sweetie gets a little excited at the vet's office. That's why we're here. Our last vet was afraid of Sweetie. Can you believe that, a veterinarian afraid of a little kitty?"

Based on the sounds coming from the carrier, I found it quite believable.

I analyzed the situation before me. It was obvious that getting the cat out to be examined would be quite a challenge. The door was narrow. There was no way to take the carrier apart without dynamite, and the critter was wedged behind multiple cat toys, a sweater, several handfuls of treats and a litter pan. I called for assistance and one of my technicians appeared with heavy gloves and a towel.

Sweetie's owner was horrified. "Oh those won't be necessary doctor. I can get him out; he'll behave for me."

I knew it was a lie. Unfortunately, Mrs. Hollonoggin opened the door, thrust her hand deep into the carrier and within seconds was bleeding on my nice clean, clinic floor. As she was escorted to another room to wash the wounds, she was quick to share her theory that Sweetie must behave that way because he was abused by someone when he was young.

In her absence, we got all the junk out of the carrier and piled it on the floor. It looked like Sweetie was about to hold a garage sale. Just when we got the 24-pound bundle of meanness restrained on the table, Mrs. Hollonoggin returned with another theory. "You wouldn't believe it doctor. He is not the same cat at home.

He is the nicest cat I've ever owned. My husband and I think he misbehaves at the vet's office because something must have gone wrong when he was neutered." (We've all heard that one before.)

Fortunately, the reason for the visit became obvious as soon as I got a good look at the cat. There was a cyst on the side of his neck that was so big that it looked like he had two heads. It was hard to assess the extent of the lesion because Sweetie was thrashing, kicking, biting and generally going berserk. He was clearly criminally insane. Had he been born a human, I have no doubt that he would have been a serial killer.

> ...it looked like Sweetie was ready to hold a garage sale.

> "Personally I don't mind the expense, but my husband is fit to be tied..."

Mrs. Hollonoggin helped by yelling. "Calm down! Calm down, Sweetie! Mommy won't let them hurt you."

Surprisingly, that didn't help the situation much. Luckily she had another suggestion. "Try handling him without gloves. I think they are scaring him."

When I ignored that brilliant proposal, she had another. "He likes to have his ears rubbed. Try rubbing his ears and he will probably hold still to be examined."

I preferred to go with my method, and had four people clamp him down until he was helpless. Then I explained that Sweetie would need preoperative blood tests, anesthesia, surgery and a biopsy. I think she was a little taken aback by the price she was quoted. She headed for home vowing to think about my recommendations.

Not an hour later, she was on the phone. "Doctor, when my husband saw the estimate for Sweetie's surgery, he just about had a conniption. He was furious. Now, he wants to know why we need those preoperative blood tests. Couldn't you do the surgery under a local? Then testing and general anesthesia wouldn't be necessary. Wouldn't that cut the costs?"

I was forced to explain that there was no chance of going that route.

"I just don't know what to do then doctor," she said. "Personally I don't mind the expense, but my husband is fit to be tied. Can't you come up with some other suggestion?"

Actually I could. "You say your husband is throwing a tantrum over this estimate," I said. "Try rubbing his ears."

July 2004

You're fired!

Irate client's verbal assault has Dr. O retrenching

My receptionist looked rather frazzled when she delivered the message.

"Doctor O. There is a guy on line one who insists on talking to you. He won't give his name or tell me what it's about. I thought it might be a friend of yours because he called you by your first name."

Against my better judgment, I picked up the phone. After all, how long could it take to say, "I don't need any more life insurance," or "I don't have any money to invest right now."

As it turned out, neither of those two responses would prove appropriate. The caller was on the attack. His verbal assault began the moment I took the call.

"Well, Puddin is not one bit better. Those pills you gave me last month didn't help him at all. Besides, I couldn't get him to take the darn things. I'm getting pretty fed up with this situation, and it's about time for you to face up to your responsibility and do something about it."

Several questions popped into my mind: Who the hell are you? What are you talking about? and Why me, Lord?

As my assailant continued, I recognized his voice. It was Hugh Dunit. I sent someone to get the medical records while Mr. Dunit went on and on.

"Puddin was fine until you put him on those antibiotics last year after he had his teeth cleaned. They gave him diarrhea. Now it keeps coming back every time we give him pork. That medicine of yours made him sick, and you should be responsible for fixing the problem."

I glanced at the record. The diarrhea problem had been going on since long before the dental work. In addition, I saw a notation that Hugh Dunit once blamed a 1998 lameness episode on the routine 1995 neuter surgery. Apparently, he felt he should not be charged for the X-rays because the lameness was obviously my fault.

When his tirade slowed so that I could get a word in edgewise, I suggested that he stop feeding pork, and that we may need to check a fecal sample and run some blood tests if that doesn't stop the problem.

"Don't try to blame his diet, Doc," he said. "Those antibiotics caused the problem. You need to fix it, and I don't think we should have to pay you one penny."

I was strongly tempted to quote Donald Trump's now-famous line, "You're fired!" Instead, I politely offered to forward his records to another hospital, one in which he might have more confidence. He declined, of course. Lousy clients usually do. He vowed to give those pills another try before putting poor Puddin through any further expense.

My next phone call, though somewhat amusing, was no less aggravating.

"Hello, doctor. This is Sharon D. Guilt. I breed Chihuahuas and I'm very upset with you. Mr. and Mrs. Newpet were in to see you with their new puppy and you

> Several questions popped into my mind: Who the hell are you? What are you talking about? and Why me, Lord?

> God must love stupid people. He made so many of them.

told them that it is cryptorchid and has a heart murmur. There was nothing wrong with that dog until you told them that it was sick. Now, they want their money back. I think you should pay me for half the cost of the puppy."

I glanced out the window to confirm my location. As near as I could tell, I was still on planet Earth. Therefore, the conversation served to prove something that I had long suspected. This planet serves as the insane asylum for the universe.

As the conversation continued, Sharon D. Guilt was quick to explain her logic.

"You know, doctor, they paid me $500 for that puppy. If they return him, that money comes right out of my pocket. You made about $50 on that office call and it cost me $500. Does that seem fair?"

Actually, it seemed fair to me. She couldn't see it from my point of view, though. In fact, if she were any dumber, she would have to be watered twice a week.

Between her phone call and the one from Mr. Dunit earlier, I was brought to a very important realization that day. God must love stupid people. He made so many of them.

June 2004

Chapter 5:
Dumber

One clear thought deserves another

Decoding needed when trying to assess some patients' needs

I have known Puzzle for years. Furthermore, I enjoy seeing the little pooch now and again even if his owners are a little wacky. (Aren't they all?) However, his most recent visit to my office did not go as smoothly as usual.

The first surprise came when I entered the exam room and found a whole new person at the other end of Puzzle's leash.

"Hello, Doctor," said the young lady serving as doggie escort of the day. "I'm Ann Biguous. My uncle couldn't bring his dog in today so he asked me to do it for him. There's something wrong with Puzzle's ears. They look dirty. I just noticed it while bringing him over here, but that's not what he's here for."

Beginning to notice a trend in the conversation, I tried again by inquiring as to whether there were any new problems to be brought to my attention.

"Puzzle just doesn't seem to get around as well as he used to and it looks to me like he's lost weight, but that's not what he's here for today."

Hoping that some reason for the visit would become obvious, I proceeded to examine the dog. He seemed to be in great shape. This was no surprise since I had just seen him a few days earlier for his annual physical and vaccinations. (That's right. I still believe in annual vaccination.)

It was time to try again.

"Why is he here?" I asked.

"He needs his nails trimmed, but that's not why I brought him in."

> "What should I tell my uncle?" Ann asked.

The floors had just been cleaned. So, cutting my wrists was not an option.

"Well," I said. "Tell your uncle that Puzzle looks good to me and have him call me if he has any specific questions."

"Oh! I almost forgot," she announced. "My uncle sent a note."

(Now we're getting somewhere.)

She handed me a piece of paper that had a few squiggly lines on it. It was the note from Hiram Glyphics. It may have been written in English. It was hard to tell. It looked like it was written by someone who held a pencil between their toes while receiving shock therapy.

I tried to read the first line. As near as I could tell, it seemed to say:

"Bog turtles throw pomegranates at the Lone Ranger."

This made no sense to me since turtles can't really throw very well. So, I decided to try again. After staring at the squiggles for a few minutes, I decided that it might read:

"Dog breathes through snorkel of the lost Beagle."

Now we were really getting somewhere. Obviously the sixth word was "the." Unfortunately, after many more tries, the other seven words didn't become any clearer. It was time to call in an expert. If anyone could decode this note, it would be my receptionist, Dee Cipher. She faces similar tasks each day when she tries to read my handwriting. I handed her the note.

Unfortunately, Dee had met her match. We were left with no idea what Mr. Glyphics wanted.

"What should I tell my uncle?" Ann asked.

"Don't worry about it," I said, "I'm going to write him a note."

I took a piece of clinic stationary and jotted down a few lines. Then I handed it to Ann and sent her on her way.

Afterward, Dee wanted to know if I really expected anyone other than her to be able to read my handwriting.

"Of course, not," I replied, "But if he can figure it out, he's going to wonder why I wrote, "Lobsters' skis tend to tangle in their parachutes."

February 2004

Know when to call in specialist

Taxidermist last, best hope for tumor with cat attached

I could see the problem the moment I entered the exam room, but, just for fun, I decided to wait until Mr. Obtuse pointed it out to me.

I didn't have to wait long.

"Look at this, Doc," he said. "I was petting Dakota yesterday and I found this lump."

Now, normally, when a pet owner asks you to look at a lump they insist on getting their hands in the way and making it impossible for you to do your job. That didn't happen this time, though. The lump was too big to hide. Dakota had developed a growth the size of Mount Rushmore. (Not the whole thing, just Lincoln's head.)

"We're sure it wasn't there three days ago, Doctor," he said. "We are always grooming him and petting him, and he was fine on Tuesday."

I tried to point out that this had probably been developing for several months, at least. The right rear leg was barely functional and the mass incorporated much of the thigh and pelvis. However, they continued to plead ignorance, a plea that seemed to fit them very well, and since there was no point in arguing with them, I continued to assess the situation.

Unfortunately, before I could complete my exam, we were interrupted by a knock on the door. I answered it immediately. You see, I operate on the theory that a knock on the door in the middle of an office call could mean that one of my staff is bringing me a jelly doughnut. True, this never actually happened, but I choose to cling to the hope.

In this particular instance, however, it was just one of my receptionists coming to announce that Mr. Putoff was on the phone.

"Doc, I have a problem with Old Gravid. She's real pregnant," he announced.

It was a typical Friday afternoon phone call. I could have predicted what was coming next. "I think she needs a caesarean, Doc. She has been in labor all day yesterday and today."

> Dakota had developed a growth the size of Mount Rushmore. (Not the whole thing, just Lincoln's head.)

"There goes my chance of getting home on time," I thought to myself.

Then, in a futile effort to save a future Friday night, I tried to explain that the dog should be spayed during the surgery. She was 12 years old. Only one puppy survived from her last litter and she had two caesareans already. He wouldn't listen.

"No, I just want the pups out of her and that's all. I think I can get one more litter out of her," he argued.

I told him to bring her over and headed back to my office call where we proceeded to discuss the options for Dakota. There was no chance of a surgical cure, but there were other choices to consider.

Their next statement was quite predictable.

"You know, we can't afford to get involved with a lot of expense here."

Nonetheless, I went over our best two options. One was just to take a few pills to reduce pain and swelling until Dakota would have to be put to sleep. The other was to take X-rays, submit biopsies, consult an oncologist, and possibly proceed to chemotherapy.

They had an important question.

"Will the biopsies, X-rays and treatments cost more than the pain pills?"

I informed them that the aggressive approach was the more expensive of the two. Not surprisingly, they opted to do as little as possible.

We were interrupted by another knock. Sensing that this just might be the day, I jumped for the door only to be disappointed once again.

"Sorry to bother you, Dr. O," said a technician who was quite obviously not carrying a doughnut, "but Mr. Balming is here and he said he needs to talk to you."

M. Balming is our local taxidermist. He has been after me for years to get me to offer our clients taxidermy as an alternative to cremation when a pet dies.

"We have a whole new system that you'll be anxious to offer your patients," he announced with seemingly great pride. "We call it biological preservation. I brought in a new partner, Dee Hydrate, and we have a whole new technique. We changed the name of our company to Eternal Companion Memorials and we even have a great new motto, 'It's not your father's taxidermy.' Can I put up brochures in your office?"

I told him that I'd consider it for certain cases only and took a handful of brochures to keep on hand.

A minute later, I was back in the exam room, ready to develop a plan of action for Dakota who was essentially more tumor than cat. Several predictable questions came my way.

"Doctor, is there a university or research institute that might want to fix Dakota for free so they could learn how this happened so fast in just two days? Or would you be interested in doing experimental surgery for your own knowledge?"

I was not able to give them any encouraging answers. However, the questions continued.

"Doctor, this big lump looks so ugly that we can hardly stand to look at it. Besides, it hurts so much that the poor guy can hardly walk. Isn't there a specialist who can keep Dakota looking and feeling better?"

Luckily, I knew a specialist who could, and in fact, I had some of his brochures handy.

January 2004

Sock-pilfering pooch uncovers hanky-panky
Tears of joy greet news that wayward sock found in nosey mutt

With little more than a glance at the first X-ray, Flora knew the diagnosis. Still, she took a few minutes to study both views carefully just as she always instructed her students to do. She knew all too well that her years of experience had not granted her immunity from mistakes. Then, satisfied that the films showed no evidence of less obvious problems which would prove to be embarrassing if discovered later, she headed for the privacy of her office to make the phone call. Many of the other staff members shared offices, but as a perk of seniority, she had her own. The door was clearly marked RADIOLOGY, Dr. Flora Scope, Head of Department.

She pushed one button on the intercom, and seconds later a phone rang on the third floor. There, the door read: SURGERY, Dr. Ruppert Glove, Head of Department. Ruppert was an expert in his field as well, and following a brief conversation with Flora, had a phone call of his own to make.

Across town, behind a door marked: No Peddlers or Solicitors, a third telephone joined the parade. Dee Ception answered the call. She heard the vet from the university say something about an obstruction in the intestine and that surgery would be necessary to fix the problem. True, the vet said that the dog would be fine after surgery, but she hated the thought of spending their hard-earned money on her husband's stupid mutt.

The dog hair had always been somewhat of a nuisance, but the recent vomiting on the rugs was unbearable. She decided to relay

the bad news to her husband on his private line at the office.

Mr. Ception's door simply read: CORPORATION PRESIDENT. He listened quietly as his wife gave him the bad news. The dog might not live and even if it did, it might never be normal. The vet had suggested euthanasia as a way to avoid needless suffering. He had his secretary call the university. Ruppert's telephone rang and the cycle was completed.

Shortly into the conversation, the two men realized that they were on different wavelengths concerning the dog's condition. Mr. Ception was delighted to hear the favorable prognosis and immediately authorized surgery. He nervously asked some questions about after care and was particularly hopeful that the dog would be able to hunt and point well by next pheasant season.

Ruppert was reminded of the old joke about the man who, needing surgery on his hand, asks the surgeon if he'll be able to play the piano after the operation. When the surgeon informs him that he will, the man says, "That's funny, I could never play the piano before." Under the circumstances, though, Ruppert thought it best not to share the joke with Mr. Ception, who was obviously upset about the dog.

A routine enterotomy took place just a few hours later. Apparently, the dog had swallowed a sock. Though it was a beautifully monogrammed expensive sock, it proved to be no more digestible than a cheap one. Ruppert, who is a classmate of mine from veterinary school, made two telephone calls after surgery.

The first was to Mrs. Ception. However, his conversation with her contained such unexpected twists and turns that he felt the need to call me to relay the entire story. Dee Ception's reaction surprised him.

"Oh, Doctor! This is such good news. I've been worried sick over this. You don't know what a relief it is."

He could sense her tears of joy over the phone. Ruppert was confused. This lady didn't seem to care about the dog yesterday. Now, the discovery and removal of the sock seemed to be a high point in her life. Her next words were even more surprising.

"I'm coming right over for that sock, Doctor. I don't want my husband to see it. He would be furious if he saw what you got out of the dog. I've been searching for that sock for three days."

Again, the situation seemed to have turned around. Mr. Ception obviously had had great love for his dog. Ruppert decided to ask if she really thought he would be that upset just because the pooch gobbled up a sock from the bedroom floor, even if it was an expensive personalized sock with his initials on it.

"Get with the program, Doctor," she said. The initials on that sock are not my husband's!"

September 2003

'Wallet lockjaw' found to be contagious

Clients have the disease, but veterinarians suffer ill effects of shallow pockets

Vera Stingy was so upset that she rushed one of her dogs over to see me after waiting just three days longer than she should have. (Usually, she waits until death is imminent.)

"I hope you can help us, Doctor," she said. "Please tell me what to do. You know how I am when it comes to my animals. I'll do anything. They are my precious babies."

I described my plan for diagnosis and treatment. I was even able to offer a relatively good prognosis. I knew, though, that I was wasting my breath. Her response was just what I expected it to be.

"A hundred and twenty dollars for a dog! You've got to be kidding! I can get a new dog for less than that!"

You see, Mrs. Stingy suffers from a disease that I call Wallet Lockjaw, also known as Chronic Pursitis. She is highly allergic to spending money. She did have some ideas, though, concerning ways to provide the needed medical attention for the pooch.

"Do you know anybody who might like to buy my dog?" she asked. "I'd be willing to give them a good price since he's sick. Then they could pay the vet bills to

get him well again. Geezer is only 14 years old. I've heard that dogs can live to be 20. Besides, I think he's one quarter purebred."

I had some bad news for her. It seems that in my practice, we don't see a lot of demand for sick, elderly dogs.

She was undaunted. "What about you, doctor?" she asked. "You know his medical history. Couldn't you use another dog at home? Instead of paying me anything for him, you could treat

> The real problem arose at the conclusion of the visit ...

my other animals for free."

I must admit that I was tempted. Tempted to laugh out loud, that is. Still, while turning down her generous offer, I managed to keep a straight face and let the conversation proceed to where I knew it was going.

"Well," she said. "I think I'll take him home and think about it for awhile. I'd hate to think that you are going to make me put him to sleep."

Then, after a 20 minute office visit, she actually asked, "Do we owe you anything for today, doctor?" (She did.)

Her case was not all that unusual. We all see examples of Wallet Lockjaw on a weekly, if not daily, basis. It is interesting to note that the client has the disease, but it is the veterinarian who suffers the ill effects. (Unfortunately, in this case, the pet suffers the most.) You may recall that last month I documented two other client diseases from which we suffer. They were "verbal diarrhea" and "information constipation."

Unfortunately, there are numerous other examples. For instance there is Mr. Video. He calls me several times a year with important observations concerning his cat's behavior. His last call went something like this:

"I think I'd better bring Kitty over to see you. There must be something wrong with him. When I got up this morning, I found that he had chewed up the phone cord. I think he was trying to tell me to call the vet."

The time before that, he was convinced that his cat was having migraines because it had refused to eat liver that day. (Of course, the cat had never eaten liver before, either.)

Mr. Video suffers from "Lassie Syndrome." He thinks that each pet gesture is a cryptic message in need of decoding. At any rate, his last visit was the worst ever. The very long phone call was followed by an even longer office call. As usual, I was unable to find anything wrong with his cat even though he was sure that "Kitty was trying to tell us something."

The real problem arose at the conclusion of the visit when Mr. Video himself began to exhibit a change of symptoms. It seems that his friend, Vera Stingy, told him that he should expect a discount if I fail to make a diagnosis. (Apparently, Wallet Lockjaw is contagious.)

December 2002

Client talking doesn't necessarily guarantee information

I entered the exam room and introduced myself as I always do with new clients.

That was before I realized that Mr. Siesta was fast asleep. His two dogs, Hale and Hearty, were wandering around the room. I repeated the introduction a little louder.

"Uh, hello, doctor," he said. "I guess I must have dozed off."

Since it was obvious the Mr. Siesta was not going to move from the chair, I picked up one of the pups and put it on the exam table.

"What brings you here today?" I asked, but when I looked back in his direction, he was gone again. I called a technician to help with the office call and made sure to do so loudly enough to wake him up. I repeated the question.

"I guess there must be some problem with the dogs, Doc. Didn't my wife tell you when she made the appointment?" he asked.

His answers to my next three questions were, "I don't really know," "Beats me," and "How should I know?"

This is what I call, in my office, "tenesmus history" because it's hard to squeeze any facts out of the owner. Still, I was able to diagnose the problem with ease. It was a case of "information constipation." (Mr. Siesta had the disease, but I was the one suffering from it.)

Under normal circumstances, with a quiet but knowledgeable client, the disease can be cured by putting a stethoscope in your ears. However, in this case, a phone call to Mrs. Siesta was in order. Unfortunately, I was forced to modify my original diagnosis. This was a case of the somewhat less common form of the disease known

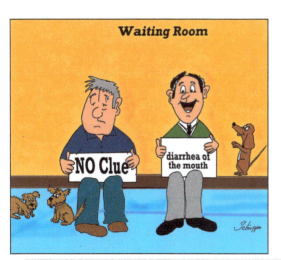

> Here it is: both of the diseases I have just described are incurable.

as "familial information constipation."

After further interrogation, I was able to glean that one of the pups wasn't acting right and the other "wasn't himself." It turned out (you are never going to believe this), that they had the two almost identical dogs mixed up. Someone had put the wrong collars on after their bath.

My technician and I showed great restraint in holding our laughter until they were out the door. Then I just about passed out I laughed so hard.

Not 20 minutes later, I found myself facing another diagnostic challenge.

This time it was Mr. Thesis with his Dachshund, Long Boy. Thesis doesn't understand the difference between a "true" or "false" question. Every answer goes on and on and on. He suffers from a severe case of "chronic verbal diarrhea." (One of the few things that cannot be fixed with duct tape. Although I have often been tempted to try it.)

Each time he finished one of his diatribes, I would try to change the subject.

"I'm sorry to hear that your marriage is not doing well, but let's get back to Long Boy and his problems," I said as I attempted to get a word in edgewise.

My next two responses were:

"Yes, that's an interesting story. That dog you had in the '60s must have really been something, but what about Long Boy?" and "No thanks. I don't need to see the scar from your hernia operation. Can we get back to Long Boy and his problems?"

Did you notice the recurrent theme in my part of the conversation? Mr. Thesis didn't. The office call lasted just 10 minutes short of forever. When it was over, one unpleasant task was left for me to accomplish. I would have to give you, the practicing veterinarian, some horrible news.

Here it is: both of the diseases I have just described are incurable.

They are responsible for one of the ironclad rules of veterinary practice (you may write this down.)

There is no correlation between the amount of talking that a client does and the amount of useful information that you are able to get out of it.

Novmeber 2002

Chapter 5: Dumber

Home diagnoses add new dimension to medicine

I entered the exam room confident that I would soon see the same old problem and would administer the same old treatment.

I was wrong.

Instead of their usual moaning about the dog's chronic rash, Mr. and Mrs. Eureka were beaming with pride.

"We figured Papule gets this rash every summer," Mr. Eureka announced. "It's not fleas like you thought, Doctor. It's his food. The rash started in June right after we changed to the new food, Mutt Muffins. After you fix his rash this time, we are switching back to Poochie Porkers."

I asked why, if he thought the food was causing the problem, they hadn't stopped using it yet. I could have predicted the answer.

"We want to use it up first, Doc," he said. "We still have a lot left."

I wanted to ask how they could explain the last six years of seasonal rashes based on this year's diet change.

I wanted to ask if they couldn't see the fleas crawling all over the way I do.

I even thought of jokingly asking if I was on Candid Camera.

In the long run, I thought it best to avoid further questioning. After all, we were going to treat the problem the usual way. Furthermore, it would probably get better. Last, but not least, the rash would surely recur, at which time they would hopefully see the error of their theory.

I was reminded of an old saying that applies very well to many of our clients' attempts at home diagnosis. It goes something like this, "For every complicated problem, there is a simple solution and it's wrong."

My very next office call that day illustrated the same point. It was Mr. Logic with his dog, Psycho.

"Remember how baffled you were as to why Psycho has been lame lately?" he asked. (I wasn't baffled. The pup had an interdigital pyoderma that you could smell from across the room.) "Well, we figured it out. Psycho was watching TV with us two weeks ago and he saw that show about the cowboy's dog getting injured. He prob-

ably saw how much sympathy that dog got and now he wants some."

I listened politely, but I also made Mr. Logic promise to continue his antibiotics.

Both of these incidents remind me of another case of home diagnosis that a colleague from Maryland once told me about. It seems that Mrs. Stepinit was having trouble with her cat, Bombsite. Each morning she would find bowel movements on her bedroom rug as opposed to being in the litter pan where they belonged.

In fact, more often than not, she would find them with her foot as she got out of bed. And so, in order to rule out a physical problem, Alice Stepinit took Bombsite to our colleague to be examined. However, she didn't expect anything to be wrong. She already suspected the true cause of the bad behavior.

"I think Bombsite is just reacting to the ghost cat," she announced. "Sometimes, in the evenings, I catch a glimpse of a shadow out of the corner of my eye. It is nothing clear, mind you. It's just a hint of motion or a dark area. I think there is a ghost cat that influences my guy to misbehave."

Our colleague was very tactful. He didn't react like my friend, Abe, would have done by saying something like, "Are you nuts? You need to get either your eyes or your head examined, lady, preferably both." Nor did he handle it with sympathy, feigned interest or total silence, such as would have been my way. Instead, he lent credence to her theory, but politely suggested that the sighting of vague or unclear shadows might indicate that a visual exam would be in order. After all, what could it hurt?

Mrs. Stepinit, as it turned out, was grateful for the suggestion. Our colleague even got a thank you note. It said, "Doctor, I can't thank you enough for suggesting that I consult with my optometrist. He discovered some astigmatism that was causing the blurring in my vision. Best of all, I can see the ghost cat much more clearly now." Sincerely, Alice Stepinit.

August 2002

Chapter 5: Dumber

Hugh Betcha, Augusta Wind blow in with helpful hints

Mr. Betcha is one of the most cooperative clients you could ever hope to have.

At least that's his opinion.

In truth, I find that dealing with him is a little frustrating. His last phone call serves as a good example.

"Hello, Doctor. This is Hugh Betcha calling about my dog, Puddin. We were in to see you a few weeks ago, remember? Well, those pills you gave me didn't do a bit of good. She still has diarrhea. What do you think we should do next?"

A glance at the record revealed that the dog had been treated over four months ago and that only eight days worth of pills had been dispensed. I asked if there had been any improvement while Puddin took the pills.

"They only helped for a few days, Doc. Do you think I should try them again? I have plenty left."

The record showed that the stool sample he had promised to bring in never arrived. Also, the follow-up office call that he was going to schedule never happened. Foolishly, I asked if he had made the changes in Puddin's diet as I had recommended.

"Your know, Doctor," he said, "We haven't gotten around to that yet. I didn't want to do it while he was on the pills, and now I want to use up all of his old food first. In the meantime, can't we do something about this diarrhea? You must have some ideas. You know me; I'm willing to do anything you advise. After all, you're the expert. Just tell me what to do and we'll work together to get this problem resolved."

I made several very specific suggestions for examination, diagnostic testing and treatment. I carefully explained the necessity for each part of my plan. Mr. Betcha agreed enthusiastically with each and everything I said.

Unfortunately, I knew from experience that he would develop amnesia the minute he hung up the phone. The man loves advice. He absorbs it like a sponge. However, since he never follows it, I wish that he'd get his advice elsewhere.

Later that same day, I got a

> Unfortunately, I knew from experience that he would develop amnesia the minute he hung up the phone.

call from Mrs. Wind. In fact, Mrs. Wind calls just about every day.

"Hello, is this the Doctor?" she asks every time. "Augusta Wind here. I have an idea to share with you concerning that stiffness in Starchy's back legs. I checked in my cat book and with my neighbor who used to own racing pigeons. We think it could be hairballs. The symptoms seem to fit. He threw up once last month and I have seen him lick at himself. What do you think?"

Naturally, I didn't share my true thoughts. In fact, I never had the chance to because Mrs. Wind doesn't believe in letting others get a word in edgewise. Her geyser of knowledge continued to erupt (Or is that Geezer of knowledge?)

"While we're on the subject of ideas, Doctor, I've been thinking about those heartworm pills that dogs take every day. Did you know that you could get bitten while giving pills to a dog? Why don't you vets wise up and tell people to give them as suppositories? They'd probably work just as well."

As the conversation continued, she repeated many of the ideas that she shares with me each time we talk. (Actually, she talks and I pretend to listen.) Most of her brainstorms are ridiculous. For example, she once discovered a way to use hand-held hair dryers on cats without scaring them. Her solution? Don't turn the hair dryer on. Another time she theorized that ear mites could be prevented by putting yogurt on a cat's feet daily. I forgot to ask what flavor she recommended. I'm sure that she would have had an answer, though. She has an answer for everything.

Her phone calls serve as a great source of amusement and, lately, we have found a way to extract real value from our association with Mrs. Wind. We gave her Hugh Betcha's phone number.

July 2002

Can anyone explain pet owner economics?

Which one would I choose: the glazed, the powdered, or my usual favorite, the jelly donut? I gazed at the box the way a teenager stares into an open refrigerator, hoping for inspiration. Just as I was about to stop anticipating and begin masticating, my receptionist rudely interrupted.

"Doctor O, would you please talk to Mrs. Rossity on line one?"

The call went something like this:

"Dr. Obenski, this is Jenny Rossity. I'm afraid I have some bad news for you. Tiger passed away last night."

Naturally, I expressed my regret that we lost such an outstanding citizen of the animal kingdom and asked if there was anything I could do to help in the way of arranging burial or cremation.

"No, Doctor," she said. "We are going to bury him in the backyard. The reason I'm calling, though, is to ask if you'd be willing to refund the money we spent for his treatment. After all, he did die."

I explained that granting such refunds is not my usual policy (believe it or not).

"I don't want the money for myself, Doctor," she replied. "But I thought you could make a donation to the Animal Spay Society. It would be a gift from me in Tiger's memory."

Why would a gift from *her* to *them* come out of *my* pocket? I somehow failed to follow her line of economic reasoning. This is nothing new for me. You see, 35 years ago, as an undergraduate student at Penn State, I took an economics course. Some of the people in the class (I swear I am not making this up) actually seemed to understand what was going on. I choose to believe that those same people now spend their days slowly thumping their heads against the wall of a rubber room somewhere.

As for me, I learned nothing during the course and apparently managed to pass by spelling my name right on the final exam. Perhaps that is why I have so much trouble dealing with the specialized branch of science known as Pet Owner Economics.

Having spent several decades observing this peculiar mental phenomenon, I would like to take this opportunity to explain exactly how it works.

Unfortunately, I have no idea. So, let me give you a few examples and see if you can figure them out.

Vera Obtuse, head of the local sterilization vigilante organization, wants to know why I charge so much for spays.

"Now see here, Dr. Obenski," she says, as if lecturing to a third-grader. "According to my calculations, you should be able to do spays for our organization at $30 apiece and still make a nice profit. Even if you lose money on each one, as you claim, you could make up the loss in volume. If we brought you 10 per day, that's $300."

Her logic escaped me. Of course I could do spays at her price and make a nice profit, if it were 1965; but not today.

Another example would be provided by Mrs. Wacky. She also called last week to complain about our prices.

"I can't believe you expect me to pay all that money for spaying and shots," she argued. "I just paid the breeder $800 for this puppy. I'm not made of money you know. Besides, I still have all those medical bills from our previous dog, Prince. Do you remember that?"

Of course I remembered. She came to me for a second opinion after running up a big bill elsewhere. It seems she "wasn't satisfied." Then, in a typical display of pet owner logic, she expected me to find the problem, render a second opinion and save the dog, all without spending any more of her money. Her total bill with us was less than $80, and we haven't seen the first penny of it yet.

Her request went something like this, "When someone has spent as much money as I have on their pets, you should start giving them a break on the costs."

Is there a veterinarian out there who can explain to me just how our clients come to these financial conclusions? Is there a veterinarian out there who can give me the precise meaning of the statement, "Do anything you can for him, Doc. Money is no object." The intent always seems to change rather abruptly about the time the bill is presented. I'd love to meet the person who can explain these things, but that probably isn't possible. Even if such a person was to exist, I doubt that he or she would be allowed out of the rubber room.

January 2002

Dreams of retirement fleeting

I left the exam room for just a few minutes to get a shot of penicillin for her dog. By the time I got back, Mrs. Quibble was hopping mad.

"I have a bone to pick with you, Doctor," she said. "While you were out, I looked at Porky's record. Last year, you wrote down that he weighed 67 pounds and that he should go on a diet. That's no longer true and I want that entry removed from his record."

I felt sick. How could an experienced practitioner like myself make such a rookie mistake? Everyone knows that you never leave an open record where the prying eyes of the client can read it. (I should be put out to pasture.)

"Porky only weighs 65 pounds this year," she continued. "You just said so yourself. I think you should cross out what you wrote last year."

Foolishly, I tried to explain the error of her thinking. The entry was correct at the time it was written. However, Wanda Quibble has never been one whose train of thought follows the track. To say that she suffers from insanity would be inaccurate because she seems to enjoy every minute of it. Seeking the easiest way out of the situation, I decided to draw a thin line through last year's entry and move on with my life. (Retirement sounds better every day.)

Waiting to see me next was the Eureka family. They had called earlier that morning to let me know that their dog, Logjam, had not pooped in two days. As I entered the room the entire family spoke at once.

"Logjam has an ear infection! We just noticed it while we were waiting for you to come in. We found a lump also. He didn't have it when we left home."

It turned out, of course, that the ears were perfectly normal. Furthermore, a five-minute game of "Where's the lump?" produced nothing other than normal anatomic structures. I gave the plugged up pooch a laxative and sent him home.

For some reason, people like the Eurekas often seem compelled to give their dog a physical exam while waiting to see me. I guess they feel that they are being helpful. In many cases this is followed by grooming the dog and depositing as much hair as possible on the exam room floor. Bolder clients often open a cabinet and borrow my comb to aid in their mission.

Another on the list of typical examination room antics involves the electronic scale. We have one in each room. The average client intends to help me by weighing their pet before I arrive. However, none of them seem to be able to work the thing. Those few who do figure out how to read it usually present me with a number equal to the weight of their own hands added to that of their dog or cat. (God must love stupid people. He seems to have created so many of them.)

One more office call and the day would be over. (I'd be one day closer to that retirement I'm always dreaming about.)

It was Mr. and Mrs. Swab with their cats, Trickle and Cascade. Both cats were in one carrier. There was no towel or other absorbent material in with them. It was high tide. Naturally, the Swabs were anxious to get the cats out of the carrier and onto the exam room floor as quickly as possible. They had urine smeared from wall to wall. One cat was getting a bath in the sink. There were now 300 of my paper towels in the bottom of the carrier. I entered the room wearing new shoes with leather soles. There was an immediate reenactment of my first experience on roller skates. I called for back-up.

Luckily, all good things must come to an end. So 20 minutes later, I was driving home. It had been one of those days. Once again I found myself thinking about retiring. It can't happen soon, though. I still have too many dependents relying on my financial support. This year, the principal one being my Uncle Sam.

Decmeber 2001

Chapter 5: Dumber

You can't win in pill stampede

Last month, I received a phone call from Mr. Maykit concerning his dog's rash.

The call came in just before the end of his scheduled appointment. You see, once again, Kent Maykit had failed to show up for his office call.

"I can't make it to your office today, doctor," he said. "My car is in the shop. But my dog's rash looks awful bad. Could you give me some pills or something to make it better for a few days until I can bring him in? It's the exact same thing that he had last time and the pills worked fine then."

I had heard this scenario before. Mr. Maykit's record showed that, the last four times this problem occurred, he simply stopped by for some Rashaway Tablets, and in spite of his promises, I never did see the dog. What I can't understand is why are there so many people who can't make it in for an office call, but have no trouble driving over to pick up medication? At any rate, it was such a busy day that I complied with his request and headed for the pharmacy to get the pills ready. That's when the game began.

Games begin

You see, getting those pills would afford me the opportunity to play my favorite veterinary hospital game, Pill Hockey. This game is a true test of concentration, speed and dexterity, not to mention level of sanity.

I reached for the Rashaway Tablets only to discover that the bottle was virtually empty except, of course, for the one remaining still floating in the small sea of pill dust that all such bottles have at the bottom. Undaunted, I threw it in the trash and reached for a new bottle. It is at this moment that the game usually begins.

The drug company has an impregnable plastic collar around the top of the jar and the lid. Apparently, this is designed to keep the freshness in and the doctor out. Next, comes the round paper freshness seal, which was glued to the rim of the jar with the same indestructible glue that they use on "easy open" cereal boxes.

Finally, there is the two cubic

feet of cotton compressed into the one cubic inch space above the pills. If you make it this far, you have reached the first plateau and, the excitement begins. You see, as the cotton is removed, some of the pills attempt a bold escape. They do so by hiding in the cotton until it is removed from the jar then bolt for freedom. As they drop to the countertop and roll, it is your job to corral each wayward wafer and keep it from getting away.

Rollin', rollin' rollin'

With lightning speed and dexterity you attempt to grab each one, thereby knocking over the open bottle and setting off a pill stampede. Some will roll into the sink while others race toward the edge of the counter and head for the floor. Renegade tablets have unbridled enthusiasm. Anyone familiar with the laws of physics knows that perpetual motion is impossible. However, anyone who has chased a pill stampede knows that once a tablet is loose, it can roll forever.

If there is an open box containing little foam packing knurdles in the pharmacy, some of the pills will dive into it and be irretrievably lost. In fact, anything smaller than a Buick can be lost in a box of foam packing knurdles. They represent the Bermuda Triangle of the packing industry.

Many pills will find an immovable object to roll beneath. This is usually a refrigerator, a radiator or a bottom shelf. Such things are usually designed with a space underneath just small enough so that your hand won't fit and just big enough so that anything else will.

It is at this point that I usually realize that, if little fuzzy balls of pet hair were worth anything, I could retire immediately. (During this most recent game, I saw several toenails, a cookie, two rabies tags and several M&Ms scattered under there.)

Once you have salvaged as many of the little discoid daredevils as possible, you begin counting them out to be dispensed. When you are almost finished, your secretary gives you an urgent message.

"Mrs. Forty called. You know, the one who was in four days ago with three dogs. Two of them vomited six times. Can you call her in the next 12 minutes?"

In spite of having seen every episode of *Sesame Street*, you lose count and have to start over again.

Once the pills are safely counted out into the dispensing bottle, the game ends but the frustration can go on and on. Such was the case with the Maykits. Ten minutes before closing time, Mrs. Maykit called.

"Doctor this is Gerta Maykit," she said. "The dog looks awful. I think his skin is infected. I've got to bring him right over."

It seems that people who live 20 minutes away always call 10 minutes before closing. This usually necessitates a delay in my supper. As I waited for her to arrive, I seriously considered unbending a coat hanger and retrieving that cookie and those M&Ms from under the refrigerator.

August 2001

Chapter 5: Dumber

Hey, what's in a name anyway?

There were three identical-looking spaniels on the exam room floor. Coincidentally, there were three neatly folded patient records in my hand. (Let the games begin.)

"Who wants to go first?" I asked.

"Let's do the bad guy and get him over with," she said.

"OK. Which one is that?"

"This one."

What's his name? "We call him Pooky."

A glance at the three records revealed no such name. I was forced to continue the interrogation.

"What name would we have for him on our records?"

"We rarely use their official names, Doctor. Anyway, we're here today with several problems. Snooter has a terrible wheeze. He might need an X-ray."

"OK." I said. "Let me see what it sounds like." I grabbed my stethoscope and began to listen.

"Doctor," she said. "That's not Snooter. Snooter is the one over there. The one on the table is Pooky, remember?"

I had an important question for her.

"Who's on first?" I asked.

She didn't get it.

Finally I showed her the three records and asked that she point to each pooch when his name was called. It worked. Foolishly, I thought the communication difficulties were over.

"Let's just talk about the dogs one at a time as we look at them," I suggested, and began the first exam as she continued to share information.

"The last time we were here, you gave us some medicine for that coughing. Do you remember? Well, it's only a little better.

153

Could we get some more medicine while we're here?"

The dog's record showed no history of a cough; a fact which I mentioned to the owner.

"Not this dog," she said. "Phlegmy is the one with the cough." (Here we go again.)

"Which one is he?"

"He's not here today. He's at home."

As the communication problems continued, the office call wound up taking three full days to complete. (Actually, it was only an hour according to the clock, but it sure felt like three days.)

As she left, I found myself hoping that I had entered the information on the proper records, but there was no way to be sure. Anyway, there was no time to worry about that, because according to my receptionist, there was an important telephone call waiting.

"Doctor O," she said. "You have a call on line one from a guy named Ian. He says it's a personal call. He won't say what it's about."

Defying all rules of common sense, I picked up the phone.

"Hello, Dr. Obenski," he said. "This is Ian Cognito calling on behalf of the Retired Fruit Peelers Association. How are you today? Last year you helped us out with an ad in our annual booklet. I hope you can help us again. We have several categories you might be interested in. First, there is the full page ad. We call it the Golden Banana Sponsorship. That's a thousand dollars. Then there is the half

> Forget about global warming. We should all worry about global name depletion.

page. We call that the Orange Appeal. The next level is blah, blah, blah …"

As you might guess, I stopped paying attention shortly after his speech began. Finally, I opted for the lowest level, the one I call the Hang Up and Save option.

Let that be a lesson to you. Never pick up the phone when the caller will not give your receptionist his or her name.

A little help here, please

My next phone call proved to be no less frustrating. It was Mr. Cryptic calling about his dog, Cipher.

"Well, doctor," he said. "He's at it again."

"You know, he's doing his thing again. His you-know-what."

Actually, I did not know what.

"And this time, Doctor," he said, "It's on the rug."

Now I had a hint. To quote Shakespeare: *"What's in a name? That which we call a rose, by any other name would smell as sweet."*

I had a feeling, though, that we weren't talking about roses. With a little coaxing, I got him to switch to more scientific terminology. It seems that Cipher left a "jobby" on the rug. We agreed that he would drop off a sample of "number two."

Later, as I left for lunch, it dawned on me that names are not only important, but that they could be getting scarce. We keep changing the names of the viruses and diseases. Every time there is a new product on the market or a new company is formed, a new name is required. Pretty soon we could run out of combinations of letters and we would have to start recycling names.

I decided to stop by my old friend Arnie's clinic and tell him about my fears. Forget about global warming. We should all worry about global name depletion.

"Do you realize, Arnie," I said, "that you could go shopping for a new car and find that since they ran out of names, they had to start using terms from other areas? Would you want to buy a new sports car called the Ford Fistula, or would you prefer something a bit more roomy like the Chevy Adenoma?" (Personally, I have my eye on that new SUV, the Chrysler Pyometra.)

Arnie laughed right in my face.

"As usual, your ideas are half-baked and half-assed," he said. He would have gone on mocking me, but we were interrupted by his secretary.

"Dr. Arnie," she said, "There is an important call for you on line three. It's a man named Ian. He won't say what it's about, only that it's a personal call."

"You'd better get that, Arnie, "I said. "It sounds important."

May 2001

DVM degree just doesn't cut it

In 1972, Dr. Birdseye had just graduated from veterinary school and entered the world of private practice. He was brimming with both enthusiasm for his profession and confidence in his abilities.

Like many new graduates, he had the tendency to feel defensive when clients questioned his judgment concerning their pet's diagnosis or treatment. After all, hadn't he just completed seven years of scientific study? His brain was crammed full with the latest knowledge in the veterinary field. Surely, there was no one whose abilities were more up to date.

The last thing he needed was a client like Mrs. Fullovit. Somewhere among her friends, her encyclopedia, the newspaper pet care column and her own imagination, she always managed to find a reason to question the doctor's judgment.

When they first met, she had a puppy that was suffering from a severe case of distemper. He gave her a grave prognosis, which fell on deaf ears. It seemed that her *World Book Encyclopedia* said that distemper was easily curable through the use of immune serum. She stomped off in search of a more competent veterinarian.

Over the years since then, she has been in his office many times. In fact, Dr. Birdseye's clinic has become a regular stop on her schedule of rotating through every veterinary office in town. Each problem with any of her pets winds up requiring several opinions before she is satisfied with an answer.

When her dog, Scratchy, had a rash, she went to six different veterinary hospitals. The first five wanted to use cortisone. She knew from the newspaper pet care column that cortisone was no good so she kept rotating hospitals. The sixth vet fixed the dog without cortisone. He used something called prednisone. Whatever that is, it sure did the job.

When Gimpy, the tomcat, came home limping, several foolish veterinarians told her that the leg was merely infected and that there was no fracture. One had actually taken X-rays and failed to see the break. Finally, she found a clinic where the doctor agreed that a splint would

do no harm as long as Gimpy continued to take his antibiotics.

Due to these instances, as well as many others, all the veterinarians in town soon became accustomed to her occasional visits and notorious lack of cooperation. That is why Dr. Birdseye was so surprised the last time she was in to see him. Her cat, Snowball, was very sick. His emaciation and anemia led to a tentative diagnosis of feline leukemia. This was quickly confirmed with a blood test and led to a very poor prognosis. That's when the surprise came. Even though this was the cat's first visit to a veterinarian for this particular problem, she decided to seek no other opinions.

"I've been reading about this disease, Doctor," she said. "I'm afraid that the only thing to do might be to put Snowball to sleep. Could we do it today and get it over with?"

He agreed that it was a logical course of action.

"Also, Doctor, could you hold him in the freezer at your clinic for me until the final arrangements are made? I'd feel uncomfortable having him in the one at home."

> *The last thing he needed was a client like Mrs. Fullovit.*

And so, a case that ordinarily would have taken two weeks of visits to veterinarians seemed to be resolved in one day.

A week later, Mrs. Fullovit was on the phone inquiring about the final arrangements for Snowball. First of all, she had a question.

"Do you think the virus is dead yet, Doctor?" I have read that freezing kills the virus but I don't remember how long it takes. I don't want to thaw Snowball until the infection is gone.

You guessed it. She was off on the road from clinic to clinic again, in search of a veterinarian who could perform a simple procedure like properly thawing a frozen cat back to life. She hauled Snowball to four more hospitals.

February 2001

The customer is always right

One day last week, I met a man who looked very familiar even though I knew we had never met. His name was Mr. Bluster and he had tagged along with his wife when she brought their cat, Puppet, in to see me.

"This cat just hasn't been right since he was here for his rabies shot a few weeks ago," she said while wearing a scowling expression that I imagined was usually reserved for slow waitresses.

"Ever since then, he has been mopey and his coat is very dull. He was perfectly healthy when we brought him in here. So, we figured out that he must be sick from that shot or from the flea medicine you sold us."

I glanced at the record. The infamous rabies vaccination visit had been seven months earlier.

Mr. Bluster took over.

"Puppet has been losing weight ever since we used those flea drops on him. We got them from you. He was perfectly healthy before that. Now all he does is drink water all the time."

I watched the man speak. Where did I know that face from? He had bushy, white, animated eyebrows and a dour expression of confident superiority. Suddenly, it hit me. He was the spitting image of Phineas T. Bluster, the sometimes villain from the old *Howdy Doody Show*. (Some of you may be old enough to remember it.)

I was fascinated, but thought it best not to mention to Mary Annette Bluster that her husband not only looked and sounded like a character from a 1950s puppet show, but even had the same last name. Nor did it seem wise to launch into a tirade in defense of Flea-Away Neck Drops. Instead, I decided that it was time to take a look at the cat.

Puppet was not a happy camper. Getting a hand close enough to the carrier to undo the latch required heavy gloves. Mr. Bluster, thinking himself quite clever, volunteered to extract the cat. He then proceeded to pull the towel that the cat was

Chapter 5: Dumber

This procedure was of very special interest to me and I watched intently.

sitting on, assuming that the fractious feline would slide right out with it.

This procedure was of very special interest to me and I watched intently. You see, I have never forgiven myself for a mistake that I made on a July evening in 1969. Everyone in America, except me, stayed awake half the night to see Neil Armstrong walk on the moon. I slept through the event. Oh, sure, I saw replays of it a zillion times, but that's not the same thing as having witnessed the live broadcast. So, if a cat ever slides out on a towel the way owners always seem to think they will, I don't want to miss it.

Following my predicted disappointment, we dismantled the carrier and attempted to examine the cat. He was obviously in poor condition.

I recommended some blood tests, but Mr. Bluster had a better idea.

"Can't we just rinse him off? He's probably just sick from that flea medicine that you sold us. He was fine before he got those drops."

His accusatory tone was becoming annoying. Patiently, I explained that something more serious appeared to be at fault. Then, along with several brave members of my staff, we took Puppet back to the treatment room. Once out of sight of his owners, we planned to use several pair of gloves and a restraint pole to obtain blood samples.

Mr. Bluster offered a typical client-type suggestion.

"If he tries to bite, just keep your hand in his mouth. He'll hold onto you, but he won't do any real harm."

We gave the suggestion all the consideration it deserved and proceeded with our original plan.

Naturally, I had ordered the tests not only in search of a diagnosis, but also in quest of vindication for my clinic and for Flea Away Neck Drops, vindication that would come when I could demonstrate the presence of some disease that was responsible for that cat's condition. Happily, I met with success on both counts. Puppet's blood glucose level was higher than the price tag on a new sofa. The cat was sick, but I would be able to make him well again and that's all that really mattered.

I gave the Blusters some information about diabetes and kept the cat in the hospital to start him on insulin. Unfortunately, their hardline accusatory attitude did not lessen as I had anticipated it would. In fact, Mr. Bluster demanded to know why I persisted in keeping Flea-Away Neck Drops on hand now that his cat had proven they can cause diabetes.

September 2000

Chapter 6:
Dumbest

'Just one more thing, Doctor...'

When I get to my office in the morning, the first thing I do is glance at the appointment book. Then, I delude myself into thinking that I know how the day is going to go. This allows me to foolishly predict just how quickly I will have to work in order to keep from falling behind schedule. My biological speedometer is set for the day.

Such predictions are, of course, usually worthless. Last Friday, however, my prediction accurately matched the day's hectic pace. It was obvious that I would have to hit the ground running, skip lunch, and keep the throttle wide open until closing time.

Unfortunately, I ran into a roadblock early. It was Mrs. Tyme. Her cat, Onemore, was in a cardboard box with rows of holes punched in the sides. In my practice, we call this type of cat carrier an "Al Capone" because the box looks as if it has been machine gunned.

Growling and snarling noises emanated from the box. It sounded as though she could use an exorcist rather than a veterinarian.

"He's just here for his annual shots, Doctor. Can you reach in and give him the vaccinations while he's still in the box? He can be so nasty that our last veterinarian refuses to see him anymore. That's why we came to you."

After assuring her that my hands were not going to be sacrificed, I called for assistance. It took four of us but we managed to inoculate the cat and get him back into the box with no fatalities. Of course, Onemore managed to spray something from every orifice in the process but no permanent damage was done.

"While he's here, do you suppose that we could check his teeth?" she asked.

I should have predicted that she would make such a request. Owners of nasty animals always wait until the fight is over to remember that they want something else done. I called my crew back for round two. I figured that it wouldn't be as bad since he had probably used up all of his excretory capacity during round one. I was wrong.

Chapter 6: Dumbest

While we fought for our lives, Juanita Tyme said things such as "Don't hurt him!" "Be careful that he doesn't get his fur dirty," and, of course "We think that someone must have abused him when he was neutered at the other vet's office and that's why he gets so upset."

No sooner was he back in the carrier than she produced a list from her purse and read off another request.

"This is going better than it usually does. Do you think we can get his nails clipped today?"

"Just one more thing, Doctor. Can we weigh him?"

"Just one more thing, Doctor. He isn't using his litter pan. What can we do about that?"

"Just one more thing, Doctor. What can we use to clean the rugs?"

"Oh, by the way. Before we leave, I brought a stool sample. It's out in the car. Can I bring it in now?"

By the time that marathon was over, I was hopelessly behind schedule. Unfortunately, my next office call was not much better. It was Avery Whichway and his dog, Hawser. The 20-pound mutt was hauled in at the end of what we call a "Titanic" leash. This is a term we use for any rope of chain so large that you could pull an oceanliner with it.

I tried to elicit some sort of logical history, but Mr. Whichway couldn't follow any particular train of thought. The man's mind was a beanbag full of unrelated thoughts. He told me about the dog that he used to have and about his neighbor's cat. When we did talk about the pooch in question, he gave me every irrelevant detail from 1992 up to the present. Somehow, he skillfully avoided divulging any facts which might prove useful. I asked questions and I got answers, but they didn't match. I was tempted to go out into the parking lot and check his license plate to see what planet he was from. Eventually, I had to phone Mrs. Whichway in order to find out why the dog had come to see me.

By the time he left, it was evident that, between the two of them, Juanita Tyme and Avery Whichway had managed to just about destroy my morning. I wouldn't wish clients like these on anybody.

A few days later, I called my friend Arnie to ask how he handles time-consuming people like these in his practice.

"I don't mind most of them, Mike," he said. "But, when I get a really bad one, I politely point out that they might be happier going elsewhere. In fact, that's exactly what I did with Juanita Tyme the last time she came to see me."

"I salute you, Arnie," I said. "And, by the way, I'm using America's favorite single-digit salute."

August 2000

Idiots, grass rolls cause logjam

Logjam was a very sick little dog. Lying on the exam room table, he looked as if he was about to gasp his last gasp. While panting heavily and looking very uncomfortable, he strained weakly as if trying to deliver puppies. His exhaustion from the constant straining was evident.

(With his energy drained, the poor pooch was spent. His get-up-and-go had got-up-and-went).

Mr. and Mrs. Feeder had no logical explanation as to what had happened to their dog. They had plenty of half-baked theories and stupid guesses, though. And, of course, each time one of them came up with an idea, the other disagreed.

I examined the pup while the dueling histories continued. Even though their incessant yammering was a bit of a distraction, it only took a few seconds to figure out that Logjam was constipated again. It happens practically every month.

"If only he could talk," Herb Feeder said. "Then he could tell us what's wrong."

Like all pet owners, he felt that his dog would be a master of self-diagnosis if only he had the ability to communicate his findings with us.

(Herb wished that the pooch could talk, but it couldn't. I wished that Herb would shut up, but he wouldn't.)

One of my technicians came in to hold the dog and I proceeded to ascertain the extent of the problem.

(There were lumps in the dog, and I could detect 'em. So I put on a glove and checked out the rectum.)

I decided to admit Logjam to the hospital for the day and get to the bottom of his problem. Later, as I worked at getting his colon unblocked, I found the same problem that had occurred in previous months. The dog had such large amounts of grass in his stools that he was pooping out what seemed to be adobe bricks!

Later, when Mrs. Feeder came to pick up the dog, I explained my findings.

"It must be the grass rolls, Doctor," Flora Feeder explained. "Logjam loves grass, so whenever my husband mows the yard, we save some of the grass. We roll it into bunches, tie each bundle with string, then save them in the refrigerator for Logjam. He goes nuts over them! Usually, he gobbles down the whole thing, string and all!

I tried to explain that feeding the grass rolls should stop. I knew, though, that she wasn't listening. Just to be sure, I turned on my imaginary sound-detecting super vision and watched as my advice rocketed in her direction, then went right in one ear and out the other.

"But doctor! He loves grass rolls! We can't stop giving them to him! It will break his heart. My husband and I get such a kick out of watching Logjam enjoy the rolls. Isn't there something else we can do?"

She called her husband who was waiting in the car, so that he could share the bad news. I explained it again. Feeding grass would have to stop. Somehow, I knew that they had no intention of following my advice.

(Their eyes looked glassy, their corneas glistening. I was giving advice but no one was listening.)

Within three weeks they were back in the office and, you guessed it, the same

> *Somehow, I knew they had no intention of following my advice.*

old problem had recurred. Naturally, I asked if they had been following my advice concerning the feeding of grass. They had a rebuttal.

"Isn't it true, Doctor, that eating some grass is good for dogs? We heard that it helps to clean out their system."

I treated the problem again. It was the fourth time this year. I'm sure it won't be the last.

(They just will not stop the feeding of grass rolls. The reason is simple. These people are idiots).

June 2000

'Hooked' on human/animal bond

When my receptionist brought me the telephone message, it didn't seem all that unusual. Someone had called who was too upset to describe their problem or even to give their name. But they were rushing over with some sort of emergency. There was nothing to do but wait.

Within 10 minutes, Mr. and Mrs. Angler came bursting through the front door of the clinic with their dog, Albacore, clutched in Mrs. Angler's arms. Tears were running down her cheeks. She was hugging the dog with all her might and started crying every time the pup moved the slightest bit. Her husband was not much calmer.

"You've got to help us, Doctor," he said. "My wife is really attached to this dog."

I assured him that many of my clients are strongly attached to their pets, but he seemed to feel that his wife was an exceptional case.

"You don't understand, Doc. Barb is really hooked on this dog. I don't know if you'll be able to get them apart."

We headed for the examination room, but when we got there, she wouldn't let go of the mutt. They insisted that I try to get a look at the problem while she held onto the dog. That's when the situation went from strange to bizarre. Snugly wedged between Albacore's face and Mrs. Angler's breast there was a small fish hook.

It was time to get some answers.

"OK. Mr. Angler," I said. "I know that your wife is hooked on this dog, but what is the specific problem today?"

"That *is* the problem, Doc," he said. "Can't you see that fishing lure that's caught between them? My wife and the dog are stuck together."

Closer examination revealed a three-pronged fish hook positioned such that

> *This was clearly the strongest case of a human/companion animal bond I had ever seen. It was, of course, up to me to sever that relationship.*

one point was in the dog's lip and the other had skewered Mrs. Angler, while the third waited patiently for a veterinarian's finger.

As we all know, fish hooks are barbed and do not come out easily. In this particular case, you could say that the hook was barbed and Barb was hooked!

This was clearly the strongest case of a human/companion animal bond I had ever seen. It was, of course, up to me to sever that relationship. Once Albacore was sedated, it was easy enough to cut the hook. The harpooned human was sent to the hospital emergency room for treatment and Albacore stayed with me for a little follow-up care.

The next day, when they came to pick up their dog and what was left of the troublesome fishing lure, I made them promise to be more careful with fishing equipment.

"It's all my husband's fault, Doctor," Mrs. Angler said. "He's always teasing the dog with those fishing lures. I warned him that there would be trouble if Albacore actually got hold of one."

"Baloney!" he said. "You caused the whole problem by hugging the dog when you could see that those sharp hooks could get you. Learn to handle things like fish hooks with respect and accidents like that won't happen."

With that, he picked up his lure with its one remaining hook, told his wife to grab the pooch, and headed for home.

She brought Albacore back within two minutes.

"Could you keep him here a little while longer, Doctor?" she asked. "I have to take my husband to the emergency room to get that fish hook that he respects so much removed from his hand."

May 2000

Why eat only one foot when you have two?

It was an honest mistake, a simple misunderstanding. It could have happened to anyone.

Unfortunately, it didn't happen to just anyone. It happened to me.

I had been treating Mrs. Bund's dog, Mory, for chronic kidney failure. The old pooch had been hanging on for weeks, but we all knew that the end was near. So, it came as no surprise when a very fearful Mrs. Bund called me on that particular morning. Her voice was barely audible.

"We won't be coming in for our appointment this morning, doctor. My dog died."

What she actually said was that her dad died.

So, operating under a completely wrong impression, I proceeded to put my foot in my mouth. "I'm sorry to hear that Mrs. Bund. How long have you had the old boy anyway?"

Her response sounded a little confused. I guess she thought I was kidding. Not realizing that one foot was consumed already, I began munching on the other.

"This must be very difficult for you. We tend to get so attached to them if we have had one for a while."

I couldn't make any sense out of her side of the conversation. She seemed to be having trouble communicating. Still unaware of the fact that I was on the wrong wavelength, I proceeded to go for the self ingestion record.

"Please let me know if there is anything we can do to help. If you should decide not to bury him in the backyard, I could cremate him for you."

She promptly hung up the phone. I found out about my mistake the following week from my friend, Arnie, her new veterinarian.

My reason for mentioning this incident is to appease those of you who feel that I pick on our valued clients

too much. I am throwing you a bone. Now, having cleared my conscience by picking on myself, I feel that clients are, once again, fair game. So, since we're talking about misunderstandings, let me tell you about Mr. Dermic and his dog, Hypo.

While he was in the hospital under our care, Hypo's diabetes had come under control nicely. He was stabilized on six units of insulin daily. When we were ready to send him home, one of our technicians spent a long session training Mr. Dermic in all aspects of diabetic care. We had him give several practice injections into an orange until we were sure that he could measure and administer dosages accurately.

Unfortunately, when we sent the dog home, his condition went out of control and, within three days, he was back in the clinic. Apparently, something had gone wrong with the treatment at home.

We had Mr. Dermic bring over his insulin, syringes and testing equipment so that he could show us exactly how he had been doing things. His ability to measure the urine sugar was fine. There was no problem with measuring the insulin

> *I couldn't make any sense out of her side of the conversation.*

dosage. He even brought along an orange so that he could show us how he administered injections.

We had no clue as to what was going wrong, especially since the dog's condition had improved immediately when we treated him in the hospital. Mr. Dermic had an idea, though.

"I think it might be that he isn't getting the entire dose of insulin," he said. "Hypo doesn't really like oranges, and, sometimes, he doesn't eat the whole thing."

Yes, you guessed it. He had been injecting insulin into oranges and feeding the oranges to the dog.

April 2000

'Sticker shock' almost kills Purstring and Dr. O

Prudence Frugality has been bringing her pets and their problems to me for more than 10 years.

Our most recent encounter was last month when Purstring the Poodle wasn't feeling well.

"I'll bet you don't have many people who come here with problems as often as I do," she said. "It seems like I'm here all the time. If it's not the dog, it's one of the cats. I should buy stock in this place."

I glanced down at the records of her six animals. Like most of my colleagues in veterinary practice, I have learned to appreciate those great clients who want to take good care of their pets, follow my directions, and even pay their bills on time. Every veterinarian hopes to have a significant portion of his or her clients fit into this elite group. Prudence Frugality, however, would not qualify for membership. All of her pets put together accounted for 12 office visits in 10 years.

There were no routine vaccinations listed. In fact, there was a notation on one of the records indicating that she had refused inoculations for the animals on several occasions. Her argument had always been that they don't go outside and therefore shots would be a waste of money. She also loved to use the old backup cliché about animals not getting vaccinations when she was a kid on the farm.

Prudence also has a history of letting problems go too long before seeking our help. Such was the case with Purstring. The dog was emaciated, covered with huge mats and could hardly move. His lungs made more noise than hotel plumbing. I had to remark that things didn't look too good.

"Are you sure it's that bad, Doctor?" she asked. "He was perfectly fine yesterday." She and I both knew that was a lie.

I recommended an X-ray, but she had a rebuttal.

Isn't it true that X-rays don't really treat anything? I'd hate to put him through that expense if it won't do any good. You can't guarantee that it will diagnose the problem, can you?"

When I suggested some blood tests, her response was similar.

"He just had some blood tests a few years ago. Can't we check those before we run up a big bill doing them all over again?"

Once again, I was forced to point out that the dog was very sick and that something would have to be done. Her response this time surprised me.

"I was thinking, Doctor. Instead of me spending a lot of money to fix him up, maybe I could sell him. He is a purebred Poodle. I'd be willing to sell him real cheap and the new owner could pay to get him back on his feet. Do you have any clients that you think might be interested?"

While exhibiting great self-restraint by not labeling her suggestion as idiotic, I informed her that Purstring was not likely to attract any buyers. She was undaunted.

"What about you, Doctor? Wouldn't you like to buy him? It wouldn't cost you anything to treat him. I'd give you a good deal."

Tempting as it was, I declined. Then with a little effort, I managed to get the conversation back to a more normal plane. I explained the tentative diagnosis, my plan for confirming it, and, most important of all to Mrs. Frugality, the costs.

That's when I saw it. An expression of dismay came across her face. It was as though she lost her best friend and her life's savings at the same time. It was the look of potential financial drain, and it only lasted for a moment.

My staff and I are very sensitive to the fact that a person's financial status can play a key role in whether a pet is cured or put to sleep. In this case though, my compassion was dulled by the knowledge that Pru-

His lungs made more noise than hotel plumbing.

dence could well afford to treat the dog if she wanted to. It all turned out for the best, though, as she eventually saw things my way and pulled the pooch through.

As coincidence would have it, I was destined to see that look of shock once again that day. After work, my wife had dragged me to the local furniture store to see a sofa that we just had to have. I glanced at a mirror on the wall, and that's when I saw it. The look of dismay was on my own face. I had just seen the price tag on the sofa. It was $2,000.

Just as I hope that each of my employees is capable of rendering compassion and empathy, I hope that each employee in that furniture store is capable of rendering CPR.

November 1999

Ow! Ooh! Ouch! Nothing hurts as much as a rubber check

I could hear a woman's voice coming from the exam room down the hall. "Ow! Ooh! Ouch!"

A quick glance at the record in my hand confirmed my suspicions. It was Mrs. Pincushion with her cat, Velcro.

Whenever I see this lady, she looks as though she just fell into the proverbial briar patch or, perhaps, had a run-in with a nest of killer bees. Her neck and arms are usually covered with inflamed welts and little red puncture wounds.

Her skin condition is a direct result of a congenital abnormality known as lack of intelligence. She has seen our waiting room sign stating that all pets should be on a leash or in a carrier. However, she knows in her heart that it doesn't apply to her. She wears her cat around her neck. (She is very attached to her cat and vice versa.)

And so, a typical visit began. I asked her to put Velcro on the table.

"Ow! Ooh! Ouch!" She put him down in front of me.

As soon as I turned around to get the thermometer, he was back on her shoulders. So, I asked for him again.

"Ow! Ooh! Ouch!" We got him down and took his temperature. I reached for the stethoscope. You guess it!

"Ow! Ooh! Ouch!"

And so, a 15 minute office call took half an hour due to the need for a total of eight difficult cat-from-owner extractions.

I chuckled to myself. Only 15 minutes behind. As long as I don't run into a nutcase like Mr. Loosegrip this morning, I'll be able to make up the time easily.

That was, of course, a big mistake. By saying it out loud, even though only to myself, I somehow caused my worst nightmare to come true.

Within minutes, I was standing in the other exam room with Mr. Loosegrip and his dog, Yo-Yo. All office calls with these two start out the same. I ask him to put the pooch on the table and he starts rehearsing his trained dog act for the *Ed Sullivan Show*.

"Up, boy! Jump up!" he yells while smacking the tabletop.

The dog ignores him completely.

"Come on, boy! You can do it! Up! Up!" he continues.

The dog has no idea what his owner is yelling about so he pees on the floor.

On this particular occasion, I lifted the dog onto the table as I always wind up doing, asking Mr. Loosegrip to hold him and began my exam. You know, of course, how things progressed from that point. Every time I turned away, Yo-Yo jumped down again. The fourth time I picked up the pooch, I called for a technician to come in and hold him.

As you may have predicted, this prompted Mr. Loosegrip to burst out somewhat indignantly with, "I CAN HOLD HIM!"

I felt like saying, "When do you plan to start?" However, there was no sense in aggravating the man. Happy clients are good for business and I still have one kid to get through an expensive college.

After what seemed like a mere eternity they were merrily on their way. I decided not to jinx myself again. So, I headed for the next appointment while keeping my big mouth shut. It didn't do any good, though, because there waiting for me in the hallway outside the exam room was Mr. Rubberneck and his dog, Snooper.

I led them into the room and began to look at the dog. When I went over to the pharmacy, they both followed me.

I led them back to the room. When I went to the lab to check the fecal results, they followed me.

I led them back to the room. By the time their visit was over, they had been reintroduced to the exam room a total of five times. An hour later, when I finally got to go to lunch, I kept an eye on the rear view mirror of my truck, half expecting to see them in pursuit.

At any rate, these incidents occurred on a strange morning over two weeks ago and had almost faded from my memory until yesterday. That's when my office manager told me that there was a problem with Mrs. Pincushion. Apparently her check bounced.

"Ow! Ooh! Ouch!" That was me this time.

October 1999

Flip-flop syndromes invade clinic

It was sleek, black, over-powered and expensive looking.

Naturally, it assumed that those spaces between the lines were placed there for use by much less regal vehicles and decided to park itself in the walkway area by the front door. After practically sliding to a stop at a rakish angle, its chrome prow almost blocking the waiting room entrance, the mighty power plant shut down with a mechanical sigh and the pilot disembarked.

It was Mr. Pompous and he was obviously in a great hurry. His usual self-important swagger suffered devastating alterations as he rushed quickly to the reception desk and declared his intention to see the doctor (that's me) immediately.

After giving his name and being told that he could have a seat, he decided instead to hang over the reception desk and demand to know exactly when he would be seen. Every few minutes he felt compelled to remind my staff that he had an appointment. Somehow it must have slipped his mind that he was almost an hour late because he didn't mention it once. Naturally, he could have been seen almost immediately if he'd shown up on time.

As you might guess, the climate began to get ugly. When they are not getting their own way, clients like Mr. Pompous have a way of finding fault with everything from your appointment system to your wallpaper. They also tend to be loud and create nasty waiting room scenes. My staff wisely hustled him into an exam room.

That's when the second miracle occurred. Sometime between his entering that room and my arrival, he had undergone attitude metamorphosis. It happens in veterinary offices every day. Technicians and receptionists see one side of the client, and the veterinarian sees another. It's called the veterinary office flip-flop and Mr. Pompous does it every time he comes to see us. This particular case was an example of a furious flip-flop but there are many other types.

Take, for instance, the falsification flip-flop. This occurs when Dee Ception calls to make an appointment. She understands that the office is busy, but just isn't sure that the pooch will live until tomorrow. This history is vague but ominous. The receptionists squeeze her into the already over-crowded schedule. As you enter the room during what was supposed to be part of your lunch hour, you get the real story.

"It's those pesky worms again, Doctor," she says. "I just hate the thought of those things around my house. Anyway, it's a good thing you could see me today because tomorrow my car has to go into the shop."

Another example would be the fiduciary flip-flop. This occurs when Otto Funds comes to pick up his cat. Just by coincidence, his arrival, which is two days late, just happens to coincide with the doctor's day off. Naturally, he is surprised to learn that the doctor forgot to leave written instructions to the effect that he is always allowed to charge. Then, after being turned down, he leaves without the cat and vows to return the next day and inform the doctor as to the inexcusable behavior of the staff. Instead, he shows up two hours later and quietly pays the bill.

Occasionally, multiple flip-flops can occur during one office call. Such was the case with Mr. Pompous. In the exam room with me he was a quiet, polite, pet owner.

"This dog is just like a member of the family, Doc," he said. "Please do anything you can for him. Money is no object."

It came as no surprise, of course, that his attitude changed when it was time to pay the bill.

"You want how much?" he asked the receptionist. "That's robbery! This dog costs me more than my kids."

> *As you might guess, the climate began to get ugly.*

While reversing the furious flip-flop that he executed earlier, he simultaneously exhibits a financial flip-flop as he angrily slams his VISA card down on the desk. This last type of flip-flop is one of the most disappointing that we see. One minute you are proud to be helping a concerned pet owner. The next, you are accused of being a heartless mercenary. In my office, we have a special name for this particular type of client behavior. We call it the Dr. J syndrome. It doesn't have anything to do with the former basketball star. It stands for Doctor Jeckyl and Mister Hide-the-wallet.

August 1999

Guy Macho turns to Tinkerbell

Many situations can be either aggravating or amusing, depending on your frame of mind at the time.

Nowhere is this more true than in a veterinary hospital, where the zany antics of our clients can provide us with an unlimited supply of chuckles on one day, then turn around and deliver a full load of ulcer fuel on the next.

Please wait for one of the good days before attempting the following:

Park your carcass on a comfortable lawn chair under the shade of a tree and spend some time watching your clinic parking lot. You see, the study of veterinary client behavior is not restricted to the confines of your building. The stupidity begins outside.

One of the most common things you will see is that many clients take five or 10 minutes to get out to the car once it is parked. Some of these are waiting for the end of their favorite tune on the radio, some are trying to catch the cat, but most are spending last-minute quality time with their pet.

They are explaining the need for surgery or treatment to their animal. The conversation is laced with reassurances that everything will be all right. They are actually trying to convince themselves.

You may see this activity as an important bonding episode between human and animal. In my office, however, we call it: waiting to be late.

A recent example from my office is best exemplified by Guy Macho, who was bringing in the family cat for an examination.

He sat in the car talking to a wooden box for 10 minutes. It took him another five minutes to get the box into my office.

It was a homemade cat carrier that must have weighed 60 pounds. Except for the door, which was steel, the entire thing was of one-inch-thick planks on a frame of construction of two by fours. We call this type of cat carrier a Ka-Boom, because it looks like the kind of box that you would expect the bomb squad to use.

Mr. Macho seemed a little put out that he had to bring the cat in. "It's my wife's cat," he said. "She's worried because he's been limping a little lately. You know how women are. I told her it was just a cat, but she insisted that I have you take a look."

When I asked the cat's name, he put on a look of disdain before answering. "It's Tinkerbell," he said. He felt the need to add an explanation. "The kids named him. I wanted to name him Fang."

He continued to put on the tough guy act as though his subscription to *Huntin 'n Shootin* magazine would be canceled if word got out that he liked the cat.

After mentioning that he was more of a dog person than a cat lover, he ran through several other clichés like: "When I was a kid, we never took cats to the vet;" and, "For a free cat, he sure costs us a lot of money."

As I looked at the infected foot, I warned him that it might be a little messy. He gave me a quick lecture on his experiences as a hunter and trapper. Moments later, as a little pus oozed from the leg, I pretended not to notice when he fell back into a chair with his face turning various shades of green.

We kept the kitty in the hospital for treatment, a course of action that pleased Guy Macho, because, as he put it, "my wife wouldn't be able to handle the sight of anything gross." He added, "You know how women are."

He wobbled off to his car.

The next day, as he wrote the check, my receptionist got a lecture on the stupidity of spending money to treat a cat. After all, "You can get a new one for free anytime," he declared. "I could have just put him to sleep myself, you know. But, my wife insisted that we get him treated. You know how women are."

He barely glanced at the cat when we brought it out to him, but we could hear the baby talk start as soon as he went through the front door. Then he sat in the car for a few minutes hugging the cat before starting the motor.

Moments later, his wife was on the phone checking to see if he'd been in yet and if everything was OK.

I told her not to worry. The cat would be fine.

"I'm not worried about the cat, Doctor," she said. "It's my husband. He had that cat before we were married, and he was up all night last night worrying about it. He wouldn't admit it though, claimed he had an upset stomach, but, he didn't. You know how men are."

I made no comment, but I did make a notation on the medical record: "If check bounces, threaten to call *Huntin 'n Shootin* magazine and tell them about the baby talk and hugs."

July 1999

Racket hits exam room

I could hear the growling and snarling even before I opened the exam room door. Soon, I would have to confront Mrs. Crescendo and her dog, Racket, a pooch who had, more than once, tried to interfere with my ability to count to 10. I looked at my hands. A quick inventory revealed that all fingers were present and accounted for. "Ten going in, let's try to have 10 when we come out," I said to myself and peeked into the room.

Having the distinction of being my loudest client, Mrs. Crescendo was quick to live up to her reputation.

"HELLO, DOCTOR!" she bellowed, in a voice that sounded much like that of an opera singer who just had her fingers slammed in a car door. (It was her normal voice.)

"I HAVE AN IDEA THAT WILL MAKE TODAY'S VISIT EASIER. RACKET HATES WHEN YOU TOUCH HIM. CAN'T WE JUST GIVE HIM THE VACCINE QUICKLY AND SEND HIM RIGHT HOME WITHOUT TOUCHING HIM MUCH?"

It sounded like a great idea to me. Just give a quick shot. Handle the dog as little as possible. Then send them on their way before the dog has a chance to detonate his explosive personality. My technician came in with a pair of gloves. In two seconds the shot was done, and, as planned, it was time to let them hit the road.

"AREN'T YOU GOING TO WEIGH HIM?"

It was a minor setback. Still, we would be done soon. Two technicians and a pair of gloves were required, but soon I was able to announce the news: "Twelve pounds and 6 ounces."

It was the easiest office call I ever had with Racket. A few seconds to vaccinate, a minute to weigh him and it was time to let them ...

"CAN YOU CLIP HIS NAILS?"

It was becoming obvious that the speedy office call I had anticipated was not going to be a reality. With two technicians, two pairs of gloves and a muzzle, the job was completed in record time. (It was a long record, not a short one.) Still, it was finally over. The vaccine, the weight, the nails and finally, it was time to let them hit the ...

"HOW ARE HIS TEETH?"

This time it took my entire staff, the gloves, the muzzle, and our restraint pole just so that I could claim that I got a cursory look at the teeth. She never even noticed that my oral exam was completed without removal of the muzzle. With my exhausted staff still restraining the frothing canine, I asked if there was anything else she needed us to check.

She looked at her list.

"THAT'S ALL I HAVE WRITTEN DOWN," she said

Chapter 6: Dumbest

This caused me to announce that we would let the writhing pooch up and let Mrs. Crescendo and her dog hit the ....

"AREN'T YOU GOING TO EXAMINE HIM? I THOUGHT THIS VISIT INCLUDED A PHYSICAL EXAM?"

We proceeded with a cursory physical examination. It was, of course, mostly an act on our part because it was almost impossible to do much with the critter who, if he were a person, would no doubt be labeled as criminally insane. Like many dog owners, Mrs. Crescendo helped by squealing at the dog, "CALM DOWN! CALM DOWN! CALM DOWN, RACKET!"

If OSHA inspectors ever figure out how pet owners try to calm their pets, we will all be forced to provide ear plugs for our employees.

Time flies when you're having fun. It was hard to believe, but the entire office call took only 45 minutes (it could have been worse).

This most recent Crescendo fiasco left me a half hour behind schedule. Nonetheless, I had to take a little more time so that I could ask about her original plan.

I thought that we agreed we would handle Racket as little as possible today," I said. "Instead we did all of the usual things and he was just as upset as ever."

"THAT'S YOUR FAULT," she said. "YOU SHOULD HAVE TRIED TO DO THOSE THINGS WITHOUT TOUCHING HIM SO MUCH."

Mrs. Crescendo is one of the reasons my staff doesn't allow me to carry a weapon in the office. The temptation would be much too great.

June 1999

A lesson in counterintelligence

It was the beginning of a brand new day.

Waiting for me in the exam room was a new client who had come in for routine annual vaccinations. What could be a better way to start the day? It would be a high profit, no brainer of an appointment. Or so I thought.

Actually, it was an ambush. No sooner had I strolled into the room than I found myself targeted by what appeared to be a cross between a dog and an alligator. His name was Blitzkrieg, and he almost took a piece out of me.

Once safely back in the hallway, I could hear his owners laughing. They were probably laughing during the attack, but having exceeded the speed of sound during my retreat, their voices took a moment to catch up with me. In fact, I may have actually exceeded the speed of light, in which case it is possible that I arrived back in the hallway before I left it.

Anyway, while working on a battle plan for my re-entry to the danger zone, I was interrupted by the need to take a phone call. It would be a reprieve from the anxiety. Or, so I thought.

It was Hugh Mustadunnit, calling about his cat, Upchuck. He had a chip on his shoulder and a stain on his rug.

"This cat has been vomiting once a week ever since he was boarded at your hospital last year," he said. "I'm sick of cleaning up the mess day after day. Your people must have done something to him while he was in there."

His accusation was, of course, pure bull. Nonetheless, the bull was charging and I had to sidestep quickly to avoid being gored. A quick glance at the cat's record showed that the vomiting had been going on for six years. The reason being that the entire Mustadunnit family had never been able to follow any of the prescribed courses of treatment.

A short battle of wits followed. Since he had come unarmed, I was able to declare victory for my side (the good guys) and headed back to the confrontation with Blitzkrieg.

With the help of a restraint pole, four people, and a lot of determination, we managed to get vaccinations into the pooch. His owners, Mr. and Mrs. Theory, said two things which I had easily predicted in advance and so would you if you would have been there.

The first was, "While we're here could you clip his nails?"

The second, and most typical of all was, "He has always behaved like this. We think that somebody abused him when he was young."

Nowadays, it seems that people cannot face a problem without finding someone else to blame. Every criminal in the court system is able to cite childhood abuses, drugs, mental instability and strange voices from outer space as valid reasons for going astray. Every excuse from, "The dog ate my homework," to "the devil made me do it," is used to avoid personal responsibility. Our clients simply take this trend a step farther by providing excuses for their pets, or, worse yet, blaming me!

Several more examples of this trend littered my appointment book later that same day. Mr. Fumblethought was in with his cat, Lucifer (another product of early age abuse, according to his owner). The cat had several typical fight wounds. Or so I thought. His nails were worn down to the bone. Mr. Fumblethought had a theory as to how it happened.

"Lucifer scratched the neighbor's dog last year. They weren't too happy about it. I think they grabbed him and cut his nails too short so he couldn't scratch anymore."

This was, of course, a ridiculous premise. If anyone grabbed this cat outdoors, there would be pieces of their shredded body all over the neighborhood and their biography would be featured in the obituary column.

I tried to explain that to him, but he liked his own version of the probable events better than my fight theory. I had to admit to myself that he had a fertile mind. In fact, the area between his ears was a dark, empty space lined with manure and would probably be an excellent place to grow mushrooms.

He left my office vowing to spy on the neighbors and report back to me if they tried to clip Lucifer's nails ever again.

His ideas were the most ridiculous of the day. Or so I thought at the time.

Within an hour, Mrs. Latrine did him one better. She was in to see me with Piddle the Poodle. The diabetes was out of control once again and she thought she knew why.

"Doctor, I think someone sneaks into my apartment some nights and gives Piddle an extra shot of insulin. Wouldn't that explain why he's always urinating too much?"

Her theory was, of course, both wrong and medically backward at the same time. I admitted the dog for some tests and she left with a half-baked plan to set up a surveillance of her apartment and catch the insulin culprit.

The fact that Mr. Fumblethought and Mrs. Latrine both planned to go into the spy business made perfect sense to me. After all, they both seemed to exhibit a great deal of what I would characterize as counterintelligence.

May 1999

Bungling Bundles botch office visit—twice

Mr. and Mrs. Bundle charged through the front door of my hospital beaming with pride and self satisfaction.

They were squealing with delight in their accomplishment.

"We did it! We did it! It was quite a battle, but we finally got Smokey into the car and got him over here for his shots."

They both had their arms wrapped around a large bag that looked as if it contained a month's supply of laundry.

Mr. Bundle kept talking to the bag.

"Stay calm, Smokey. We'll be home soon. It's just a little shot. This won't take long."

Mrs. Bundle was anxious to tell everyone in the waiting room how the capture had been accomplished.

"We waited until Smokey was asleep on the bed. Then, I threw a coat over him and wrapped the blankets around it. Then we stuffed the entire thing into the laundry bag and here we are. Smokey never knew what hit him."

We all headed for the nearest exam room, closed the door and proceeded with the ceremonial unwrapping of Smokey. The laundry bag was removed, the blankets unfolded, the coat unrolled and, as I might have predicted, Smokey was not there.

Mrs. Bundle thought that we should search the exam room, but I assured her that the room in need of such a quest was in her house and not in my hospital. Slightly chagrined but vowing to try again, the Bundles headed for home.

As it turned out, that office call set the tone for the rest of my day. It was a day that I spent trying to find things. Of course, I couldn't find Smokey, but that wasn't my fault. He wasn't there. My search during the next office call was easier.

The Prim sisters brought their cat, Logjam, in to see me because of a strange anomaly that they discovered. They seemed reluctant, however, to describe the problem. Sensing a little embarrassment on their part, I patiently waited for one of them to get up the nerve to explain.

"Doctor, our cat doesn't seem to have any anus. My sister called the problem to my attention yesterday. We looked carefully, but can't seem to find an opening. Do you think that it might have healed closed?"

I fought the urge to ask them what brought on the anal quest in the first place and, within moments, was able to demonstrate the presence of the evasive orifice by harpooning it with a thermometer. On top of that, I was able to accomplish the entire task while maintaining a straight face. They went home secure in the knowledge that Logjam was anatomically functional. To the Prim sisters, such security is well worth the price of an office call. Unfortunately, my next client was not as amiable.

It was Mrs. Carp with her dog, Tubercle. She was worried about a strange lump that had been developing on the dog's side. Naturally, she was unable to find the lump when the time came to show it to me. Like most pet owners, she ineffectively fondled random areas of the pooch and lamented over the apparent disappearance of the lesion, while simultaneously demonstrating an uncanny ability to keep me from examining properly. At any rate, after an extensive bipartisan quest, no lump was found.

Can't you do something to find it?" she asked. "It seems to me that you ought to be able to do a biopsy or something to find out what it is."

> *"Doctor, our cat doesn't seem to have any anus ... Do you think that it might have healed closed?"*

I tried to explain that you have to find something before you can do surgery on it. However, she was able to see right through my flimsy excuse and, having uncovered my incompetence, left in search of a better veterinarian.

The rest of my day followed along similar lines. I won some. I lost some. Still, I had a better day than the Bundles. They called me about an hour before closing time with good news.

"We caught him for sure this time, Doctor. "He's in a cat carrier that we borrowed from our neighbor. We just live a few minutes from your office. We'll be right there."

Five minutes later, the Bundlemobile roared into my parking lot. Mr. Bundle was beaming with pride once again. That is, until he realized that in his haste to get to the office, he had run off and forgotten to bring Mrs. Bundle and the cat along with him.

April 1999

Hey, doc, Izzy Dunyet?

I was having one of those mornings where there wasn't much work to do, but I seemed to be having a rough time getting it done.

Such days tend to go from bad to worse, so I wasn't surprised when the office reported that Mr. Dunyet wanted to talk to me before he dropped off his cat for surgery.

Of course, when I went to the reception area to talk to him, he didn't actually have anything to say. I wound up explaining, for what seemed to be the millionth time, that there would be some preoperative blood tests in the morning followed by surgery in the afternoon. If all went well, he would have his cat home before we closed at 7 p.m.

"We'll be waiting by the phone, Doctor," he said. "We'll be anxious to hear about his surgery, and, of course, we'll want to pick him up as soon as possible."

Within 20 minutes I was informed that Izzy Dunyet was on the phone inquiring as to the status of his cat. He insisted on talking to me personally. We were now up to one million and one by my count. He told me that he'd be waiting for any news.

As the morning progressed, several of my other clients decided that it would be a good day to subject me to torture by telephone. It's not that the calls were all that unusual for a veterinary office, it's just that there were more of them than we usually get. As a result, I fell farther and farther behind schedule.

Duey Hafta called about his dog's diabetes.

"Do you think those shots are really necessary? He seems fine. Maybe he's cured. Why don't we quit for awhile and see what happens?"

No sooner did I finish his refresher course in physiology than Ann O'Rexic called about her dog's weight problem.

"Can't we do something to slim her down?" she whined. "She seems to be so fat that I can't bear to look at her. I'm afraid she's going to have a heart attack."

I explained that the pooch looked normal to me the last time I saw her just a week earlier. It wasn't the answer she wanted to hear.

An hour later, Mr. Corpulent called. He wanted to know if I could talk some sense into his sister-in-law, Miss O'Rexic. It seemed that he felt her dog was wasting away and that I should prescribe something to beef the mutt up a little. I explained about the pooch looking normal to me. It wasn't the answer that he wanted to hear, either. The entire incident just goes to show that everything is relative.

You may wonder why I would let a barrage of inane phone calls throw my morning off schedule like that. The logical thing to do would be to concentrate on my work and refuse to take the calls until I was caught up. Unfortunately, I don't work that way. I have always followed an insane policy of trying to be available when my clients feel the need to talk to me. I realize that you may see this as a demented, self-destructive behavior. You are probably right.

At any rate, should I ever decide to commit a crime, I will simply plead, "Not guilty by reason of insanity." The fact that I have always been willing to talk to anyone on the phone will serve as certain proof that the plea is accurate.

The telephone assault on the day in question did eventually slow down and I even made it to lunch on time. Izzy Dunyet caught me at the diner.

> *You may wonder why I would let a barrage of inane phone calls throw my morning off schedule ...*

"I'm glad I found you, Doc. The girls at your office told me that you were out to lunch so I thought I'd come over here and ask you when we can pick him up."

Once again, I told him I would call, and once again he said that he would wait by the phone.

He called again at 2 p.m. and 3 p.m. but, mercifully, I was busy in surgery and couldn't talk to him.

By 4 p.m., my surgeries for the day were finished. The Dunyet cat was awakening in the recovery area and would be ready to go home soon. I called the Dunyet house. You guessed it! No answer!

March 1999

Mrs. Bungle's lager-loving pooch still has those pesky fleas

Mrs. Bungle was at her wit's end. (In her case, the proper term would be half-wit's end). After exhausting her vast knowledge of home remedies, she was ready to let me have a crack at the problem.

"I just don't know what to do anymore, Doctor," she said. "I've tried everything and Tipsy still has these darn fleas."

This lady had been coming to me for years. I knew from painful experience that she never follows directions correctly. However, since it was a slow morning in my office and I was in the mood to be amused, I asked what she had done so far to get rid of the fleas.

"Well, Doctor, first of all I gave Tipsy a sponge bath with warm water. I didn't get her too wet, though, because it would take too long for her to dry. You know, when I was done, there were still fleas running around on her. Did you ever hear of such a thing?"

I told her that I had seen cases of the plain water sponge bath failing to kill off fleas, and that something else was often necessary.

"That's what my neighbor, Mr. Blunder, said. He told me that I would have to spray around the house to get the fleas that weren't on my dog. He recommended Lysol spray because it freshens the air as well as surfaces where you spray it."

Obviously, she was providing the fleas with a germ-free and pleasant-smelling environment. However, unless some of the fleas died laughing at her, their population had not suffered any great loss.

"You know, Doctor, those darn bugs were still around. That's when I decided to get tough with them. I got a perfume mister and filled it with my husband's mouthwash. Then I sprayed a little on Tipsy's fur. My neighbor, Mrs. Blooper, gave me the idea. It made Tipsy smell nice, but I don't think it killed many fleas."

I pointed out that the fleas were now, no doubt, minty fresh. Unfortunately, mouthwash was never really intended to serve as an insecticide.

"Now you tell me," she said. "Anyway, the problem seemed to be getting worse, so I did some research on the Internet. That's where I heard about the beer dishes. A dog breeder from Brainstorm, Michigan, by the name of Kent Holdwater, told me about the beer dish theory. He says that if you put dishes of beer around the house, the fleas will jump in and drown. I tried it and I think it might have worked, too. But Tipsy keeps drinking the beer. Now I'm afraid the problem is getting much worse. Those darn fleas must be making her sick because she acts weak sometimes."

I was forced to point out that the pooch was undoubtedly half pickled due to her new status as a lager lover and that her access to beer should be cut off.

"If you say so, Doctor. I just don't know what else to do, though. How will we ever get rid of the fleas without the beer dishes?"

I outlined a simple plan. Mrs. Bungle's role would be to do nothing. I would have the dog stay with me for a few hours for flea treatment. An exterminator would treat the house. There was no reason why we could not have the problem solved within the day.

"I just don't get it," she said. "What if your plan doesn't work? Does anyone ever have this much trouble getting rid of a few bugs? Why won't the darn things go away? Why do they seem to like my house so much?"

"Are you kidding?" I asked. "You've given them a clean place to live. And, as if that wasn't enough, you have each of them smelling minty fresh, which has undoubtedly enhanced their little flea sex lives. Then, after all that, you give them an intoxicated dog, which serves to provide them with a cocktail at each meal. They don't want to leave! In fact, they are probably thinking of electing you 'Woman of the Year.'"

Obviously, she was providing the fleas with a germ-free and pleasant-smelling environment.

February 1999

Does anyone lease pets? Client Izzy Worthitt may be in market

It all started last Thursday when I made a stupid mistake. Kelly was taking an X-ray, Donna and Nancy were drawing blood for a leukemia test and Barbara was out to lunch.

I wasn't busy. The phone was ringing. And so, during an episode of what I can only describe as temporary insanity, I answered the phone myself.

This was, of course, a stupid mistake. I've been in practice for decades. Disco came and went while I was treating animals, and I'll probably still be in practice when people don't even remember Monica Lewinski. I should have known better. But, by the time I came to my senses, it was too late.

The caller was Izzy Worthitt. He had an important question for me. "How much is an operation?" Naturally, I was forced to inquire as to what procedure he had in mind.

"I don't know, Doc," he said. "Harley has been real sick, and my cousin, who used to work in a pet store, said that sick dogs might need an operation."

You can guess what happened next. I told him that I'd have to see the dog to determine what was needed and he was prompted to ask the next obvious question. "Will there be any charge for that?"

I didn't hear from him again for four days. Then, yesterday afternoon, he showed up at the office (no appointment of course), with a mighty sick looking dog.

The exam revealed that I would need an X-ray of the dog and some blood tests.

His reply? (You guessed it!)

"Will there be an extra charge for that?"

Within hours, I had the diagnosis, treatment recommendations and prognosis ready. This prompted multiple questions from Mr. Worthitt.

"Doc," he said. "I need to know how much all of this will cost and how long you think Harley might live if we do all these things."

I was able to fill him in on all of these details. (I took a guess.)

Then, it happened. His gaze turned to a glassy stare. There was a look of slight contortions to his face. He looked helpless, and possibly unable to move. At first, I thought he might be having a seizure. Then, I thought I noticed a wisp of smoke coming from one of his ears. It dawned on me that Izzy was simply undergoing a new experience. He was trying to think.

"Gee, that's a tough one, Doc," he said finally. "The way I figure it, that comes to almost a hundred dollars a year."

Actually, it would work out to $120 a year, but I didn't tell him that.

> *Wisps of smoke were definitely coming from both ears now as he had a brilliant idea.*

"Maybe I should think about getting a new dog," he said. "In the long run, it would be a lot cheaper. Don't you think?"

His emotional attachment to Harley was heartwarming. He was faced with a choice that often puzzles car buyers. Do you buy a used car and inherit someone else's troubles, or do you buy a new car and make a payment each month that would be enough for any major repair on your old car? Following the same analogy, I asked him if he ever considered leasing a dog. That way he could avoid maintenance expenses. The sarcasm went over his head (like most everything).

Wisps of smoke were definitely coming from both ears now as he had a brilliant idea.

"Do you think we could send away to the Animal Pals Organization and get one of those low-cost certificates to pay for this?"

I informed him that they only pay for spays and neuters. This made no sense to him since his dog needed a more important operation.

"Well then, Doc, do you think you could do a little better on the price? You know, the name is Worthitt, not Rockenheimer." (He meant Rockefeller, but I didn't bother to tell him.)

So, in the long run, he figured that it would be best to get a new puppy. Harley would be, in his words, "better off if we put him to sleep."

That just left one more question.

"Will there be a charge for that?"

October 1998

... Because the clients helped

If you're anything like me, there is a stack of journals on your desk that you plan to look through any day now. Somewhere near the middle of the pile, you will find the issue of this magazine from November 1996. I'll wait while you go and read the story entitled "Bozo finds the equipment."

Can't find it? Then I'm going to have to drag you back in time to when I was 8 years old.

Our family car was a snazzy Studebaker, my favorite TV show was *The Honeymooners*, and my most prized possession was a phonograph record entitled, "Bozo Under the Sea." This little 78 rpm beauty told a story about Bozo the Clown (believed by many to be the ancestor of most veterinary clients), and was accompanied by a book of illustrations that allowed you to look at the pictures as you listened to the story.

Now, pay attention, here comes the interesting part. As I accompanied Bozo on his deep sea diving adventure, the record made an occasional "beep" sound so that I would know when to turn the page.

What an idea! The Bozo people created an interactive children's record. This seemed like an idea worth stealing.

So let's return to the present where, unless you come to your senses immediately, you are about to participate in another one of my interactive magazine columns.

Here's how it works. Every time you come to the simple **, insert the phrase, "because the clients helped."

And now, on with our story, "Bozo Proves A Point."

Mr. and Mrs. Inept came to see me one day last week. It seemed that their cat, Fishhooks, needed his nails trimmed. This should be a simple procedure requiring two or three minutes at the most. Unfortunately, a technician and I took 15 minutes to finish the job on this cat. Why? **

The incident reminded me of the time that I was treating a sick dog for Vera Helpful. Members of the family kept calling with different and conflicting pieces of history. Friends and neighbors of the family kept calling with different and conflicting pieces of history. Friends and neighbors of the family called in half-baked theories of their own. Some of the callers had never even seen the dog. I had so many pieces of conflicting information that a simple diagnosis was made difficult **.

Furthermore, every phone call included a request for some new blood test, X-ray or diagnostic procedure that Vera agreed would be wise. The result was that the bill was much higher than necessary **.

The point I was going to make in this column was that, when things go wrong, it is often **. However, something happened this week that turned out a little differently.

Every time you come to the simple **, insert the phrase, "because the clients helped."

It all started when Dr. Newvet called to tell me off. He gave it to me with both barrels.

"As a new graduate, I am insulted by the way you are always making fun of our clients." he said. "Clients are the lifeblood of small animal practice. Maybe you should try treating them with respect instead of belittling them all the time. I'll admit there are a few wackos out there, but those things you write about are obviously just a bunch of made up ridiculous stories."

What could I say? Would I dare burst his idealist bubble? ... Sure, why not?

I invited him to spend the afternoon in my office. Soon, I had him convinced that there are more than a few wackos out there, and that strange things can happen faster than you can count them.

Not only that, but I taught him these lessons without any effort on my part at all **.

September 1998

Mrs. Lotsavets proves plenty of 'stray' clients still roam streets

Some office visits seem to stick in my memory more clearly than others. A case in point would be the first time that Mrs. Lotsavets brought in her dog, Rover. Although the office call occurred over two years ago, I'll never forget it.

Come to think of it, I'll never forget her last visit to my office either. In fact, it was the same visit.

She had been looking for a new veterinarian to take care of her pets. Apparently, I seemed to be a viable candidate for the job.

"I'm just not happy with the vet that I have been using," she said. "Whenever we have a problem at night or on a holiday, he acts like it's an inconvenience to be bothered outside of his regular office hours."

Naturally, her statement caused a faint alarm to go off in my head. Apparently, she was the type of person who expected a great deal of extra service.

She continued, "The vet we used to go to was always worried about money. He seemed more concerned with getting paid than with caring for animals."

Alarm number two went off, loud and clear.

I glanced at the record in search of other bad signs. They were all there. The address was a post office box, and there was a notation that the client did not have a telephone. (Alarms three and four went off simultaneously.)

Mrs. Lotsavets was quickly shaping up to be a four-alarm loser, but I had no choice but to proceed with the examination. As it turned out, Rover was pretty badly banged up. There were some minor cuts and bruises, a luxated hip and a laceration that would need suturing. After hearing the recommended course of therapy, my new client had some further history to share.

"You know, Doctor, Rover isn't really my dog. He's a stray. I've just been feeding him and felt sorry for him when I saw this injury. He doesn't belong to anyone, but if you wanted to fix him up, I would consider keeping him. I feel bad that this had to happen since I don't usually let him outside except on a leash. I guess one of the kids must have left the door open."

We discussed the expenses that would be involved and she borrowed the phone to call her husband at work. From 25 feet away, I heard his reply roaring out of the telephone: "We ain't spendin' no money on that stupid dog! He's been nothing but trouble since the day we bought him."

She took Rover and left, apparently seeking a more compassionate veterinarian—one who would treat a poor, homeless stray "for the good of the animal."

It seems to me that people use the word stray expecting it to have a profound affect on us. Our knees are supposed to go weak with compassion as we realize that the client is a selfless good Samaritan who has gone to great lengths to bring a pathetic situation to our attention. Meanwhile, the patient is to be seen as needy, homeless and in desperate need of assistance.

We are expected to be so overcome with emotion that we will be anxious to do something to correct the situation, something to alleviate pain and suffering. Something to help the good Samaritan in his or her quest for animal welfare. Something dramatic, and most important of all, something free.

Just for fun, I approached this subject one day last month while having lunch with a few colleagues. I was curious as to how other practices handle clients with so-called strays.

Arnie told us about a lady who called him to inquire about spaying a dog.

"Doctor, do you ever do spays for free just for the good of the animal?" she asked.

"There's this stray dog that keeps having puppies, but she's not really ours. Would you like to spay her sometime?"

After he politely declined, she had another question.

"Well, do you have a bulletin board in your hospital where we could advertise the puppies for sale? The notice wouldn't have to be up very long, because we've never had any trouble selling her puppies before."

Abe Raisive had a story of his own to tell.

Once, when a client identified her dog as a homeless stray, Abe asked how long the dog had been hanging around in that neighborhood. Her answer made us all chuckle.

"We brought him with us two years ago when we moved here from South Carolina."

Apparently, the lady thought that, unless she gave birth to the dog herself, it was a stray.

For the most part, we all agreed that

> *From 25 feet away, I heard his reply roaring out of the telephone...*

client use of the word stray is basically motivated by the desire to keep costs down. The notable exception being Dr. Newvet who felt that we were all too cynical.

"How much could it cost to treat a few strays for free?" he asked. "It seems to me that the goodwill would be worth it."

I immediately offered to help build the goodwill of his practice by referring all such cases to him.

"That won't be necessary," he told me, "our practice is growing just fine. Why, only yesterday I saw a client who started coming to us because she heard that we don't worship the almighty dollar as much as other hospitals do. In fact, when I asked her about her previous veterinarian, she mentioned you. Her name was Mrs. Lotsavets."

"I am happy for you," I told him. "But the truth is, she's not really my client. She's a stray."

August 1998

Mechanical Caesarean cures cat carrier dystocia

I entered the exam room just in time to see the Tazmanian Devil chasing Roadrunner around the base of the examination table.

Mr. Potatohead stood in the corner with a glazed, disinterested look in his eyes. Olive Oyl had her nose buried in a magazine that she had brought in from the waiting room.

Admittedly, it was a strange combination of individuals. However, I call them as I see them and on this particular day, I was having fun comparing my clients to fictional characters. Since I had seen this family many times before, my knowledge of their personalities and physical characteristics allowed me to assign their nicknames very quickly.

Olive, for example, is so thin you have to close one eye to get a good look at her. Her husband's name seemed to be a good match also, not only due to his amazing resemblance to the famous vegetable character, but also due to his mental abilities. If he did have a tuber for a brain, I don't see how it could make much of a difference in his I.Q. Their children, of course, acted like children.

At any rate, their cat had to be treated, and so it was time to stop daydreaming and get to work. It was one of my least favorite types of office calls, an obstetrics case. It would be a difficult delivery. The patient was nasty. The presentation was breech. And worst of all, the owners wanted to help. Having taken care of their cat before, I knew just how much help they were going to be.

Just last week they were in with their other cat. He was in a bad mood, also. Like most people, they found the cat's aggression highly amusing. Once, when the cat lunged at me, Mr. Potatohead laughed so hard that he almost unfolded his arms and helped the kids hold the cat. (Almost).

The rest of that office call was filled with the typical antics that we have all learned to expect from cats and their owners. Every time I turned my back, they let the cat jump down from the exam table. This, of course, caused more squeals of laughter.

While I was in the pharmacy getting his distemper shot, they let him climb into the sink. If they laughed any harder, I was going to have to put them on oxygen.

A few minutes later, I went to the lab to check the results of a stool sample. By the time I got back, the fractious feline was in one of my cabinets knocking bottles over. The family was enjoying a group convulsion of hysteria.

However, this was a new day. The things that occurred on their previous visit wouldn't necessarily mean that they couldn't be a lot of help this time. So, I considered the idea of letting them assist. Fortunately, I quickly came to my senses and called a technician in to help. When they began to reminisce and giggle about their last visit, there was no doubt that the right decision had been made.

The procedure was tedious. We would deliver a foot or a tail, and a minute later we would lose it. One minute we would have a posterior presentation, but, the next minute it would be anterior. I found myself wishing that I had paid more attention to obstetrics when I was in school. The knowledge would have come in handy. But who would have guessed that a small animal practitioner would face cases like this one at the rate of several per day?

Finally, I was forced to recommend a mechanical Caesarean section. The only way we were going to get him out was to remove the bolts and take the cat carrier apart. Then we could give him his vaccinations and bolt him back in.

Yes, we were treating a case of cat carrier dystocia, a common prelude to feline office calls. It is a subject that should certainly be given more attention in veterinary schools; along with, perhaps, a course on how to resuscitate people who have laughed themselves unconscious.

June 1998

Client monkeyshines leave a doubting Arnie

I once heard it said that an infinite number of monkeys playing with an infinite number of typewriters, would eventually reproduce every great novel that has every been written.

However, that was quite some time ago and I would hazard a guess that monkeys use word processors nowadays. Nonetheless, the basic tenet still holds true and with some slight modification, could be applied to our profession.

It should say that a whole bunch of veterinarians dealing with a whole bunch of pet owners will eventually face just about every type of crazy circumstance you could imagine. Now, if you are a practicing veterinarian, the truth of this statement is self-evident.

On the other hand, if you are not a member of our profession, but simply someone who happened to pick up this article to line a bird cage or to wipe off the dip stick from your car, then you may need some examples. Well, it's your lucky day because yesterday I had so many examples, I hardly know where to begin.

It all started when Vera Picky stopped in while on her way to work, so that she could visit her cat, Fuzzy. Following a few hugs, kisses and a little baby talk, her red wool jacket was covered with cat hair. She viewed the situation as a catastrophe. Frantically, she began to wipe the jacket with her hand. This proved to be a futile effort, so she put the jacket on one of our exam tables and performed hair removal surgery for a full 10 minutes. Finally, she "borrowed" two rolls of adhesive tape and dabbed away every single remnant of hair that was left. The jacket was restored to its original splendor. Then, in a move that surprised us all, she picked up Fuzzy for a last hug and walked out of the office looking, once again, as if she had been tarred and feathered.

I hardly had time to recover before Ann Fibian called with an important question.

"Doctor, I found a frog in my backyard. The kids want to know what kind it is. If I hold it up to the phone, can you tell me?" I informed her I couldn't.

"Well, Doctor, could you at least tell me if it's a frog or a toad?"

"I have no way of knowing," I said.

"Then just tell me how to tell if it's a male or a female."

"That's easy," I explained. "Just watch when it catches a fly. If *he* eats it, it's a male. If *she* eats it, it's a female."

She vowed to begin an immediate fly hunt.

Moments later, Mr. Wingnut was on

the phone with a big problem of his own.

"Doctor, there's something wrong with my dog, Ouija. He wanted me to call you."

Foolishly, I asked how the dog got the message across.

"This morning Ouija chewed up the telephone cord. I think he was trying to tell me to call you."

I informed him that the only problem was almost certainly just that Ouija was bored, and moved on to my next office call.

It was the entire Wacko family with their dog, Frenzy. The scene was all too typical. The dog, who had just taken his annual car ride, was excited and nervous. He sniffed every area that the length of his leash would allow. He pulled against his choke collar with almost enough force to render himself unconscious. He panted and whined until his owners finally realized what he wanted.

"Doctor," said Mr. Wacko. "Frenzy is thirsty. Could you get him a bowl of water?"

Knowing it was a waste of time, I went for the water anyway. However, what happened next was truly amazing. I witnessed a miracle. The dog actually drank the water!

When they left, I was still so excited that I had to tell someone. Naturally, my first thought was to call my friend, Arnie. I told him all about the Wacko dog and how I planned to write this column and share the news with our colleagues.

He didn't believe that such a miracle could really happen or that anyone would take me seriously if I wrote about it. In fact, all he would say was, "Monkeys with word processors? So that's it! I always wondered how you turn out that silly column of yours!"

March 1998

Queen of the Clueless takes defective reasoning to new heights

I hate to be interrupted when I'm on vacation. Furthermore, my private yacht can only sleep 28 people comfortably.

Still, I understand that it is quite an honor to win a Nobel Prize. So, I told the prize committee that I would accept if they would present me with the award aboard ship. All they would have to do is charter a seaplane and meet me at a predetermined spot in the Caribbean.

The ceremony started out beautifully. Unfortunately, my secretary interrupted right in the middle.

"Sorry to have to wake you, Doctor, but it's one o'clock and Mrs. Post Opp is here with her two Cocker Spaniels, Cauze and Efect."

As soon as I heard the client's name, I knew that I was about to be treated to a demonstration of pet owner deductive reasoning. (Known as "defective reasoning" in my practice.)

"Doctor," she said. Efect seems to be having trouble making wee-wee. He strains for a long time when he goes. This never happened before he was neutered. Did everything go all right with his surgery?"

I knew that she would ask that question. Her dogs were neutered in 1992 and every problem since has been blamed on the surgery. I checked the entries on her pets' medical records.

September 1994. Both dogs had fleas. "Could they have gotten them when they were in for neutering?"

August 1996. Cauze had a sore leg after getting loose and staying out all night. "Could it be that something went wrong during his surgery?"

February 1997. Both dogs were sneezing. "Could they have picked something up when they stayed in the hospital?"

After assuring her that cystitis rarely takes five years to manifest itself, I treated the dog and sent her home.

At that moment, I was sure that Mrs. Post Opp was my most clueless client. Moments later, I was proven wrong.

Mrs. Sleuth was waiting to discuss the condition of her cat, Sherlock. It was an easy diagnosis. Sherlock was painful and swollen around the right shoulder. I explained to her that the cat had been shot. At that point, most clients would have gotten excited. Many would say things like, "Who shot him?" or "How can we find out who did this?" But Mrs. Sleuth said nothing. I showed her the X-rays. There was a bullet in the soft tissues. I had her palpate the skin by the side of the neck where the bullet could be clearly felt. I showed her the clean, round entrance wound three inches away from the projectile.

She looked at her well-ventilated feline, then looked at me and said, "So, Doctor, do you think it could be a bite wound?"

We had a new champion. Move over Mrs. Post Opp, you are no longer queen of the clueless. Mrs. Sleuth had taken pet owner defective reasoning to new heights.

And yet, as it turned out, Mrs. Post Opp was not about to take this coup lying down. She tried one more time that same day to regain her title. She called to tell me about a new problem. It seems that Cauze had developed some diarrhea and, *guess what?* He never had it before his neutering surgery!

> *And yet, as it turned out, Mrs. Post Opp was not about to take this coup lying down.*

I told her to come over to pick up some diarrhea medicine. I should have told her to bring a stool sample, but I didn't. I was afraid she'd show up with a Tupperware container full of shinola.

January 1998

Time on their hands, trouble on their minds, a mess in their wake

Desperate times call for desperate measures.

And so, I found myself sneaking down the hall of my own hospital and hiding in the closet at the end of the corridor.

From there, with my stethoscope held to the wall, I could determine what was being said to my clients as they were being ushered to the exam rooms. It was all part of my on-going investigation into client behavior.

As footsteps approached, I listened carefully for the voice of my receptionist.

"The doctor will be with you in a moment," was all she said.

I waited anxiously for her next line, but it never came.

I was half expecting her to say something like: "Make yourself at home." "Feel free to roam the halls while you wait," or "Please amuse yourself by playing with all the equipment in the room until the doctor comes."

You see, if such statements were made, either as innocent chit chat or, perhaps, deliberate sabotage, it could help to explain the way my clients behave whenever they are left alone in a room. However, I am pleased to be able to report that my staff,

My initial reaction was one of surprise. After all, I thought I had seen everything.

and probably yours as well, is not at fault. According to my research, they do not make such statements. Apparently our clients are responsible for their own misbehavior.

Take for example, Mrs. Preen. I am sure that no one tells her to, and yet she always feels the necessity to groom her dog while waiting to see me.

"Oh, Doctor, I hope you don't mind," she says, "But I borrowed this comb out of your cabinet."

Like many clients, she might

not comb that mutt for two years at a time. Then, all of a sudden, in my exam room, purging the pooch of loose hair becomes a dire emergency. By the time I arrive, she is piling loose hair on the floor next to her dog. Why does her compulsion to borrow my things include use of the comb, but not use of the trash can?

Mr. Spritz represents another case in point.

I would venture a guess that no one said to him, the last time he was in to see me, "Why not bathe your cat in the sink while waiting for the doctor?"

And yet, he managed to get water all over the floors, walls and countertops. He used six ounces of surgical scrub, "borrowed" two pair of latex exam gloves, and concluded by drying the cat with five dozen paper towels!

These and other examples of typical exam room misbehavior are seen by all of us. Often, we wonder how our clients could be so similar. Then, once in a blue moon, someone will come up with an entirely new antic. So, stand by and hear about my encounter with Mrs. Dingleberry.

I could hardly believe my eyes as I entered the exam room. And yet, there it was. There was no mistaking it. A brand new, original, crazy veterinary client stunt was in progress.

My initial reaction was one of surprise. After all, I thought I had seen everything. Apparently, I was wrong. My furniture had been rearranged. The trash can was in the center of the room with the chair next to it. The exam table (200 pounds) was moved over against the wall. Mrs. Dingleberry (also 200 pounds) was seated in the chair. Her son, who was not wearing any clothes, was seated on the trash can. It took me awhile to catch on. She was potty-training the kid using my waste can as the potty.

Frankly, I didn't know how to react. What would motivate someone to do such a thing in my office? I have no idea. I am sure of one thing, though. No one on my staff said, "While waiting for the doctor, why not have your kid poop in the wastebasket?"

October 1996

Mr. Punster wears out welcome; Dr. O would like to just 'barium'

Will Dawdle was a great veterinarian in the 1970s. In fact, he still is. But Will never quite found high gear. In all the years I worked with him, he never seemed to finish his work on time. Such was the case one evening in 1973 when he asked me for a favor.

"Mike, would you see my last office call for me?" he asked. "I'm running behind and it's almost closing time already. Besides, you'll like the guy. He's been a client for years. It's just some little lump to check on the dog. You'll be out of there in no time."

I entered the exam room and met Mr. Punster and his dog, Scooter.

"Scooter's been rubbing his back end on the floor, Doc," he said. "I know it can't be a *terminal* illness. Scooter has never even been to the airport!"

He proceeded to laugh like a hyena at his own joke. Unfortunately, he had more.

"I guess we can't do a *CAT* scan. Scooter's a dog."

At this point his face was turning red. His eyes began to water. I had never seen a client laugh so hard except, of course, for those cases where a beloved pet tried to bite the veterinarian.

I tried to continue and, since the pooch had a history of stomach problems, asked if there were any G.I. symptoms.

"He might have some colic in him, Doc. Now that you mention it, I never did know who his father was and the neighbor down the street has a *colic* named Laddie. Anyway, the last time he was sick, they were going to take an X-ray and use barium. I said, 'We can't *barium*! He ain't dead yet!' "

The laugh-fest continued. Closing time came and went. Through the window I saw Will Dawdle's car leave the parking lot. I started dreaming of ways to get even.

As the exam continued, I pointed out a small tumor near the dog's rectum.

"You say there's a lump there, Doc? I *node* it, I *node* it," he said.

Where did I go wrong?

"But, I only see one lump. How come you said there's *tumor*?"

Visions of my dinner getting cold kept me swimming upstream in a sea of stupid puns. I explained that surgery so near to the rectum could be a problem due to the local blood supply. The volcano of corn erupted again.

"First of all, don't worry about that *artery*," he said. "Scooter don't know a thing about paintings. Furthermore, she's a humble dog. There's nothing *vein* about her. I am worried about the location, though. My friend's dog had a lump there and it was serious. It *rectum* all right. It dang near killed 'em."

The conversation, if you can call it that, continued.

Mr. Punster had a comment for everything I said. And, each one of those comments was followed by one of his time-consuming fits of laughter.

"Did you see the look Scooter gave you when you talked about stopping the bleeding? You really *cauterize* when you said that! And I don't know how you're going to clean out that rectum. She has lots of friends, but she's never had an *enema*!"

Eventually, I managed to schedule the surgery for a day later in the week, and, within minutes, was hustling Mr. Punster out the door. Unfortunately, he had a few parting shots, which he managed to shout in my direction as he headed for his car.

"I won't be able to sleep a

> *Visions of my dinner getting cold kept me swimming upstream in a sea of stupid puns.*

wink worrying about this, Doc. I always get *euthansia* when I'm upset. I haven't thought about a *post-operative* recovery this much since my mailman was in an automobile accident."

The next morning Dr. Dawdle gave me quite a smirk.

"How did you like Mr. Punster?" he asked.

I was compelled to tell him that it made me feel a great deal like an elevator.

"Really?" he asked. "Is that because a visit with Mr. Punster has its ups and downs?"

"Not at all," I said. "It's because I got the shaft."

April 1996

Chapter 7:
The World We Live In

How do you treat acute pet owner stupidity?

Are you ready to take a surprise quiz?

Well, sharpen your pencils boys and girls because in a few minutes, we're going to put your knowledge to the test.

First, however, I have to tell you about my latest encounter with Hawkeye Pursewatcher and his wife Myopia. As usual, they found the prices at my clinic to be unconscionable. This time it was Myopia who was particularly distraught.

"You have got to be kidding me, Doctor," she said. "$55 is a lot of money just to worm three dogs. Isn't there a cheaper way to do it? Besides, bringing them in for injections is very difficult."

Since her dogs were regular patients of mine, I was able to assure her that I could dispense tablets that would do the job for a fraction of the cost. Somehow, my statement induced her to have another attack of pet owner stupidity.

"I can't give them pills," she answered. "Can't you take a few minutes to teach me how to give injections? Then, you could give me the medicine to treat them at home. Wouldn't that cost about the same as giving me the pills?"

For some reason, I failed to jump at this golden opportunity. That was OK because she had another idea.

"You know, Doctor, we only live a few miles from where you live. How about if we buy the pills as you suggest, and then you stop by our house and give them to the dogs for us? That would be a nice goodwill gesture on your part. If people knew that you would go to their houses and give medicine to sick animals, you would sell a lot more pills. Wouldn't that be good for business?"

Naturally, I was touched. Her kind offer to help build my practice almost brought a tear to my eye. I must be

crazy because I declined to accept her humanitarian gesture. Undaunted, she stepped up to the plate and prepared to go for strike three.

"Doctor, I have another idea," she said. "When we brought our first dog to you over on Old Street, it only cost $4 to worm a dog. Do you remember?"

Of course I remembered. That was in the '70s. I waited patiently for her train of logic to derail again. It didn't take long.

"Why don't you check in the back of your cupboards, Doctor?" she said. "Maybe you have a bottle of that cheap worm medicine still sitting around somewhere. You could use that to worm our dogs. You wouldn't charge us, would you? After all, that medicine is probably outdated by now."

Much as I hated to disappoint such a good client, there was no choice. If I didn't tell her, she would find out sooner or later. So, I gave her the bad news: Prices have changed since the '70s.

And now, it's time for our quiz. It is one of those math questions presented in the form of a story, just like the ones you hated so much in junior high.

Part 1: Shortly after Mike graduated from veterinary school, he and his wife bought their first house. It was a three-bedroom, split-level home with a two-car garage. It had an acre of land and a 30-year mortgage.

Part 2: Last year, Mike bought a new truck. It was an ordinary GMC truck with a seven-foot snowplow.

Question: Which one costs more each month?

Take your time. Use any reference material that you would like. Remember, at no point were words like Mercedes, Cadillac or Rolls Royce mentioned in the problem. Calculators are permitted.

(Note: If you are under 30 years old, you may wish to be excused at this point.)

Finished? Due to your undoubtedly cynical nature, you probably guessed by now that the truck costs more (a lot more).

I guess I should have asked the truck salesman to check the back parking lot to see if there were any brand new leftover 1975 model trucks available.

August 2006

Politics in the exam room can get heated

Ideologies largely are emotional, which makes them good topics to avoid

Every now and again, a fight breaks out in my hospital waiting room. Usually, it is because a patient got out of its carrier or slipped off its leash. However, the last skirmish we witnessed was different. It was the people who were fighting, not their pets.

Libby Rail and Ken Servative were screaming at each other. Each addressed the other as either "Dumbo" or "Jackass." They argued about everything from the national economy to the local school board election. When I entered the room, they both tried to get me to join the fray.

However, the last thing I needed was to take sides in a heated political discussion. For some reason, it seemed like a good time to quote Will Rogers. "I tell you folks," I said, "all politics is applesauce." They wanted to know what that meant. "I don't have a clue."

I told them, "I just thought it sounded folksy and wise." They chose to ignore me after that. So, I decided to say folksy things more often.

"Here we go again." I thought to myself. Election day is coming and controversy over who should have won the presidential election still rages on in Florida, where many people there still feel that Dewey should have beaten Truman in 1948. If they ever get that settled, they will re-examine the election of 2000.

Hopefully, such places that use unreliable paper ballots will move up into the 19th century.

You see, the voting machine was invented in 1868. I know this because I checked with our research department, which is

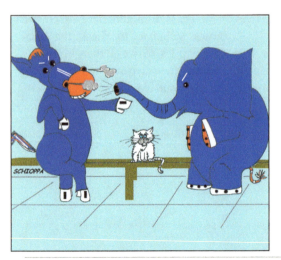

> I told them, "I just thought it sounded folksy and wise." They chose to ignore me after that. So, I decided to say folksy things more often.

located on the second floor of my home. The entire department consists of an almost complete edition of the 1979 World Book Encyclopedia. (The M book is missing, and S-Sn volume has had the cover chewed off by the dog.)

Using the E book, I found out that the vote counting machine was invented by none other than the Wizard of Menlo Park himself, Thomas Edison.

That's right, before the phonograph and even before the light bulb, old Tom had this country's election problems covered.

Anyway, from now until the election, I plan to avoid getting into political discussions with clients. No good can come from it. I learned that lesson four years ago, and I learned it the hard way. It happened when I pointed out to Mrs. Ballot that politicians all know they can catch more flies with honey than they can with vinegar, but they also all know that they can catch the most flies with a shovel full of manure. How was I to know that she was running for re-election as county supervisor at the time? She stormed out vowing never to return.

She was back a month later though. It seems that after she left my office, she went to see my friend, Abe Raisive. He really turned her off by sharing his election-day philosophy. He pointed out that politicians are a lot like diapers. They need to be changed frequently, and for the same reason.

October 2004

Computers: friend or foe?

For the 'electronically challenged,' pencil and pens worked just fine, thank you

As you undoubtedly know, computers have revolutionized our ability to store and retrieve information.

However, they are not really capable of displaying independent thoughts or emotions.

(Note: the preceding statement is blatantly false.)

As proof that computers can and do display emotions, I would like to point out that our office computer does not like me. It likes younger people, people who don't remember slide rules, vinyl records, Howdy Doody or rotary dial telephones.

It may be that our relationship got off on the wrong foot four years ago when certain members of my staff talked me into installing one of the evil contraptions. I was pretty sure that I knew how to work the thing. After all, I had seen every episode of *Star Trek*. So, I sat down next to the new machine and had a long talk with it. The conversation was one-sided. The beast failed to answer my questions. It seemed to me that there must have been some problem with the way the thing was working because, the way I remember it, whenever Scotty talked to the computer on the Starship Enterprise, they would banter back and forth like old buddies. I tried yelling at it and when that didn't work, I was forced to break the bad news to my staff.

"I think the new computer is deaf," I told them.

When they got done laughing, they explained that our computer had to be operated with a keyboard and a mouse. Over the next month or two, several of them tried to show me how to work the thing. It didn't make any sense to me.

It would do things that defied logic. For example, one day it had a seizure. There were little pieces of multi-colored pipes and wheels gyrating all over the screen. I called one of the younger people over to have a look at it. (Note: My entire staff is made up of younger people.) They told me that I was looking at a screen saver and that the computer was supposed to do that. They went on to explain why, but it didn't make any sense to me.

Soon, we were getting e-mail, which is a really fast way to get information that you don't want or need. (Although I do enjoy the jokes, which seem to comprise most of the e-mail floating around in cyberspace.) We were also able to surf the Web and to play card games without the burden of having to have an actual deck of cards.

My office manager tried to explain why these things were important, but it didn't make any sense to me.

You see, I never really understood why computers were so popular. I had always maintained that they were a fad, much like the Hula Hoops that everyone had when I was a kid. You don't see them now, do you? I figured if I waited a few years, computers would disappear. Apparently, I was wrong. So, I have had no choice other than to accept them as a necessary evil in my world.

I'm not sure, though, why computers and I don't get along. My clients seem to love the things.

Many of them will show up for an office visit with 40 pages of crapola that they downloaded from the Internet. This is so they can tell me what to diagnose and what

> I was pretty sure that I knew how to work the thing. After all, I had seen every episode of Star Trek.

to treat it with. It goes without saying that they are almost always wrong, but the computer saves them from having to get their bad advice from well-meaning friends, newspaper pet advice columns or pet psychics. (Note: I prefer they get their advice, good or bad, from me.)

Anyway, I'm still trying to learn to get along with my electronic friends. My grandchildren tried to explain the great benefits society has reaped during the computer era. Apparently, they are indoctrinated with stuff at school. It didn't make any sense to me. We all got along just fine in the pencil and paper era.

The guy from petpillpushers.com tried to convince me that his outfit could benefit me and my clients by saving me the trouble of dispensing medications and having to haul all that unwanted profit to the bank. It didn't make sense to me. I asked my accountant why businesses were so bullish on installing these things. After all, I had to lay out a good deal of cash to computerize an office that was already running just fine. He showed me what happened after the computer was installed. Gross income went way up. Accounts receivable plummeted. Profit skyrocketed. All of a sudden, it made perfect sense.

July 2003

Do-it-yourselfer redefines medicine
The medical records showed three visits and 83 telephone calls from this client

As my receptionist handed me the cat's medical record, I was immediately impressed with the size of it. Clearly, it was one of the thickest files ever compiled at my clinic.

Along with it came the bad news. Mrs. Dingaling was on hold waiting to talk to me.

"Doctor, do you have Goner's medical record with you?" she asked. "He hasn't been himself lately, and I thought you could read his record and tell me what's wrong with him."

Hefting the inch-thick record, I was tempted to ask if I just couldn't wait for the movie to come out. Instead, I took a moment to skim over the two-pound document. It chronicled eight years of Goner's life, including just three visits to my office and 83 telephone calls.

"This," I thought to myself, "is not the type of client who pays our overhead."

Nonetheless, I politely inquired as to the problem.

"Goner is really sick this time," she told me. "He's lost a lot of weight and he won't eat a thing. Sometimes he seems so weak that he can hardly walk. What do you think it is? I don't have time to bring him over to your office. Can you tell me something that I can do at home?"

That was April 1. After I explained the potential seriousness of the situation, she rushed right over, arriving on April 30. I'm not sure why she bothered to come at all. The cat was in terrible condition, but she wouldn't let me do anything.

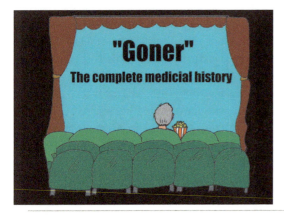

"Isn't it true that he might die?" she asked. "It doesn't make any sense to spend money on tests or treatments if he might die anyway. I'm going to take him home and let nature take its course."

The next day, she was on the phone with a request.

"I figured out the problem,"

she announced. "It's in his ears. Can I come over and get some ear drops to treat him with?"

> **For once, I said "no."**

Not seeing what harm it could do, I foolishly complied. However, this only led to another call the following day.

"Those ear drops you sold me aren't any good. I think they make him dizzy. Anyway, if the infection is deep in the ears, wouldn't it make more sense to give antibiotics by mouth? I'd like to come over and get some."

Foolishly, I complied again. (I'm detecting a pattern here.)

One day later she had a new diagnosis.

"I have the problem figured out," she said. "It's in his throat. I think those antibiotics you gave me caused a fungal infection that makes it hard for him to eat. I'm going to try force-feeding him."

Surprisingly, there was no improvement the next day.

"I can't believe this is happening," she said. "Isn't there anything you can do? I find it hard to believe that in this day and age, nothing can be done to help this poor animal."

Once again, though, she refused to consider any of my suggestions for diagnosing or treatment. Two days later, however, she surprised me by actually showing up at the office. Unfortunately, she left Goner at home. She came to discuss his force-feeding schedule. She had pages of charts and graphs. They showed the feeding schedule as well as documentation of everything the cat did each moment of the day. It was an impressive array of paperwork. Never have I seen anyone go to so much trouble to do a half-assed job. (Excluding politicians, of course).

The diagnosis du jour went like this:

"I think he's constipated, Doctor. Can we try laxatives mixed in with his food?"

Against my better judgment, I let her try it.

The next day, when the much-anticipated recovery failed to materialize, she had a new question.

"Goner looks like he won't make it much longer. Do you know of any research institutions that might want to do an autopsy for free? Since we couldn't figure out what was happening to him, they might be interested in him as a scientific study."

I told her that I didn't know of any source of free autopsies and explained the costs involved with doing a complete postmortem exam. She almost swallowed her telephone.

A week later, the inevitable happened. Goner passed away. His owner had one final request.

"Can you tell me, over the phone, how to do a simple autopsy at home?"

For once, I said "no."

May 2003

Enough blame to go around

Each of us receives the occasional "thank you" note or letter of praise from a grateful client.

If you are anything like me, you have a drawer full of them somewhere. The one I saw recently, however, was too good for the drawer. It was suitable for framing.

Even though the writer's cat had died while in my care, the letter had a glowing tone that would make you think that my mother had written it. Apparently, according to the letter, I could do no wrong. If my efforts failed, then surely no one else's would have been more successful. I was hailed as a miracle worker and a should-be role model for all veterinarians. Unfortunately, I'll never know who the letter was from because it didn't actually exist. Before I finished reading it, my receptionist woke me up to tell me that Mrs. Inkort was on the phone. Apparently, I had been desk dozing, something I often do for 10 or 15 minutes between lunch and afternoon office calls.

"Hello, Doctor," the dreaded phone call began. "This is Althea Inkort calling about my cat, Docket. I'm sorry it took so long to get back to you, but I wanted to consult my attorney before deciding how to proceed. You know, Docket was perfectly healthy when I brought him in there, so I just couldn't believe it when you told me he died."

At this point, I wondered what planet she was calling from. The cat was a seriously ill, unstable diabetic whose kidneys were failing.

When she dropped him off, he had one foot in the grave and was standing on a banana peel.

Her monologue continued.

"I think you should do an autopsy to see if you did anything wrong. My lawyer suggested having one done elsewhere, but if I do that, they might charge me for it. I figured that you would be willing to do it for free since his death was probably your fault."

I briefly explained my view of the situation to the party of the first part and went to see my first office call. It was Mrs. Tofu with her dog, Scratchy.

"Doctor," she said, "Scratchy has a sore foot. I think it's your fault. Another vet told me that you shouldn't have given him cortisone for that rash last summer. Cortisone isn't good for dogs."

One glance at his foot showed that he had two ingrown nails due to a simple case of owner neglect. I asked if the other veterinarian had seen the foot.

"Well, I didn't actually talk to him," she said. "I read it in the newspaper. It was in the pet advice column by Justin Inkslinger, DVM. He said that you veterinarians use too much cortisone and that we should have treated the rash with a high fiber diet and oatmeal soaks. And he ought to know because he is a real veterinarian even though he doesn't practice."

I explained the foot problem in terms that even she could understand. It didn't matter, though, because she wasn't listening.

No sooner had I recovered from her visit than Mr. Void was on the phone.

"Hello, Doctor, this is Warren T. Void calling," he announced as if I should be honored.

"It's about my kitten who died in your hospital last week. I think I know why she got sick. When I asked the pet store to replace her they said that she was too young for those vaccinations you gave. That's why they never give shots to the puppies and kittens in the store. You should have waited until she was 6 months old."

I had heard that line before from people who purchased animals at Pricey Pets, a less-than-reputable local pet store run by Alice Buylow and her partner, Tanya Markitup. Somehow they always find a way to renege on their guarantee. Once, they told a client of mine that their puppy got parvovirus because I said it was OK to feed Poochie Platter after they advised feeding only the Yuppie Yummies available exclusively at their store. I informed Mr. Void that he should insist that they honor their commitment, because, quite frankly, they were wrong and I was right.

Later than evening, I found myself glad to be in my own home where I seldom get blamed for things. And, when my youngest son's homework prompted him to ask, "Dad, who shot President Kennedy?" I was able to look him right in the eye and say, "It wasn't me."

September 2002

Old habits die hard

I used to have a handle on life, but it broke. At least that's what my friend, Arnie, says.

If your practice suffered greatly from the February doldrums and you had nothing better to do with your time than to read my column, then you may recall what he said about me last month. He called me a "dinosaur—an old Fogysaurus." He formed his opinion just because I refuse to embrace the metric system. I don't see why the rest of the world can't think in terms of pounds and inches, while letting their water freeze at 32 degrees. Furthermore, I know that many of you agree with me whether you are willing to admit it or not.

Nonetheless, Arnie is known for his wisdom. So I have given some serious thought to his criticism. There are times when I seem to be out of step with the rest of the world (I don't see where that is necessarily a bad thing.)

For example, last week, Mr. Keyboard was in to see me with his cat, Bytes. It seemed that the fractious feline had a choking cough. I was not looking forward to examining this particular cat's throat, but I knew I would have to. I expected to find a foreign body in the pharynx, probably a piece of someone else who foolishly got too close to this cat's mouth. However, Mr. Keyboard informed me that there was no need to examine the throat. According to his "research," the cat was suffering from diabetes. "All the symptoms fit, Doctor," he said. "I read about it on the Internet. I brought you the printouts from my home computer in case you want to learn about it. Did you know that cats can get diabetes?"

His home diagnosis was, of course, completely wrong. As I sedated the cat to remove the chicken bone, I found myself longing for the good old days when people got their bad advice from friends, neighbors and newspaper columns (no equipment was necessary.)

That same day, Mrs. Wideload called about her dog, a Chow Chow named

Yum Yum. (Don't blame me, I didn't name him.)

"Doctor, is there anything we can do to get some more weight on Yum Yum?" she asked. "He seems so thin. Do you think I could change his diet?"

I asked what she had been feeding the dog up until now.

"We have him on Earth Blend Goodie Brand Special Dental Formula, Sensitive Stomach Urinary Health Diet for Less Active Mature Dogs." (How do they fit the entire name on the bag? I remember when there were two foods available—dog food and cat food.)

I advised her to try plain old "Dog Food." She didn't like the idea because they don't sell plain old "Dog Food" at her favorite pet supply store, "The Yuppy Puppy."

These two examples aren't the only areas in which I find myself to be out of step with the rest of society. Take last summer for instance. I was at the local amusement park with my children and grandchildren. You wouldn't believe what it cost to get in. (I'll give you a hint. It's not $2 anymore.) My family had a good chuckle when they saw my shock at the price of admission. A few minutes later, I had them squealing with laughter. It happened when we passed a soda machine and I reached into my pocket, pulled out

> A few minutes later, I had them squealing with laughter.

a couple of quarters and asked if anyone wanted a soda. My son laughed so hard he almost swallowed his tongue. (Apparently, sodas aren't a quarter anymore. Are you ready for a shock? The machine wanted $2 for each can! I remember when they were 5 cents.

Yesterday, I decided to call Arnie and tell him that he was right. I am a dinosaur. Many of my ideas are old fashioned and so are my values. I have resisted many of the modern trends that now permeate our society in general and my profession in particular.

"I'm glad to hear you admit it, Mike," he said. "You have a lot of antiquated ideas and now that you have confessed, you can start thinking about changing."

"You don't understand," I told him. "I'm not confessing. I'm bragging."

March 2002

Just how far can you stretch a dollar?

Mr. Dollar had absolutely no intention of skimping on anything as important as the health of his pet.

"Bottom is the best dog I've ever had, Doc," he said. "Let's get this problem figured out. Run any tests or take any X-rays that you think you need. I don't care about the cost. Bottom is my best friend. Money is no object."

On the surface, this may appear to be an ideal situation. However, any experienced veterinarian knows that the client who professes to be a big spender is the same client who demands a half-hour explanation of the charges after the pooch was admitted to the hospital. I made a mental note to itemize and justify all the charges carefully, then moved on to my next office call. It was Mrs. Frugal with her cat, Budget. This was their first visit to my office.

"Doctor, I hope you can help us. Budget is very sick, but I just can't afford a lot of high vet bills."

I examined the cat and explained the tests and treatments that I thought were indicated. Unfortunately, further discussion revealed that she had no money whatsoever with which to help her cat. I wound up offering to provide basic medical treatment for free.

"Oh, thank you, Doctor," she said. "I'm so glad we came to you. By the way, you'll probably want to update him on his vaccines while he's here. Also I'll be very anxious to hear about his blood test results, especially the ones for leukemia and FIV. Please keep him with you until you're sure he's well. Then, when he comes home, I'll need copies of his records, including X-rays and tests, so that my regular vet can keep them on file."

I wasn't a bit surprised. I've been in practice too long. So, I gave her a quick lecture on the limits of free treatment, sent her home and went to answer a

waiting phone call. It was Al Paloosa calling about a problem with his barn cats.

"You know, doctor," he said. "The stables where I keep my show horses have a lot of cats. They always seem to be breeding. If I can catch them one at a time and bring them over to you, can you spay them or neuter them or whatever you call it? I know that you vets are concerned about animal overpopulation. Do you ever do things like this for free, just for the good of the animals? After all, they're not actually my cats. They're just strays."

I told him to check into the low cost programs that are available through the local animal shelter. I also suggested that he might send away for reduced cost certificates that are available from the Friends of Gonad Removal organization. These are just two of the many national and local charities in which my clinic participates. When these are added to the list of individual clients for whom we reduce our rates based on need, my clinic comes out second to none in the bleeding heart department. Nonetheless, there is a point where we have to draw the line. With the conclusion of his call, I found that I had reached another milestone in my life. I had made it through another day.

Unfortunately, I couldn't head straight for home. I had an appointment to see my own physician, Dr. Armand A. Leg. He had been treating me for a back injury and insisted that I come in for regular rechecks. His average office call lasts about 37 seconds. It consists of a handshake, a comment about his dog, and a

On the surface, this may appear to be an ideal situation.

casual "How are you this week?" For this I pay about $1 a second.

Armand drives a new Jaguar. Each year the Allentown Chapter of the Daughters of American Wealth hold their Historic Home Tour. His mansion is featured. The most recent visit to him lasted longer than most because he wanted to ask me a few things about his new kittens.

As I drove home, I couldn't help but wonder how much I paid to sit there and answer his questions. The thought didn't bother me, though, because I was going to get a chance to recoup a little of my losses. Those new kittens were going to need shots, leukemia tests and spaying. It was all going to happen soon, too, because Dr. and Mrs. Leg had an appointment to see me the next day.

I got to my house just in time to answer a call on the home phone from Mrs. Full.

"Doctor, this is Faith Full calling about my dog. He just hasn't been himself all day long. I think he needs to be seen tonight, but your answering service said that I'd have to take him to the emergency clinic. I can't do that. You're the only veterinarian that we can trust.

> *I wasn't a bit surprised. I've been in practice too long.*

Can't you come out to your office and see him? I called the emergency clinic but they'll charge me a night fee if I go there and they expect to be paid tonight. Can you believe that? They take credit cards, but then I might have to pay some interest. If you'd see us, I figure I could charge it."

I turned her down.

The next morning I headed for the office looking forward to seeing the Leg's new kittens. I would have a new client who didn't nitpick over nickels. Even better, I would get a tiny portion of my orthopedic investment back. It would be a good old-fashioned office call where my advice would be accepted, followed and even paid for.

I was wrong.

As it turned out, the Legs didn't really believe in giving shots to cats because, as Mrs. Leg explained, "When I was a kid we had cats and they never got shots. They never got sick either. We just want to get the free exam that we are entitled to because of adopting the kittens from the shelter. And, of course, we'll want to schedule them for spaying as soon as our low-cost certificates arrive from the Friends of Gonad Removal Organization."

March 2001

No such thing as a simple question

I called the bank with a simple question.

I was sure that whomever picked up the phone would be able to answer it easily. Unfortunately, no human seemed to be available. There was a voice though. It told me in a very pleasant way that my call was important to them (but obviously not important enough to have a real person answer). Then there was some nice music followed by a list of options.

"If this is about your savings account, press 1."

"If this is about a loan, press 2."

The voice went on through several choices that didn't fit my question. I began to daydream. Just how far would one of these automated systems go if you waited long enough?

"If you ever put metal in the microwave, press 27."

"If you like Regis Philbin, press 32."

"If you think Elvis is still alive, press 96."

"You may bypass this message at any time by slitting your wrists."

There didn't seem to be any point in hanging on. So, I hung up and headed for the treatment room where some very important doughnuts were waiting. One of the technicians snagged me before I got there.

"Doctor O, Mrs. Babble is on line two," she announced.

I picked up the phone.

"Hello," I said.

It was the last word I would squeeze into the conversation for awhile.

She launched into a lecture concerning everything from her cat's diet to Al Gore's chances in the election.

"Did …?"

Again, I was cut off. She gave me the history of her family's pets from 1964 to the present. This was followed by her home diagnosis of her cat's medical condition.

I was obviously not a necessary part of the conversation. She told me when

she would call again, thanked me for the advice and hung up.

As it turned out, I was to be excluded from most conversations that day. Each time I headed for the doughnuts, I was interrupted by a phone call in which I was not destined to be an active participant. When Mrs. Fruitcake called about her dog, Chatter, I never got in a word. They had a great conversation without me.

"Chatter, your vet is on the phone. Shall we tell him how you're doing? Did you eat your breakfast? Is your cough better? Come over to the phone. Maybe the doctor will be able to hear your breathing. Well, I guess that's about all. Say goodbye to the nice doctor, Chatter."

I couldn't even figure out how she knew I was on the phone at all. There was no time to ponder that question, though. My doughnut wasn't getting any younger. I knew from experience, that a doughnut in the treatment room of my hospital would have a very short life expectancy. If I didn't hurry, someone else might attend to the matter.

Unfortunately, I was foiled again. This time it was the entire Tussle family. The conversation was in high gear by the time I tuned in.

"Dad! You're the one who left the car with an empty tank."

"So, what? It wouldn't kill you to put some gas in once in awhile."

"Mom! Tell him that I need the car to go to the movies."

> *There didn't seem to be any point in hanging on.*

Apparently, they were on several different extensions all within their house.

"Will you all shut up for a minute! I have the vet on the phone. We can talk about this later!"

"No we can't! I need that car!"

"Fine. Fill it with gas and you can use it."

I hung up. They probably didn't even realize it for another hour or so. Moments later, I arrived at ground zero only to find an empty box where several doughnuts used to reside.

As if that wasn't enough of a disappointment, one of the receptionists brought me some other bad news.

"Doctor O, there is something wrong with the telephones. When people call, we can hear them but they can't hear us. We need to get them fixed."

I had one question.

"Why?"

October 2000

Chapter 7: The World We Live In

Computers = Hula Hoops and other passing fads

Mrs. Browser carried the little bundle of joy in her arms. I have to admit that it was one cute little puppy. Mr. Bowser carried the phone book. There were first time pet owners and the joy was written all over their faces.

"We were not nervous about getting a puppy at first, Doctor," said Webb Browser. "But then, I went on the Internet and got all this information about how to raise little Byte, here."

Upon closer examination, I realized that he wasn't holding the phone book. It was a stack of information (and misinformation, no doubt) fresh from his home computer. I knew that my usual 15 minute lecture on pet care was not going to be necessary to educate this client. (Re-educating, however, would be, and it would take at least half an hour.)

"You know, Doctor," Mr. Browser went on, "Byte here is a purebred Peek-a-Poo. We got quite a bargain, too. The man at the dog farm let us have him for $400 because he is pet quality, not show quality. What I can't understand is, with all the information about dogs on the Internet, I wasn't able to find anything about this breed."

I, of course was not surprised in the least. I could have told them that, even with the vast resources of the Internet, information on the purebred Peke-a-Poo would be scarce. Nonetheless, they vowed to continue their search. I told them to hurry and do so while the Internet still exists. (I feel that its days are numbered.)

You see, when I was a kid, everybody (and I do mean everybody) had a Hula Hoop. You don't see them now, do you? I figure computers represent a similar fad and will undoubtedly disappear soon. Since I see no reason to get caught up

Where did I go wrong?

in a silly craze, I take the "head in the sand" approach when it comes to computers.

I must admit, however, that e-mail seems to have a purpose. People love to use it as a means of sending jokes and bits of trivia all over the world. The reason I know this is that people insist on sending me copies of their e-mail. They do this by regular mail at the staggering cost of 33 cents.

Here are just a few examples of e-mail jokes that crossed my desk this month:

• Did you hear the one about the guy who ran through the screen door?

He strained himself.

• Did you hear the one about the red ship and the blue ship that collided?

The survivors were marooned.

• What do you call a boomerang that doesn't work?

A stick.

• Did you hear about the two silk worms that had a race?

It ended in a tie.

Pretty bad, huh? Well, if you think those jokes are bad, take a look at some of the quotes that accompanied them:

• Apparently it was Groucho Marx who said, "Outside of a dog, a book is probably man's best friend, and inside of a dog, it's too dark to read."

• And, no one actually knows who said, "I think animal testing is a terrible idea; they all get nervous and give the wrong answers."

Those of you who have not yet thrown this magazine in the trash deserve to suffer more, so let's take a look at some very important trivia from the same source:

• More people are killed by donkeys annually than are killed in plane crashes (One more reason to be a small animal practitioner.)

• Stewardesses is the longest word that can be typed using only the left hand. (Big deal! I typed this whole column using just two fingers!)

• Marilyn Monroe had six toes.

(So what. I see cats every day with six toes.)

OK, You've suffered enough. I'll stop now. I've proven my point. Had I never seen these valuable bits of information, I feel that I could have survived just fine.

Therefore, I'm not going to spend my precious time trying to master a contraption that won't be around long. I learned my lesson in 1958. I honestly tried. I did my best. But I never could work that Hula Hoop.

February 2000

Procrastination rears ugly head

It was on a Monday morning in mid-July when Mrs. Frazzle called to report a serious problem.

"I'm very worried, Doctor," she said. "Rocket is just laying around and hasn't eaten a thing all day. I'm sure it's the heat. Is there anything we can do?"

Similar calls had been coming in for six days. We were being hammered with the worst heat wave in decades. Afternoon temperatures were flirting with 100 degrees every day. I assured her that things would get better when cooler weather arrived.

"That will make it worse! That will make it worse!" She was beginning to sound hysterical.

I asked her to explain what she meant.

"Didn't you read this month's issue of 'Healthy Health' magazine?" she asked.

I avoided mentioning that the good Lord did not bless me with the gift of vision just so that I could waste it on idiotic trash like 'Healthy Health' magazine.

"Well, doctor, you should read it. Each month there is an article by Dr. Parsley. He's a real veterinarian."

I resisted the temptation to ask her what she thought I was.

"Anyway, his article this month was all about keeping our pets safe when the winter comes. He says that there could be carbon monoxide in the heating ducts and that could make pets sick. Maybe there's some in my ducts and that's what's making Rocket lay around."

I didn't bother to tell her that Rocket is the most sedentary dog that ever lived, even under normal circumstances. The first part of every physical exam consists of holding a mirror under his nose to see if he's alive.

"Rocket doesn't feel like doing anything. According to the article, dogs are closer to the ground than we are so they feel the effects of the gas before we do."

I chose not to mention that if Dr. Parsley was ever given a good enema, he would fit in a shoe box.

"Do you think I should go out and get some of the herbs that he recommended to treat the problem? There's an herbal tea recipe right in the article. It says that I can get the ingredients at a health food store."

I glanced out the window at the bank thermometer down the street. It proudly displayed a temperature of 97 degrees. The obvious question came to mind.

"When is the last time the furnace in your house was on?"

"I checked that before I called, Doctor. My husband shut it off in March, about four months ago."

I was able to assure her that, in spite of her search through the scientific literature,

> *The first part of every physical exam consists of holding a mirror under his nose to see if he's alive.*

there was no danger of carbon monoxide in her heating ducts.

She was on the phone again an hour later.

"It's the tree. It's the tree. I think he may have been chewing the branches."

This time her explanation almost made sense.

"We keep meaning to take down the Christmas tree, but somehow we never got around to it. I think Rocket may have been chewing on it."

In disbelief, I glanced at the calendar. Surely some procrastination record must have just been shattered.

"Do you think I need those herbs now, doctor?" she asked.

I don't even remember what I told her after that. All I could think about was sharing this particular wacky client story with Arnie. As soon as she hung up, I called his hospital to share the experience. He wasn't there so I called him at home. It turned out to be my lucky day because Arnie's wife answered the phone and invited me over for lunch. I accepted the offer then proceeded to tell Arnie all about the morning's unbelievable demonstration of gullibility and procrastination.

An hour later, when I arrived at the house, Arnie's wife met me on the porch.

"Sit down and have a beer, Mike," she said. "I don't know what you said to Arnie, but right now he's in there frantically taking down the Christmas tree."

Septmber 1999

Dr. O is in deep doo-doo

Welcome to the month of December. My psychic powers tell me that you might be spending some time at the shopping mall this month.

So, while you're there, I'd like you to do me a favor. Stroll over to the perfume counter and check out the fragrances. The salesperson will tell you all about the expensive and exotic ingredients. Never, will he or she let on that they are actually talking about such things as anal gland squeezing and whale vomit. If they did, I would venture a guess that a lot less perfume would be sold.

You see, if it sounds good, it will smell good.

And so, I disagree with William Shakespeare who wrote, "What's in a name? That which we call a rose, by any other name would smell as sweet."

Shakespeare was wrong. I contend that a perfume with a name and slogan such as: "Princess Schnozola, the fragrance that launched 1,000 sniffs," is going to smell a lot better to people than something like: "eau de Whale Barf, a lot of odor for the money."

Would you be likely to purchase an aftershave called Bear's Butt Liquid? (Slogan: Stinks a long time.")

I doubt it.

Furthermore, the "Perfume Rule" carries over into veterinary practice. Mrs. Cipher provides a typical example.

The last time she called, my new receptionist didn't know what to think. "Doctor," she said. "There's a lady on the phone who wants to talk to you. It has something to do with her dog, but, I can't understand what it is she wants. The things she's saying don't seem to make any sense."

I told her that dealing with my clients would soon get her used to such calls, and headed for the phone.

Mrs. Cipher was quick to deliver a coded message.

"Hello Doctor, I'm glad you could come to the phone. Crypto seems to be having trouble with his you-know-what."

The fact is, I didn't know what and had to ask for a further explanation.

"He can't make right," she said. "His jobby is OK, but, his tinky must be out of order because he can go number two but not number one. The last time this happened, he had to get a you-know-what in his you-know-where."

I could see why the receptionist was confused.

However, since many of my clients tend to speak in such euphemisms, I was able to decode Crypto's history with very little trouble.

Nonetheless, such conversations tend to make me marvel at the power of the euphemisms themselves and the effect they have on society in general.

I am reminded of my friend, Tom

Henry, who started his trash removal business about the same time that I opened my clinic. That was the '70s and Tom's Trash, as the company was called, became successful very quickly.

The company logo had a picture of a garbage can and a refuse truck. However, in the '80s, he changed the name of the company to Henry's Hauling. As he said, "The name has a modern ring to it."

The can disappeared from the logo.

More recently, Tom felt the need for a change once again. His company is now called Clear Horizons Environmental Technologies. The logo merely shows a few snow capped mountains. It makes the entire business seem so much more pleasant.

My local telephone company has gotten the idea as well.

A recent notice from them announced that they had been granted a "community rate adjustment."

It sounds like such a civic-minded thing that you hardly notice that they are socking it to you once again.

And so, it's only natural that our clients tend to sugarcoat the things they find offensive.

A jobby certainly sounds like a nicer thing than a stool. And a stool is definitely worlds above that stuff that has become famous for hitting the fan.

It seems to me, that by removing the negative connotations from many of our expressions, the euphemism has served to take some of the anxiety out of our society, and that can't be bad.

After all, if things were any more tense, we would all be in deep doo-doo.

December 1997

Veterinary 'dream team' gets Gator by the tail, has the last laugh

The man was doubled over, clutching his chest and having obvious difficulty breathing. His face was turning shades of crimson and purple. I was about to reach for my cell phone and call 911, when he took a deep breath, grabbed his knees and relapsed into a fit of convulsive laughter.

A few feet away, there was a lady who seemed to be having a similar attack. The reason was obvious. Her dog had just attempted to turn a veterinary technician into an amputee.

"He always does that," the man screamed. "Whenever we take Gator to the vet he tries to take a piece out of somebody. You'll never get that shot into him."

Their attitude was, unfortunately, all too typical. I don't know what people find so (expletive deleted) funny about their pet's attitude toward veterinarians, but nothing will get them laughing quicker than the site of a technician or veterinarian jumping back in an attempt at self preservation.

The frustrated technician looked over at me.

"I hate these shot clinics," she said. "Now what are we going to do? I can't get near this dog."

The combination of growling and laughter was drawing a crowd of curious on-lookers. Each person waiting in line wanted to see if anyone could get the best of Gator.

I looked around to see if there was anyone to help. Luck was with me. Arnie and Abe were coming through the crowd to assist.

Gator's owners waited in gleeful anticipation, hoping that I would get close enough to trigger the menacing mutt and provide them with another good guffaw. Little did they know that they were about to face the veterinary "Dream Team." Never before had such vaccinating talent been assembled in one location.

Allow me to introduce the members of the group.

The team captain was Arnie. Known to his friends as "The Flash," no one can give a shot as fast as Arnie can. In a face-to-face dual, with each man having his choice of weapons, Arnie could give Clint Eastwood a rabies shot before Clint could snatch that big Smith & Wesson out of the holster.

His right hand man in this match would be Abe "The Grip"

> *The combination of growling and laughter was drawing a crowd of curious on-lookers.*

Raisive. Abe has forearms like Popeye the Sailor. Furthermore, Abe doesn't take any grief from anyone.

Bringing up the rear we have Mike "Ordinary" Obenski, a man with no exceptional skills at all. However, this is my article, so I got to be on the team.

We approach from three sides.

"I want to hold Gator myself," the lady says. "You three might scare him."

"Sorry, ma'am," says Abe. "But you seem to have mistaken me for someone who cares."

Arnie raised one hand, as if to catch something. That was the signal. I tossed him the syringe. Foolishly, the dog glanced upward as the vaccine flew over his head. That fraction of a second was all Abe needed. His right hand flashed out with speed and accuracy enough to make any snake jealous. The pooch was in the veterinary version of the Vulcan Death Grip.

By the time he started to struggle, it was already over.

Several people in the surrounding crowd started to applaud. The team members exchanged high fives.

"Score one for the veterinarians!" a man shouted.

The dog's owners did not share in the joy.

"You people scared Gator with that attack of yours. I'm never coming back here again," she yelled. "Next year I'm taking him to his regular veterinarian. Even though I'll have to pay full price for his shots, I don't care. I can afford it and besides, you didn't even give him an examination."

"Score two for the veterinarians!" Abe yelled back.

July 1997

'Emergency calls' foster beeper blues

There is a man on my television screen enjoying a relaxing game of golf when, all of a sudden, he is interrupted by a phone call.

You see, he has that new telephone system that allows anybody on this planet to dial one number and get his office, his home, his cellular phone and his beeper, all at once. He has the benefit of being completely accessible at all hours of the day and night.

An announcer comes on the screen and tells me that this man has signed up for PESTER-U, the incredible new system that allows people to keep in touch with him constantly.

I don't understand. Why would he do that? Is he being punished for something?

I have the strong suspicion that, if the commercial ran a little longer, we would hear the man yell into his cellular phone: "No! I am not interested in aluminum siding for my house!"

As for me, personally, I don't want to be accessible at all hours. I learned my lesson way back in the '70s when I used to carry a pager. That was before everybody and his brother had one. Heck, that was even before drug dealers and hookers had them.

The unit would give a loud, obnoxious "Beep," then announce my code number and give a voice message. It was state of the art at the time. So, a typical message would go:

"BEEP... Unit 414... Please call Mr. Miser at 555-JERK... Man has important questions about location of nearest low cost spay clinic."

One specific message sticks in my mind. My wife and I were waiting in line at the local burger place when it came in.

"BEEP... Unit 414... Please call Mr. Sprout at 555-NERD... Serious fight. Wounds involved. Caller described situation as urgent."

We forgot about dinner and rushed over to the office. It was only about a half mile away and we could call from there. The situation did, in fact, turn out to be urgent. Mr. Sprout was a 9-year-old who was working on a school report that was due the next day. I was needed for input into the following question: "If a lion and a tiger had a fight, who would win?"

Where did I go wrong?

Due to these, and countless similar "emergency calls," I have learned to protect myself.

For example, I never answer a telephone myself. This is the job of employees, family members and answering machines. These call-screeners save me from having to explain why I don't want to change long distance companies, why I am not interested in a bargain price on copier supplies, and why I don't want to invest in soybean futures.

Some people think I'm old fashioned. Dee Mandin is one of them.

"I know that Mr. Wellcat has never been sick, Doctor. But what if he does have a problem? How will I get in touch with you? I can't believe you don't have a car phone and a beeper. Everyone has them nowadays. If your clients could get in touch with you anytime, they wouldn't have to go to the emergency clinic. You would pick up a lot of extra business on weekends and holidays."

Gosh! Why didn't I think of that? That darn emergency clinic is taking away afterhours revenue!

She continued, "Besides, Doctor, those people don't know Mr. Wellcat's medical history like you do."

She was right again. They would have no way of knowing that the cat is perfectly all right, but the owner is a hypochondriac wacko.

On the other hand, I have confidence that they would figure it out within minutes.

At any rate, I was able to assure her that my home number was in the book (even though I neglected to mention I never answer the phone.) Furthermore, I assured her that, if I ever decided to drive a car with a phone in it, she would be the first to know.

As I drove home that night, I wondered where you draw the line between truth and falsehood. You see, I never drive a car and, I never give out the phone number of my truck.

December 1996

Too bad sloppy baking can't be blamed for these animal 'crackers'

Normally, I don't treat exotics. So last Thursday taught me quite a lesson. Never have I seen such animals. In the herd I was examining, I counted three zebraphants, two giraffalos, and no less than seven hippopotamoose.

I must be doing a very poor job of keeping up with the veterinary literature because I had no idea that such species even existed. Yet, there they were, spread out before me as if they were begging to be examined more closely. Had genetic engineering reached these great heights without my being aware of it? I doubted it. Then, perhaps, a more plausible explanation would be ...

Unfortunately, my receptionist chose that moment to rudely interrupt my train of thought.

"Dr. Obenski, there are clients waiting. You'll have to finish your animal crackers later."

Realizing that sloppy baking and not genetic engineering had created the herd, I dumped everybody back into the little cardboard cage they came in and headed off to exam room No. 2.

There, I ran into creatures who were no less strange. Perched on the exam table was something named Fuzzy. It could have been a dog that was part Lhasa Apso. It could have been a cat that was part Persian. It could have even been the world's first cross between the two.

Hoping that this thing was created by Mother Nature (on an off day, no doubt,) and not by a sloppy baker, I glanced at the record. Surely the name would help me to determine which it was. It didn't. The record said Fuzzy belonged to Herm Aphrodite. Was it Herman? Was it Hermione? Was it a cross between the two?

Whichever it was, he or she or it, it certainly seemed to be entertained by Fuzzy's experiences with the rectal thermometer. As for me. I just wanted to get the nondescript pooch out the door and move on to a more normal office call.

On the way, I stopped by the lounge to gulp down a few hippopotomoose. Since the bakers seemed to be into representing strange combinations, I wondered why the Flub-A-Dub was not represented in my cookie herd.

(Note to Baby Boomers: You can earn extra credit by contacting me if you know which species of animals were cross bred to cre-

> *On the way, I stopped by the lounge to gulp down a few hippopotomoose.*

ate the Flub-A-Dub. Please include two box tops.)

As you may have guessed, my next office call turned out to be no less strange. It was Mrs. Dizzy and she was very upset. Her precious pet, Figment, was not doing his "jobby" in the litter pan. There was a bundle of towels and blankets in her lap. Somewhere in the center of the bundle, Figment was waiting to see me. After much unwrapping, I was presented with the patient. He was a toilet brush. The nurse who drove Mrs. Dizzy to the clinic gave me a wink. I continued with the pseudo-office call.

Moments later, following examination and treatment, a pleased client who was convinced that Figment would feel better, was on her way home. Naturally, there was no charge.

As for me, I was glad to get home that night. You see, at my house, the cats are cats, the dogs are dogs and the only strange, inexplicable creature is me.

September 1996

Machines that go nowhere and other inducements to shape up

I could hardly believe my eyes. The man was a perfect physical specimen. He wasn't heavily muscled like a weight lifter or body builder, nor was he lanky like a runner or swimmer. Each muscle and muscle group was beautifully defined as though the man had been carved by Michelangelo himself.

Behind him, there was a strange contraption. It was made of metal tubes and large rubber bands. It looked like one of those pieces of modern art that people like me are supposed to appreciate even if we don't understand why.

Then, from somewhere off-camera, an announcer hit me with some shocking information. If I would just buy the strange-looking contraption with the rubber bands and use it for 20 minutes a day, three times a week, I could look just like the perfect anatomy guy on the TV screen.

The news hit me like a ton of bricks. I almost dropped my can of beer right into the bowl of potato chips on my lap. That guy had muscles in places where I don't even have places. That I could be transformed into him was hard to believe. On the other hand, my best friend (the 40-inch Quasar TV in my den) would never lie to me. I thought about sending for the machine but took a more logical course of action instead. I changed channels.

The next thing I saw was someone riding what appeared to be a futuristic bicycle. The seat went up and down. The handle bars went back and forth. The rider was working furiously and getting nowhere fast. An announcer casually mentioned that for $1,200, I could be the proud owner of such a machine. Then, any time I wanted, I could ride it and go nowhere. I recalled once owning an unreliable automobile that seemed to be designed along that same principle.

Furthermore, owning a vehicle that can't take me where I want to go does not stick in my mind as a pleasant experience. However, I must be alone in that thinking because, as I surfed the channels, I saw dozens of machines designed to go nowhere.

I found out that you can walk or run while standing still. You can climb stairs while not going up. Heck, you can even cross-country ski without snow.

The latest craze seems to be machines that allow you to do sit-ups without actually sitting up. There are dozens of gadgets available, such as the "Gut-Go-Way," the "Spare Tire Deflator," and the "Middle Melter" that promise to develop the tummy muscles without having to do sit-ups. I don't see what all the fuss is about. What's so horrible about sit-ups? I distinctly recall having done one once when I was in high school, and it wasn't bad. In fact, I have often considered doing another one some day.

At any rate, the commercials keep telling me that well-developed "abs" (the scientific term for tummy muscles) are the key to health, happiness and earning the admiration of others. If I had known how important it is to have lumpy rectus abdominis muscles, I'd have done that second sit-up long ago.

And so, with the fitness industry already in high gear, along comes the Summer Olympics. Countless viewers such as myself are awed by the performances and vow to get back into shape

On the other hand, my best friend (the 40-inch Quasar TV in my den) would never lie to me.

soon. We watch the personal stories of the athletes. We hear of the grueling and constant long hours of training they have endured. We marvel that we could be just as good if we had the rubber band machine and used it 20 minutes a day, three times a week.

And so, I am motivated! All this talk of fitness, combined with the fact that I'm not getting any younger, has brought me to a definite conclusion. It is time to think about putting myself on a vigorous exercise program. And, that's just what I'm gonna do. I'm gonna think about it.

August 1996

Chapter 8:
A Runaway Train

Safety's cardinal rule: Just don't get hurt

I recently read an article touting the 10 safest cities in the United States. I could hardly believe my eyes. My town was not even mentioned.

It just so happens that I live right on the outskirts of the safest city in America if not the entire world, Macungie, Pa. (pronounced: mack un'gee).

Perhaps you are thinking that my town is too small to have made the list. Well, let me straighten you out. We not only have a traffic light in Macungie, but often we have it turned on.

Our safety record is impeccable. We do not have earthquakes or tornadoes in Macungie. There are no killer bees or fire ants either. Not only that, but I have it on good authority (Kermit down at the feed store) that there has never been a fatal shark attack in all of Macungie's history. (I am not making this up.) If you recall the movie *Jaws*, you will have to admit that Macungie was not mentioned even once.

Furthermore, international terrorist organizations are completely ignorant as to the existence of this metropolis. Thus, my assessment is that we are relatively safe from attack.

I share these facts with you in order to establish my credentials as an expert on all matters regarding safety. (Just living near Macungie makes me a safety guru.)

It was this self-acquired expertise that led me eight years ago to launch a comprehensive workplace safety program at my clinic. Their very first day on the job, all employees are instructed in each and every aspect of the program. This is easily accomplished because there is only one rule: don't get hurt!

Here's how my system could be applied in your practice. Suppose Mrs. Hotpipes runs into your office and announces that her cat, Ambush, has crawled under her car in the parking lot. Naturally, she expects you to crawl under the car to get him out. If this had happened to you yesterday, you might have jumped at the chance to be a hero. Now, however, after learning my rule, you would politely decline her invitation.

Let's try another hypothetical situation.

Mr. Harebrain arrives for his appointment, but his dog, Carnage, is left waiting in the car.

"I can't get him out of there, Doc," he announces. "He will bite at anything that moves near him. The way he is wedged in behind the seat, there is no way I can even touch him without getting bitten. Can you crawl in and give him the shot where he is?"

You are probably thinking something like: "Oh, well, all in a day's work."

No, no, no. You are forgetting my rule. You need to handle this by saying something like: "Are you nuts? I'm not going in there."

Are you getting the idea now?

Let's try another.

You enter the exam room to find Mrs. Spacey and her dog, Thug. There is a 6-year-old boy holding the dog. "Thug will probably behave this time," she boldly predicts. "You won't need those gloves, the restraint pole, the muzzle and the two helpers like last time because he will behave if little Timmy holds him."

Do you follow her advice? Not if you follow mine. Send for the gloves, extra technicians and muzzle. And, don't get hurt.

To sum it all up, my rules for ensuring a long and happy existence on this planet are simple. Don't get hurt and consider moving to Macungie.

September 2006

Ghost of veterinary future delivers ultimate reminder

It seemed that everyone in the little town of Vetville had gone crazy. Arnie wanted nothing to do with them.

"Happy days, brother Arnie!" they shouted to him.

"Bah! Humbug!" he retorted, and hurried to his home.

Later that night, he tried to get to sleep, but the voices coming from the street outside his window kept him awake. The people residing in the little hamlet of Vetville were chanting with enthusiasm.

"Vitamins, pet toothbrushes, bandannas! We're saved. Marketing is our future. Marketing has come to save us."

"Bah! Humbug!" Arnie shouted at them. "You people are forgetting what got us where we are today."

Suddenly, stepping from the shadows of the bedroom, there came an apparition. It was the ghost of veterinary practice past (of course).

"I have come to show you the way it used to be," announced the uninvited spook.

"I know how it used to be," Arnie said. Now, hit the road before I call an exorcist."

The reveling in the street continued. "We're all going to specialize," the villagers shouted. "We can each be an expert at something." One gleeful student shouted: "I want to be a patella doctor."

"Bah! Humbug!" Arnie shouted again.

"You're a dinosaur, Arnie," someone in the crowd retorted. "They could take some of your DNA and create Jurassic Park. Can't you see that we have been spreading ourselves too thin. We should each concentrate on one organ or joint. Specialization is our future."

"Bah! Humbug!" Arnie repeated. (He was in a rut.)

Moments later, his second visitor arrived. Naturally, it was the ghost of veterinary practice present. "Don't waste your time," Arnie said. "I am in touch with our profession every day. It is the people who are trying to improve it who don't know their anal orifice from a terrestrial excavation."

The mass hysteria continued throughout the town. "Quality, quality; the pet supermarket people say they have invented quality. At last, the same industrial policies that put McDonald's on the map can be ours to enjoy."

"What's the matter with you people?" Arnie called. "Don't you remember the pride and satisfaction that our profession provides?"

"Who needs it?" they yelled back. "We're going to get a 30-hour work week with medical and dental benefits. Commercialism is our future."

"Bah! Humbug!" Arnie the skeptic repeated.

As you may have guessed, the spirit of veterinary practice yet-to-come arrived momentarily. Out of curiosity, Arnie accompanied her to the year 2020. Quite surprisingly, he noted that small and mid-sized veterinary hospitals were thriving.

Accompanying the spirit to his own clinic, he was pleased to see an older version of himself still happily treating patients with the kind of personal care he had always believed in. The neighborhood, however, had changed. Vetville looked different. There were abandoned buildings where their used to be fields.

The ghost explained: "Each of those buildings represents a failure in our profession. For example, that small one was the office of a colleague who specialized in elastology. His entire practice consisted of gluing little rubber tips onto cat toenails. It was a specialty that thrived when a majority of communities outlawed declawing. Those laws were repealed in 2015, though. And do you see that building across the street? In the year 2010, that building was the home of Dot.com Pet Care. They tried to provide veterinary services online. Unfortunately for them, personal care and a solid doctor-client-patient relationship never went out of style.

Arnie was elated. Perhaps he was not a dinosaur after all. There was still a place for those of us with old-fashioned caring attitudes and a deep respect for our profession.

The next morning, he called his old friend and colleague who practices down the street in the real town of Allentown, Pa.

"Mike," he said. "I have good news. I have seen the future, and it is us."

December 2005

Road to recovery still requires a toll

Bea Fuddled's incessant complaining signals larger professional issue

Bea Fuddled and her cat, Dewclaw, were my first office call of the day last Thursday. Neither of them liked veterinarians very much. Dewclaw simply threatened, but Mrs. Fuddled let me have it with both barrels.

"You veterinarians ought to get your act together," she said. "This poor cat has been limping for more than a month, and none of you seem to be able to do a thing about it. I've spent a lot of money with you people and nothing has helped."

I glanced at the cat's record. It was blank. We had never seen him before. It seemed best to start at the beginning.

"Has he had his vaccinations?" I asked.

"Don't try to sell me any shots," she countered. "I get those at the shot clinic that they hold every few months in the Poochi-Pet-food Store parking lot. The shots are given by real veterinarians, you know. Besides, we are here about the lameness, not some silly shots that he probably doesn't need anyway."

Ignoring her tirade, I moved on to the next logical question. "What has been done for the problem so far, and was there any diagnosis?"

That set her off on another fit of complaints.

"None of you vets seem to have a clue. I called all the numbers listed at (900) VET-STUFF. I listened to all the messages, and not one of them dealt with Dewclaw's lameness. All I got for my trouble was a $46 charge on my VISA card. You'd think that company would have been more helpful. After all, it is run by Dr. Holden D. Line. He's a real veterinarian, you know."

I found myself hoping that a meteor would hit the office and spare me from the rest of the office call. Just my luck, it never came.

"Has anyone ever actually ever treated the leg?" I asked.

"Of course they have," she retorted. "Do you think that I'd just let him suffer? We got medicine from the mail-order vet catalog. It's run by U. Ken Order and Trudy Mail. Their both real veterinarians, you know. Their remedy didn't work at all. There went another 26 bucks down the drain. You vets should be ashamed of yourselves."

I informed her that there were some that I was ashamed of, and proceeded to examine the cat. One of his claws was ingrown and infected. Using a nail clipper and a dose of penicillin, I had him on the road to recovery within minutes. Bea Fuddled didn't like the idea that the road to recovery was a toll road. She complained bitterly about the $48 charge.

After she left, I called my friend, Arnie, to complain, not about Mrs. Fuddled, but about colleagues who use their veterinary license as a basis for some money-making gimmick.

Unfortunately, Arnie wanted to talk about something else. "Mike, are you going to sign up to be in that new American Dog and Cat Club? It was started by a group of veterinarians. Pet owners pay a fee to sign up and get a membership card. Then, they get a list of participating veterinarians who will offer free exams and large discounts on other services. They claim that participating clinics will get hundreds of new clients."

> "Sure you will lose money on these people. But there will be a lot of them."

I already have plenty of clients who don't pay," I told him. "Why would I want more?"

"Volume, Mike," was his answer. "Sure you will lose money on these people. But there will be a lot of them."

Gently, I pointed out that he was making no sense at all, and guided the conversation back to my original reason for calling. "This just serves as one more example, Arnie," I told him. "Quickie vaccine clinics, mail-order catalogs, 900-type phone lines, etc., are all examples of our profession run amok."

"Uh-oh! Here it comes," he said. "You're getting back up on your high horse again aren't you? I guess you'll be writing another column critical of 'alternative lifestyles' in our profession."

"That's right," I told him. "I see myself as the spokesperson (politically correct term) for sanity in veterinary practice, and it seems to me that this would be a good time to speak out again."

"Why now, Mike?" he asked. "What makes this a good time to fan the flames?"

"Well, it has been months since the last time I openly criticized blatant marketing, online pharmacies, over-specialization and vaccine clinics held in parking lots," I told him. "The death threats have all but stopped."

October 2005

Ingenuity, imagination can lead to ultimate equipment bragging rights

Case in point: Consider the many uses of an ordinary wire hook and Fred Flintstone's cup

Turn to the back of any veterinary journal and look at the help-wanted ads. Hospitals that are seeking a new employee love to blow their own horns.

They imply superiority by focusing on two major areas, such as equipment and client education. A typical ad may say something like: "We have three anesthesia machines, an ultrasound and one of those little pens that you poke at an eye to measure glaucoma." Brag. Brag. Brag.

Big deal! We have equipment at my hospital, too. Better equipment.

For example, there is the wire hook. We made it out of an old coat hanger 26 years ago. (I designed it myself, and it cost a lot less than an ultrasound machine.) It is used

to hang IV bottles from cage doors or surgical lamps. However, the list of other potential uses goes on and on. It has been used to retrieve items that have fallen into heating vents or behind cabinets. It can hold the storage room door opened while deliveries are being made, and as if that isn't enough, it makes a great back scratcher.

The wire hook is kept on a shelf in the treatment room right next to our hospital's most valuable piece of equipment, the Fred Flintstone's cup. This old plastic cup joined our staff almost 30 years ago. When the peanut butter that came in it was all gone, we were left with one of the most versatile tools that the veterinary profession has ever seen. It can be used to scoop kitty litter, collect urine samples or drain abscesses. Through it all, there's still a smile on Fred's face. So, when it comes to the area of specialized equipment, let me just say that my clinic is second to none.

> Are you kidding me? You couldn't teach these people to fetch a stick.

The other area of journal ad boasting contains phrases something like this: "We place a strong emphasis on client education."

So what? Don't we all?

Let me tell you about the last time Mr. and Mrs. Dufus were in to see me. Catnip and kitty litter spilled all over the exam table as I dumped their reluctant cat from the carrier. I ignored the mess, examined the cat, and then, showing a great deal of patience and concern, I explained all aspects of the cat's bladder problem. I asked if they were following the diet recommendations that were made the last time this problem occurred.

"Well, to tell you the truth, Doc, our neighbor gets us a great deal on Notsogood Kitmunchies. So, we've been feeding those instead of the stuff you recommended."

I asked if they gave the last prescription until it was all gone.

"We would have, but our dog got diarrhea that week. So, we gave him the pills instead."

My opportunity to emphasize client education was at hand. I could be just like those hospitals in the journal ads.

I sat Mr. and Mrs. Dufus down and explained just how antibiotics work. I told them about the culture results. I made it clear that the infection might not get better unless they gave the pills according to the instructions. Then, I handed them a vial of 28 bactomycin tabs.

They looked at the vial. They looked at me. They looked confused. Then, they asked an important question. "What are the pills for?"

Client education? Are you kidding me? You couldn't teach these people to fetch a stick.

After they left, we swept up the spilled catnip and litter. It was easy because we had the right equipment. We used the Fred Flintstone cup.

April 2005

What's wrong with catalog drug sales?
Who says you need a veterinary degree to dispense, administer meds?

I patiently explained the technique several times, but Mr. Bungle didn't seem to be able to grasp the concept. There was nothing to do but keep trying.

"Now, remember," I said. "After you measure the insulin in the syringe, you have to put the needle through the skin, inject the liquid and then pull the needle back out."

Mr. Bungle proceeded to draw the appropriate amount of practice saline into the syringe. Then, for the 10th time, he put the needle into the cat, pulled it out and squirted the liquid onto the fur. After several decades of teaching pet owners how to control diabetes in dogs and cats, I was beginning to sense that my first failure was at hand.

We continued our training session using a roll of paper towels as the victim, but after countless foul-ups, I had to admit I'd met my match. I wanted things to be done in the following order: in-shoot-out. Mr. Bungle's brain would only go: in-out-shoot. Luckily, I was able to find a solution. This particular cat turned out to be one that could be stabilized on oral medication and eventually Mr. Bungle did master the ability to give the pill.

The same day as that ill-fated training session, I got a phone call from Dr. Helpful, a colleague who ran into a similar problem in her practice. It seemed that the use of intra-nasal vaccine was causing a great deal of side effects in Mr. Whaler's cattery. Being a breeder with a large number of cats and an avid do-it-yourselfer, Mr. Whaler had been ordering his vaccines by mail and ad-

ministering them himself. Unfortunately, his cats were reacting painfully to the vaccine and the noses were staying swollen for up to two weeks afterward. Dr. Helpful checked the product he had been using. It was the proper vaccine, it was not outdated and caused no reaction when she administered it to one of her own cats. She thought, perhaps, that it was an allergy of some sort that ran in Mr. Whaler's line of Persians.

Her next step was to have Mr. Whaler bring in one of his cats and administer the vaccine in her office so that one of the reactions could be observed first hand. She watched as he mixed the vaccine, drew it

Why am I telling you about these people?

up into a syringe with an 18-gauge needle, and proceeded immediately to harpoon the cat right between the nostrils. In her defense, let me say that the stabbing took place so quickly that she barely had time to react to what she was seeing, otherwise she would have stopped him from injecting the vaccine. At any rate, the reason for the sore noses became obvious at that point.

Why am I telling you about these people? Because they are just two of the millions of reasons that I believe vaccines should not be sold in drug stores, pet stores and mail order catalogs.

Need more examples? How about Mrs. Foggythought. She scheduled an appointment to have her dog examined. He wasn't having any problems. She just wanted a check-up. I pointed out that although he seemed to be in fine health, he was due for his vaccines.

"That's why we're here, Doctor," she said. "I got his shots from Polyp & Carbuncle's catalog, but the label warns that pets should be healthy before vaccination, so I thought we'd have you examine him. By the way, I don't know how to give a shot, so as long as we're here, can you give the stuff for me?"

A glance at the vaccine she had purchased, along with a few questions, revealed that it was outdated and had not been properly refrigerated. Neither of those things mattered though, since it was cat vaccine and wouldn't do her dog any good anyway.

My point is that administering injections is a very easy thing for those of us who do it hundreds of times a week. But I cringe at the thought of people teaching themselves to do it at home with essentially no qualified instruction. After all, spays are simple, too, after you've done a few thousand of them. But no one would consider marketing a do-it-yourself spay kit. (Or would they?)

October 2003

Post-Seminar Syndrome has Dr. O re-examining old habits

Exuding his usual charm, Pucker greeted me from his perch atop the exam table.

The circular tail gyrations at one end seemed to be at odds with the menacing growl emanating from the other.

A long-time patient of mine, Pucker has many of the qualities of a fine physical specimen. His head, tail, weight and coat are beautifully proportioned; that is, they would be if his skeleton had kept up. Unfortunately, his bones are too short. The end result being that he looks like a furry alligator with a short tail. (If he were to develop the temperament of an alligator, that would be an improvement.)

Medically speaking, he has been prone to problems with his skin, which is covered with more wrinkles than a cerebral cortex. (Something that Pucker seems to lack. His ears and feet are prone to infections and his back is bad. To make a long story short, Pucker is a Bassett Hound.)

On this particular occasion, I was able to get close enough to see that his semi-annual bout of eczema was right on schedule. All I had to do was to administer an injection to stop the itching and the pooch would be on his way. I reached for a vial of Cortodepazone.

The record clearly showed that the same treatment had worked wonderfully six times in the past four years. Pucker's owner, Lotta Vets, had always been very pleased. Before coming to me four years ago, she had been to several of my local colleagues. Sometimes, the dog's coat would look a little better, but the itch never stopped. All she wanted me to do was stop the scratching. I had succeeded then, and all I had to do now was to administer the same treatment.

Then, right in the middle of the office call, I became disabled. It happened somewhere between my examination of the patient and the administration of the miracle Cortodepazone injection.

I was suffering from a malady that is peculiar to the veterinary profession. A malady which most of us have experienced. Worst of all, my problem was self-inflicted.

You see, in January, I had attended a continuing education seminar. Instead of being held someplace conveniently close to home where I could enjoy the single digit temperatures as well as the stresses of being near my practice, the meeting was held about a zillion miles away on a tropical island in the West Indies. However, I wasn't about to let that stop me. So, being dedicated as I am to continuing education, I decided to go, even if it meant having to spend a week in some tropical paradise far from the joys of shoveling snow.

Much to my surprise, I attended all 24 hours of available lectures. In fact, my time was divided between stuffing knowledge into my head and stuffing food into the rest of me.

It was at some indefinite point that week that I was stricken with the bug. The precise moment that it happened is unimportant because, as it happens in all cases, the symptoms did not appear until I was back in my office. Once I began to see office calls, it became painfully obvious that I was showing

> I was suffering from a malady that is peculiar to the veterinary profession.

signs of an affliction that I call Post-Seminar Syndrome.

At one time or another, we have all experienced it. You spend a few hours in the presence of an Ivory Tower-type lecture and, the next thing you know, you are using a more scientific vocabulary, running more lab tests and, most obvious of all, using less cortisone.

Since Pucker was in my office just two days after my return from the meeting, I found myself facing a difficult choice. Would it be the usual blast of cortisone? Or, should I opt for the scientific approach with its battery of tests, its variable short-range prognosis and its lack of quick fix, client-pleasing, itch-stopping results?

Would it be better to wrestle with my conscience over the quick shot of steroids or wrestle with a sawed-off itch alligator while we tried to run tests on him?

My symptoms cleared up very quickly and so did the dog's.

June 2001

What the heck is wrong with you?

In case you haven't been keeping up with recent developments, let me bring you up to speed. It has been discovered that I am a dinosaur.

My Neanderthal-like thinking is out of place in this day and age; or as one veterinarian put it, I represent the anchor that keeps the good ship of veterinary medicine from progressing at top speed.

These are just a few of the truths that I've learned about myself over the past few months. It all started in April when I let the cat out of the bag by openly criticizing some recent trends in our profession. As our April issue arrived in veterinary hospitals, my phone began to ring.

The first call was from Dr. Rantin N. Ravin from Moot Point, Ark. He had an important question for me.

"What the heck is wrong with you? Have you always been afraid to try new things?"

It turned out that he was referring to my reluctance to back off on routine vaccination of dogs and cats. You see, I don't care if immunity might last longer than a year. I don't care if I give a vaccination that might not be necessary. I only know that routine vaccination prevents illness and saves lives. When there is proof that any medical procedure is not necessary, it would be time to stop it. This is not the time.

However, as to my reluctance to try new things, allow me to defend myself. I jumped onto the cutting edge of technology in 1957, and have remained there ever since. At that time, I was the proud owner of the first transistor radio in my hometown. It was the size of a cigar box, got AM stations only and required a separate battery pack that weighed four pounds, but it was a modern miracle at the time.

The next call was even less kind. It was Dr. Dee Tergent from Ropes End, Wisc., and she was in a lather. After asking my secretary if she could speak to "the moron who won't get out of the way of progress," she gave it to me with both barrels.

"What the heck is wrong with you? Are you afraid of trying new techniques?"

She was upset about the same column. You see, I had implied that it was easier and more effective to give a vaccination than to avoid it by running blood tests and checking antibody titers. I had come to this conclusion by using a little known principle that I like to call Common Sense.

As for trying new techniques, I am ready to defend myself again. In 1970, I had the very first Mr. Coffee in my neighborhood. Friends, neighbors and relatives gathered in my kitchen to witness the miracle as cold water and coffee grounds, like magic, turned to coffee.

> *I had come to this conclusion by using a little known principle that I like to call Common Sense.*

There were, of course, many other phone calls about that April column, there were even several veterinarians who agreed with me. Dr. Haywire from Lost Cause, S. D., was not one of them. He had an important question for me.

"What the heck is wrong with you? When is the last time you attended a continuing education meeting, the Stone Age? You need to get over some of that horse and buggy thinking of yours."

He was mad because I don't advocate having pet owners sign a consent form for each vaccination we give. He felt that I don't keep up with the times. He was wrong.

You see, I have made it a point to regularly attend the AVMA convention. You could set your calendar by my attendance. I drop everything and head to the conference religiously, once every 18 years.

As coincidence would have it, the convention is this month, and I'll be there. I'd like to hear what you have to say. So, if you feel it is time to vaccinate less and to abandon techniques of preventive medicine that have served us well for these past several decades, please look me up. I have an important question to ask.

What the heck is wrong with you?

July 1998

Bout of temporary sanity stymies Dr. O

Are you one of those veterinarians who saves all of your old journals thinking that, some day, you may need to look up some gem of wisdom from the past?

If so, it's your lucky day. Rush to the storage room and find the May 1, 1990, *Journal of the American Veterinary Medical Association*. On page 1505 you will find the following example of brilliant advice: "Bioavailability of ketamine after administration per rectum in cats is similar to that after IM administration. So, per rectum administration may be an alternative route in fractious or frightened cats."

When I first read that paragraph, I imagined a vicious tomcat fighting with my staff. Razor sharp claws sliced the air in all directions. Anxious teeth sought a human target. Leather gloves and restraint poles were of no use against the feline demon. Then, in an act of kindness, I approached with no needle visible to the cat. He calmed instantly. Moments later, he was purring with contentment while he enjoyed a ketamine enema.

In reality, I have never actually incorporated full use of U.T.B. (up-the-butt) anesthesia in my practice. Frankly, I don't plan to. I don't rush to change what works for me just because there is a new trend or fad. My friends seem to disagree.

In January, a local colleague, Dr. Gill T. Newvet, called me for advice.

"Am I in trouble, Mike?" he asked.

I told him that I had no idea what he was talking about.

"Haven't you seen the latest journals? I've been over-vaccinating my patients. On top of that, I may be guilty of wasting vaccine! Can we get in trouble by over-protecting?"

"No," I answered. "Only by over-reacting."

"But, Mike," he said. "They say we should stop giving annual vaccinations to cats. Instead we are supposed to spend more time diagnosing and treating disease. My practice is new. We need that vaccine income. There aren't enough sick animals out there to make up for that lost revenue."

"Don't worry about it," I told him. "If we stop giving yearly shots, there will be plenty of sick animals to diagnose and treat."

An hour later, Dr. Nailbiter was on the phone.

"Mike, can I borrow a copy of your hospital's consent form for administration of vaccines? I am ashamed to admit it but at my hospital, we give shots without a discussion of every possible danger. On top of that, we don't even have an informed consent form that each pet owner has to sign."

I had to let him down.

"We don't use one at our hospital, either. We once tried to make one up, but after we listed every possible danger whether real or imagined, the thing was six pages long. Why don't you try calling Arnie and ask to borrow a copy of his?"

"Do you think he has one?"

"No, I don't, but he could use a good laugh."

Abe Raisive was the next on the phone.

"Mike, have you seen the good news? Our profession is coming to its senses. Finally, someone has realized that all this vaccinating of animals is counter-productive. The emphasis on preventive medicine has been choking me for years. Let's stop vaccinating and make some real money."

"You're missing the point," I told him. "The intent is not to make more income, it is to provide better, safer medical care."

"Oh, wake up and smell the money, Mike!" he said. "We need to twist this to our advantage. That's where I need your help. Write in that silly column of yours that we all need to stop vaccinating dogs for parvo. You know, I have two kids in college and I miss the income that disease can generate."

Obviously, I turned him down.

Arnie was on the phone before it had a chance to cool down.

"Mike, have you heard new advice that makes protecting pets more practical? Instead of giving one of those nasty vaccinations, we should draw blood samples and run antibody titers every year."

This gave us both a good chuckle.

"What about those tumors that some people say come from shots?" he asked. "We give over 40,000 vaccinations a year here, and the only lump I've seen turned out to be a bee sting."

I had to disagree. "The growths are real, and I've seen a few myself," I said.

"You have to take a stand, Mike. There are actually a few misguided individuals out there who read your column and think you know something."

"I can't, Arnie," I said. "If I disagree with all sorts of Ivory Tower thinking and recommendations for change, I'll be branded as an old-fashioned thinker. Letters to the editor will pour in saying I'm unprofessional, greedy and detrimental to the future of our profession!"

"Mike," he said. "I've been reading that stupid column of yours for almost 20 years. Believe me, the only thing that you could be accused of is a bout of temporary sanity."

July 1998

Where is the on-ramp to the information superhighway?

After a local veterinary association meeting, I approached a group of colleagues just in time to hear Arnie defending himself.

"I know I'm right," he said. "If you don't believe me, go ahead and ask him yourself. Here he comes."

Apparently, I had been the subject of some controversial discussion.

"All right, I will," said Dr. Juan Armup, a local bovine practitioner. He then turned to me and asked, "Mike, what kind of hardware do you use?"

I told him that I had always been partial to Sears, and that I found you would rarely go wrong with their Craftsman brand of tools.

For some reason, this brought the group to their knees with laughter.

"We're talking computers, Mike," one of them announced.

So, naturally, I asked what that had to do with tools. The question brought fresh peals of laughter from all those present.

"You were right, Arnie," Juan said.

"I told you so," Arnie replied. "The computer age has left Mike behind."

The truth is, he was 100 percent right. The closest thing to a computer in my office is the solar-powered calculator that we got free for buying 12 dozen bottles of Pinkicillin Liquid. Two buttons are missing, but it will still add and subtract even numbers.

I once thought about getting a computer but then I figured, "Why?"

Apparently sensing the presence of an infidel, they all seemed to turn on me at once. The advantages of computer ownership were hurled at me from all directions.

If I had one, I could "surf the net." I figured, "Why?" (Shouldn't surfing have something to do with water?)

I could have access to articles that are unpublished anywhere else.

I figured, "Why?" (If the articles were any good, they would be published somewhere.)

I would be able to travel along the information superhighway right from my own home. I figured, "Why?" (Staying home means staying home, not traveling).

I left that meeting still ruminating on quite a bit of food for thought though, and two days later, I let Arnie take me to the

Apparently sensing the presence of an infidel, they all seemed to turn on me at once.

computer store "just to look." There were countless numbers of these menacing looking machines lined up in neat rows. My theory that they are deliberately taking over the earth through a well-planned secret invasion seemed very feasible from inside this store.

Arnie spoke to the salesman in some foreign language. Only occasionally, was there a word I recognized, such as Apple or Macintosh (I'm partial to Granny Smith myself.)

They started to put the pressure on. Arnie and his newfound accomplice took me over to one of the electronic invaders and introduced it to me as a good, basic computer for a beginner such as myself. I figured, "Why am I here?"

The thing looked a lot more complicated than the calculator with the two buttons missing.

Next, I got a look at the price tag. Before they show that to you, they should stand by with a defibrillator. It doesn't seem right to spend that kind of money for something when you can't kick the tires or examine the teeth.

Eventually, they got me to sit down next to the thing.

"Are you ready to join the 20th century?" Arnie asked. "Are you ready to take this baby home, adjust the mirrors, fasten your seatbelt and pull out onto the information superhighway?"

I figured, "Why not?"

September 1995

Chapter 9:
My Corner of the World

Mrs. Blastaway takes aim at those 'high' exam fees

I barely got a chance to say hello before Mrs. Blastaway gave it to me with both barrels.

"I just brought him in today for the same old shot that he always gets," she announced while slamming her little dog onto the exam table with almost cruel force.

"That unreasonable office manager of yours said I would have to pay an exam fee, even though you and I both know what shot he needs."

The lady (I use the term loosely) didn't look familiar. Neither did the dog.

I glanced at the record. It was blank. My first thought was that we had misplaced the records of an already irate client. (I hate when that happens.)

While gently picking up the petrified pooch, my technician was able to enlighten me as to the nature of the situation. "We have never seen Puddles before, Dr. O," she said. "However, Mrs. Blastaway brought records from her previous vet's office." (Now, we were getting somewhere.)

I looked at the computer printout from Downtheroad Veterinary Hospital. The last entry was dated 1998. Several notations indicated slow payment, refusal to authorize proper diagnostic testing and failure to follow directions. (Oh, goody. We have a new client.)

Unfortunately, the records did not indicate a diagnosis of any sort, nor was there any mention of the "shot" that Mrs. Blastaway demanded. She glanced at her watch, obviously annoyed that this office call was taking more than the 90 seconds she had allotted for it.

I informed her that I would need to ask her some questions and that Puddles would need to be examined. She had a question for me as well. "How much is that nonsense going to cost me?" (I was touched by the concern for Puddles.)

After a short examination of our office charges, I was compelled to point out that we might even need to run some blood tests. (She was not happy.)

"As you can clearly see from those records, I already spent a lot of money on this problem. When does it stop? The shot always made him well before. I don't see what good blood tests are going to do."

It was clear to me that the symptoms were entirely different from 1998, and furthermore, it wouldn't take Sherlock Holmes to see that this was a very sick little dog.

Following another furtive glance at her watch, she asked if there would be an additional charge for the blood tests. (In a word, yes.)

This, of course, caused her a great deal of concern, until she came up with a money-saving plan. "My cousin is a veterinary technician," she announced. "Couldn't I get her to draw the blood, and I would bring it in. That would save me the part of the cost you get for taking the samples."

When I broke the news that I was not enamored with her plan, she quickly came up with an even better one. "Why doesn't my cousin just come in here to do it? She could draw the blood, and even run the tests in your lab. Wouldn't that save me a lot of money?" (Now, why didn't I think of that?)

I was getting nowhere, and it was taking entirely too long to get there. This lady needed to be straightened out. Unfortunately, I am the world's most non-confrontational person. Situations like this call for the big guns. I excused myself and sent my office manager in to tell this lady how things were going to be. (My way or the highway, came to mind.)

Moments later, while examining a cat in another room, I heard Mrs. Blastaway storm out of the building, while loudly vowing never to come back.

That office manager of mine had just cost me a client. That's why she makes the big bucks.

April 2006

Consider a 'not my problem' department

This chairman finds it easy to evaluate many client concerns, problems

I am a veterinarian. I know this because I have a diploma from the University of Pennsylvania, which says so. At least, I think that's what it says.

The truth is, it is written in Latin so, for all I know, it could be a certificate entitling me to a free Happy Meal at McDonald's.

Anyway, just for the sake of argument, let's suppose that I am actually a veterinarian. This means that the welfare of animals, and, in many cases their owners, is of great concern to me. Unfortunately, many members of the general public seem to think that their problem is actually my responsibility.

Such was the case last Monday when my week began with a visit from one of my fussiest clients. It was Walter Wall with his Shih Tzu, Dingleberry. He got right to the point, "We have a real problem here, Doctor. Dingleberry has been leaving little doodles all over the rugs at home. It's been going on for four months, and we are leaving on vacation tomorrow. I can't come home to a house full of poo. You have to do something. We have very expensive carpets at our house."

I explained that he might have to board the dog while he was away. After all, it was unlikely that the problem could be cured in 24 hours.

"I can't afford to do that, and I can't afford new rugs," he replied. "I would cancel the vacation, but it has been planned for a long time and I can't get my money back if I don't go. Just what do you expect me to do, Doc?"

I took his question to a fictitious portion of my hospital known as the "not my

problem department." As chairman of the "not my problem department," I was able to quickly determine that the problem was "not mine."

Later that very same day, in a similar incident, Dee Linquent stopped in with her new kitten. "You know, Doctor," she said. "I don't appreciate that office manager of yours always asking me when I'm going to pay my bill. It seems like that's all she ever wants to talk about. I have a lot of dogs and cats, and as you know, I keep getting new ones. My husband and I have a deal. He doesn't mind how many animals we have as long as I am able to take care of the expenses on my own. Your office manager has to understand that."

After she left, my office manager and I checked with the "not our problem department" which is a branch of the "not my problem department." Guess what? We figured out that the problem was "not ours."

Many of the office calls that week followed a similar theme. Mrs. Broadloom, for example, was very upset with me. "If you can't do something about this cat peeing on my rug, I may have to put him to sleep." Naturally, she didn't want to follow any of my suggestions for treatment, but did want to imply that eventual euthanasia would be our fault, not hers.

> Another client, Al Truistic, wanted to know why veterinarians don't spay all strays "for the good of the animals."

Another client, Al Truistic, wanted to know why veterinarians don't spay all strays "for the good of the animals." It seemed logical to him that I would want to reward any person who took in a stray dog or cat by giving him or her free care. It turned out that he himself had three dogs and two cats that "were not really his. They were strays."

By Thursday, I was getting annoyed with the concept that I should be held responsible for the majority of the world's problems. So, I called my friend, Arnie, to tell him what a lousy week I was having. In typical fashion, he had some words of wisdom for me. "Not my problem, Mike."

August 2004

Where did I go wrong?

Losing clients can be ... satisfying

Kowtowing to bad clients can be bad for business

Mr. Bicker was making quite a scene at the front desk, so my staff asked me to talk to him. When he saw me coming, he gave it to me with both barrels.

"I have no intention of paying these high prices, Doctor," he announced. "Butterball needs to be spayed, but I'm not going to let myself be robbed. I have a paper right here that you gave me when I got her. It says that a spay is only $75."

I took a look at the paper. It was six years old. Not only that, but Butterball was clearly one of the fattest Beagles I had ever seen. I tried to explain that six years and 60 pounds alters a lot of things. He was not in agreement.

"I read about you vets in *Consumer Truth* magazine. You're a bunch of crooks. All you care about is money. It's getting so that the average person can't afford to have a dog nowadays. Poor Butterball has been vomiting and drinking lots of water since the last time she was in heat. My regular veterinarian ran a blood test and said that she has something called a "pie a meter." She needs to be spayed, and I can't afford these high prices. Believe it or not, the price he quoted me was even higher than yours. Now, are you going to honor the quote on this paper, or not?

I chose "not." Then when I tried to explain that I might need to take an X-ray and run some other blood tests, he left my office in search of a vet who wasn't so "money hungry." He took the six-year-old paper with him, vowing to show it to the Better Business Bureau.

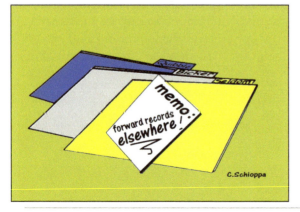

Later that same day, Mrs. Quibble came to see me with her old tom cat, Mr. Cheeks. He had a lump forming on his right shoulder. Mrs. Quibble wanted to know why we hadn't noticed it before.

"You know, Doctor. We were just in here for his vaccinations a few months ago.

> I tried to explain that six years and 60 pounds alters a lot of things. He was not in agreement.

Shouldn't you have seen this? You must not have examined him very well."

I looked at the record. She was right; it had been a few months since his last visit. Eighteen months to be exact. I pointed out that a lot can happen in a year and a half. Unfortunately, she was no more understanding than Mr. Bicker had been. The way she saw the situation, because we didn't see the lump when she feels we should have, it was now our responsibility and not hers. I was given a choice; fix the lump for free or watch her take her business somewhere else.

(Bye. Bye.)

It wasn't long before the third problem of the day surfaced. (My problems always seem to come in threes.) It was a phone call from Mrs. Seldom, and she was hopping mad about our examination policies.

"What's this nonsense about Poochie having to come over there to get a health certificate? He was just there to get neutered last year. You know he's healthy. We're flying to Florida next week, and your office person said that you wouldn't give us a health certificate unless you look at him first. That's the most ridiculous thing I ever heard."

I explained that health changes from year to year. She did not want to hear it. "I've been coming to you for 10 years. I'd think that you'd be willing to break the rules once in a while for your regular clients. If I have to make a trip way over to your office, I might just as well go to a closer vet."

It was true; she had been coming to see me for 10 years. However, she was a pain in the butt both times. Anyway, she did as promised and went elsewhere for the exam. It had been quite a day, an exciting day. I had lost three clients, three terrible clients. It was a great day.

January 2005

Cookie batter's ingredients raise concern

This cat owner emergency easily licked by speedy stool sample analysis

Things were just winding down at the end of another busy day when my secretary knocked on the exam room door.

"Dr. O," she said, "there is a lady on the phone who is hysterical. All she will tell me is that she was baking cookies and needs to talk to you right away. She keeps screaming that it's an emergency."

I took the call and was barraged with seemingly useless information. "Doctor, we were baking cookies! We were baking cookies! That's how it happened. It was all so fast that I didn't realize what was going on until it was too late. What can I do? Has anything like this ever happened before?"

After politely asking her to calm down and get her wits about her, I explained that I needed more details as to the nature of the emergency.

"We were baking cookies when Tangy, our cat, got into the kitchen." Her voice still sounded a little shaken, but she was talking with less hysteria now. "All of a sudden, he jumped up on the counter right near the dough."

Now I realized what was going on. She must have been one of those people who are so fussy that they panic over the thought of an animal being anywhere near their food. I began to explain that a few stray cat hairs in the kitchen would be very unlikely to cause any human fatalities. She quickly interrupted.

"You don't understand, Doctor!" When he jumped up on the counter, I grabbed him and put him back on the floor. I went right back to work, and that's when it happened. It was all so fast. I guess I wasn't thinking. What should I do?"

I guessed that she was upset because she neglected

Chapter 9: My Corner of the World

to wash her hands after handling the cat. Big deal! Once again, I began to explain that she probably was worried about nothing. Once again, she interrupted.

"There's more to it than you think, doctor. We were baking cookies. The cat jumped up. I moved him away. I got a little sloppy while stirring the batter. I wasn't thinking. I'd hate to tell you what happened next. It's too embarrassing."

I told her that she would have to give me a hint as to the nature of the problem.

"I licked poop! There was batter on my hand. Not thinking, I licked it off. It

> I began to explain that a few stray cat hairs in the kitchen would be very unlikely to cause any human fatalities.

> Her kids announced, "Mom ate poo."

wasn't batter; it was poop! I actually licked poop. Am I going to be all right?"

After getting her to calm down, I told her to bring me a stool sample from the cat and to call her family doctor. She vowed to rush right over, and she arrived within minutes. While we ran the fecal exam, her two children insisted on humiliating her by announcing that, "Mom ate poo," to anyone and everyone that they saw. Her attempts to quiet them went unheeded. Fortunately, owner and feline eventually checked out fine. I'm not sure about the kids, though. I suspect they got punished for teasing mom when they got home.

As a reward for our calm handling of the incident, a grateful owner delivered two dozen cookies to our office the very next day. That was two weeks ago. Those cookies remain untouched.

September 2004

Wanda Sample spurs spurious ethical dilemma

Should we actually charge for medicine or give it away?

It seemed like a routine office call until the very end. I had explained to Mrs. Sample that her kitten, Little Fussy, would have to take a dropper full of the medicine twice daily for a week.

My technician took the bottle from me so that she could apply the computer label with the directions. Unfortunately, Mrs. Sample grabbed the medicine from her hand before she could get out the door.

I began to explain that the medicine needed to be labeled before we sent her home, but Mrs. Sample had other ideas. Pulling a tablespoon from her purse, she poured a generous portion of pinkicillin into the spoon and gulped it down.

"I won't give anything to my pets that I wouldn't take myself," she said. "My cats are very finicky, and I wouldn't want any of them to hate me for giving medicine that tastes bad. This stuff is pretty good though. I don't think Little Fussy will mind it at all."

Now, for those of you who aren't familiar with either the metric system or higher mathematics, let me point out that, if liquid from a 15-ml bottle is poured into a 15-ml spoon and is then swallowed by a 15-IQ person, there will be none left.

That is where the trouble began. Wanda Sample could not believe that we intended to charge her for two bottles of medicine. It's not that she minded paying for the second one, she just didn't think that she should have to pay for what she called "the sample bottle."

I was faced with a difficult decision. Should I charge for medications or give them away for free? I decided to take the question to an imaginary part of my hospital called the "not gonna happen" department. I took a pretend walk down the imaginary hallway to the fictitious

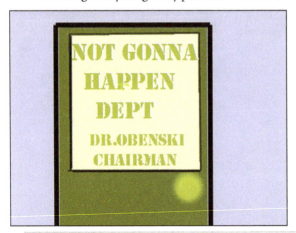

door of the "not gonna happen" department. It was the second door on the left, right next to the "not my problem" department, another figment of my imagination that I introduced to you last August.

These are my two favorite and most-often used fictitious departments. Those two doors, and in fact, all doors in the imaginary hallway are stenciled with my name in gold letters right above the words "Chairman." Guess what? After a brief meeting, during which I discussed all of the pros and cons with myself, I came to the surprising conclusion that furnishing medications for free was "not gonna happen."

Wanda Sample stormed out with no medicine and told my receptionist that she would contact Pill-a-Pooch.com for her prescription.

By the time she was out the door, I was on the phone listening to another ridiculous request.

This time it was Mrs. Needy wanting to know why I couldn't come to her house and fix a broken leg.

"You could bring one of your helpers and put a cast on Bonaparte's leg right here, Doctor," she suggested. "Do you remember how wild he gets when he has to come to your office? Why, the last time he was there, it took four people to hold him down. I wouldn't want to see him go through anything like that again. If you fixed him here, I'm sure that he would hold still for me."

Finding myself somewhat lacking in suicidal tendencies, I held another brief department meeting and concluded that a visit to her house was "not gonna happen."

Unfortunately, it turned out to be one of those days.

Not an hour went by before Izzy Serious called to ask for my help. "It's pretty cold outside, Doctor, and there is a stray cat in my neighborhood that I feel sorry for. At least, I'm pretty sure it's a cat. It might be a groundhog or a raccoon. Anyway, I've seen him prowling out in the woods behind my house, but I've never been able to get close to him. Could you go out there some night this week after dark and try to get a look at him. Take a powerful flashlight. If you could get a look at him and if he seems healthy, then maybe you could trap him for me, and I could give him a home."

This request called for a special meeting. I went all the way to the "snowball's chance in hell" department.

> I decided to take the question to an imaginary part of my hospital.

March 2005

Beware of grass moles

Every practice has them—'F' clients who 'dispense a whole 'lotta misery'

Will Rogers was a man of great perception whose homespun brand of humor and philosophy once captivated America.

Will Rogers' peaceable spirit is reflected in his often quoted line, "I never met a man I didn't like."

Will Rogers never worked in my office.

I would like to take this opportunity to confess to you, right now, that there are people whom I do not like. Who are the people on this list? They are certain of my clients, and you know who they are because you have clients just like them.

True, these "F" clients comprise a small group. Nonetheless, they cause most of our daily anxieties. In my office, they all have one thing in common. Their medical records are marked in the upper left hand corner with the "universal symbol." It is a circle with a dot in the middle and is the universal symbol for something that rhymes with "grass mole."

Anyway, when Mrs. Carping called last week to complain about our services, the symbol on her record was the first thing I noticed.

"This is Alice Carping, Doctor," she announced in her usual obnoxious tone. "I don't care what you say, there must be something wrong with Robusto. He's just not himself today, and I'm not going to pay for this visit, either. We were just there a few weeks ago, and you said he was fine. Besides, you also made me get those expensive vaccines that supposedly were going to keep him well. I think that those shots are probably what made him sick."

The dog's file clearly showed that the last visit was actually five months ago. As she rambled on, my eyes wandered over the somewhat lengthy medical record in my hand. It was a catalog of aggravating veterinary office scenarios that started with my notes concerning the dog's very first visit four years ago. It read:

"Owner wants to know why she

OFFICE MEMO

tonight after work party to celebrate 14 days ⊙ free.

has to pay for neutering. Since pet population control is good for the general public, she wants to know why vets don't do these surgeries for free as a public service."

The very next day the record noted:

"Owner cannot get here by closing time to pick up the dog. She wants one of us to stay open an extra hour so she can still pick him up tonight."

Then, quite predictably, the following line read:

"Owner refuses to pay for extra day's board. Says it is not her fault that we insisted on closing on time yesterday."

There were three places on the record where the following notation occurred: "Owner called to complain because our receptionist said that we won't dispense medications without examining the animal first. Her neighbor's dog had the exact same thing, so we should dispense the medicine that the other dog got."

One notable entry said, "Owner refuses to pay for blood tests. She says that they didn't show anything, and that we just wanted to run up her bill by doing unnecessary tests."

Another time, we were chastised for our poor surgical skills.

"Owner demands an X-ray for a swollen stifle joint. She doesn't feel she should have to pay for it since the swelling is probably related to the neutering surgery three years ago. She says she is going to call the Better Business Bureau to report us."

Most importantly, every ugly incident on the record was followed by the following notation:

"We offered to forward copies of the medical records to another hospital since owner would probably be happier going elsewhere."

Unfortunately, "F" clients like Alice Carping rarely accept our invitation to leave. They profess to be unhappy, but they just keep coming back. Luckily, they make up a very small percentage of the people who walk through my door, and yet they dispense a lot of misery.

I cringe when I see one of them listed in the appointment book. Furthermore, I hope that a receptionist or technician will be able to handle each of their phone calls, because I don't want to deal with them if I can avoid it.

Will Rogers may have only seen the good side of people, but there is another more realistic philosopher who said: "Ninety nine percent of the aggravation comes from one percent of the people."

Come to think of it, that was me.

March 2004

> Unfortunately, "F" clients like Alice Carping rarely accept our invitation to leave.

Axioms guide, as well as rule, veterinary life

Words to live by: 'Everything is funny when it happens to someone else'

It was a strange phone call, indeed. At least, that's what my secretary thought.

"Doctor," she said. "There's a man on line one who keeps yelling the number six."

I asked her if that was all he had said, and she replied that his exact words were: "Six! Six! Get Obenski to the phone. Tell him that I have a classic six!"

Sensing that it had to be my friend, Arnie, I picked up the phone to ask him what was going on.

"Mike," he said, "You know how some

dogs arrive at your office with pink stuff on their face because the owner tried to give them Pepto Bismol?"

"Sure," I said. "It happens all the time. Sometimes it's axomicillin, though."

"That's right," he said. "In fact, in this case, that's exactly what it was. These people came to me for a second opinion. It seems their dog was being treated for gingivitis. The pooch had pink smears dribbled and caked all over his face. I asked them if the dog had been giving them a hard time about swallowing the antibiotics. Do you know what they said? They said, 'Swallowing? What do you mean swallowing? We've been putting the medicine in his ears.'"

"That certainly sounds like a six to me, Arnie," I said, referring of course, to axiom No. 6 of veterinary practice.

Now, for those of you who may be unfamiliar with the 13 axioms of veterinary practice, let me point out that No. 6 states: "When someone brings a pet to your

> " ... What do you mean swallowing? We've been putting the medicine in his ears."

office, you cannot automatically assume they have any brains."

You see, there are certain universal truths that govern the day-to-day happenings in a veterinary hospital. To date, Arnie and I have documented the existence of 13 such rules. Arnie just fell victim to No. 6.

The next day, Arnie was on the phone again.

"Eleven! Eleven!" he shouted. "My six turned into an 11!"

I asked him to tell me about it.

"Well, the dog's mouth had been getting worse for weeks, and it turned out that there were some gum tumors. The owners were really upset. They love this dog. So, after giving me the usual lecture about how much they care and how money is no object, they had me operate on the dog. Surgery went great. The recovery was uneventful. Everyone was happy until they saw the bill. All of a sudden, I got a dose of axiom No. 11: 'There is absolutely no correlation between what people want and what they are willing to pay for it.' You should have heard them, Mike! 'You must be kidding!' they said. 'We thought it would be about 20 bucks. He's just a mutt, you know. For that kind of money, we could have gotten a new dog.' They went on and on, but you get the idea. It was a typical 11"

I couldn't help but laugh at the situation. Arnie, however, failed to see the humor.

"I'm gonna get beat for this whole bill," he said. "I don't know what you are giggling about, Mike, because I don't see what's so funny. I'll talk to you later when you're not so busy laughing at my misfortune."

And with that, he said goodbye.

I called him right back. As soon as his receptionist answered, I gave it to her with both barrels.

"Nine! Nine! Get Dr. Arnie to the phone and tell him it's a nine!"

I could hardly wait to point out that axiom nine had just gone into effect. It says: "Everything is funny when it happens to somebody else."

March 2003

Smooth-talking Dr. O fells unsuspecting Arnie
'You can catch more flies with honey than vinegar, but...'

It was not a particularly unusual office call.

Mrs. Latherlips was foaming on about something irrelevant while I waited for the opportunity to get a word in edgewise. I had triggered her monologue by inquiring as to the reason for her visit. This led to an avalanche of useless information.

First, she felt compelled to share an amusing anecdote about her neighbor's dog. This was followed by a description of every pet she had ever owned, an explanation of her views concerning pet over-population and an attempt to show me the scar from her recent operation.

Finally, she proceeded into what I call a non-history. She told me everything that the pooch ever did, while skillfully avoiding anything that resembled a straight answer to one of my questions. Interestingly enough, she went home apparently happy with the service at my clinic, even though I had no idea what she came in for in the first place.

My next office call was with Mr. Windtunnel. His cat came for routine vaccinations. Mr. Windtunnel came to educate me. He began with a lecture on several ways to improve my practice. A soliloquy on national health care reform followed. He then began jumping from subject to subject, solving the world's problems one at a time. It took 10 minutes to extricate myself from the conversation.

Later at lunch, I told my friend, Arnie, about these two office calls. Both were clear examples of one of the axioms of veterinary practice. In this case, it was axiom No. 3 which states, "there is

> All of a sudden, Arnie started to choke. His face was red and his eyes widened.

no correlation between the amount of talking that a client does and the amount of useful information that you are going to get out of it."

You may recall that last month, I spelled out several of the axioms (or rules) of veterinary practice. You don't? In that case, go check the bottom of your parrot's cage and review that article. I'll wait...

OK. Let's continue. Since that article appeared, several colleagues have called to ask me for a list of the 13 rules. I have decided to do the next best thing by going over a few more of them this month. Arnie is going to help me. I broke that news to him as our lunches arrived.

"Don't get me involved in any of your nonsense," he said. "I don't like being in that silly column of yours. Besides, if you got stuck with a couple of threes, that's your problem. I haven't seen a three for weeks."

All of a sudden, Arnie started to choke. His face was red and his eyes widened. There was no need for the Heimlich maneuver. What he was choking on was the realization that I had tricked him into breaking axiom No. 4, also known as Murphy's Law of the unspoken. It says: "You may think anything that you please, but if you say something out loud and it's bad, it will happen."

Merely by mentioning that he had avoided threes lately, Arnie had sealed his own fate. He was now doomed to spend that afternoon treading water in a sea of useless information. I welcomed him to the April column.

"I'm going to get even with you for this, Mike," he said. "I pride myself on having a smooth-running office. We like to avoid aggravations, and you may have just changed my percentages in axiom No. 8."

(No. 8 says: In veterinary practice, 90 percent of the aggravation comes from 10 percent of the people.)

"Take it easy, Arnie," I said. "A master client handler like you shouldn't have any trouble. I've seen you glide through situations that would tie me up in knots. Your hospital policies are so effective and your staff is so good, that you could master any situation. He seemed to calm down. I had used axiom 12 on him: "You can catch more flies with honey than you can with vinegar, but you can catch the most flies with a shovelful of manure."

April 2003

Let's set the record straight, please

Recently, I ran across a newspaper article that shook me to the marrow.

I would have shared its contents with you sooner, but it has taken awhile for the shock to wear off.

The headline was, "Did They Really Say It?", and according to the article, many of my favorite quotations are counterfeit.

I find it hard to believe, but P.T. Barnum never said, "There's a sucker born every minute." Furthermore, Leo Durocher never said, "Nice guys finish last," nor did President Abraham Lincoln utter the phrase, "You can fool all the people some of the time, you can even fool some of the people all of the time, but you can't fool all of the people all of the time." (No comment will be inserted here about recent White House residents.)

At any rate, I was shocked at seeing these astounding facts in print! Now, before you even consider disputing any of these things, please note that I did not see this in just any newspaper. It was none other than the Allentown Morning Call, so, naturally, there can be no doubt as to the validity of the information.

As I read through the article, I could hardly believe my eyes. It seems that W.C. Fields is not the originator of the phrases, "Never give a sucker an even break" and "Any man who hates dogs and children can't be all bad." Nor does Harry Truman get the credit

for "If you can't stand the heat, get out of the kitchen."

Then I remembered that you and I have discussed counterfeit quotations before. In previous columns I have pointed out to you that some of history's

> ...when it comes to handling our clients, I go by our hospital motto...

most famous sayings actually came from veterinarians.

Let me refresh your memory with an example from the year 1775.

Bill Prescott was taking his dog, Musket, to the veterinarian for vaccinations. He had a lot on his mind that day. Among other things, he had to prepare a speech on battle tactics to be delivered to his troops the next morning. While his veterinarian, Dr. Colonial, was treating the pooch, Bill jokingly asked how the vet knew where to give the shots.

"After all," he said, "Musket is so shaggy you can hardly tell which is his front end and which is his back."

Dr. Colonial had an answer.

"Colonel Prescott," he said. "I never shoot until I see the whites of their eyes."

The saying is, of course, famous. The veterinarian, unfortunately, never got the credit.

And so, I have come to an important decision. I should help to set the record straight for future generations by recording some of our profession's most quotable phrases. Naturally, this would include giving the proper credit to the originator.

For example, on the subject of clinic neatness, it was my hospital manager who said, "Everything belongs in one of two places; either where it belongs or in the trash."

On the subject of taking a clinical history, I am the one who said, "There is no correlation between the amount of talking that a client does and the amount of useful information that you are going to get out of it."

Finally, concerning techniques for handling problem clients, my friend, Abe, likes to tell them, "If you don't like our policies, there's the door. Don't let it hit you in the butt on the way out."

(Actually, instead of the word "butt" Abe uses a more colorful anatomical term.)

However, when it comes to handling our clients, I go by our hospital motto: "You can catch more flies with honey than you can with vinegar, but you can catch the most flies with a shovel of manure."

(Actually, in place of the word "manure" we use a more colorful term, also.)

Aprl 2001

Blockhead Hall of Fame competition fierce

It has been eight years since my first phone call from Ann Biguous.

She wasn't sure what was wrong with her cat, or even how to describe the symptoms, but she was positive that some horrible disease was in progress.

"My cat just isn't himself," she said. "He's acting strange. He's not as playful as usual and, he's ignoring his favorite toys." I tried fishing for some pertinent facts, but apparently her lake had not been stocked. The only bits of information that I managed to reel in were too small and had to be thrown back.

She didn't want to bring him in to see me, but promised to watch him for the day and call me by 3 p.m. if he was worse. Then, we would have plenty of time to schedule an appointment and examine him before we closed that evening.

Predictably she waited until 7 p.m. to call. The cat was no worse, and she didn't want to bring him in, but wanted my assurance that he would be all right. She began using typical night caller phrases such as, "Are you sure that he doesn't have anything that he could die from?" "Will you be on call all night in case I need you?" And my personal favorite, "Do you charge more if you have to come out in the middle of the night?" I told her we'd see the cat in the morning if there still seemed to be a problem.

By the 11 p.m. phone call, she had shown a change of attitude. It was obvious she wanted the cat to be seen. Any symptoms I mentioned became distinct possibilities. We've all seen clients exhibit this tendency to maximize a problem; it can happen any time they want to be seen at a time that is convenient for them, but inconvenient for you.

So, 11:30 p.m. found me at the office where I looked over the records of her three cats while waiting for her to arrive. I hoped she was bringing the nice one. Imagine my disappoint-

> *Any symptoms I mentioned became distinct possibilities.*

ment when I saw her show up with the whole crew.

"I brought them all," she said. "Something could be wrong with any of them. Besides, I just found out that my husband needs the car tomorrow." There was a proud look on her face as if I should be thrilled. After all, I am in the business of treating pets. So, why shouldn't I be elated to have three cats to treat instead of one? I assume that this, if anything, is what goes on in our clients' minds when they pull this sort of stunt.

Naturally, I couldn't find anything wrong with the cats. However, something positive did result from the fiasco. Ann Biguous, due to her three-for-one night call, won our hospital's "Client Antic of the Week Award." Furthermore, Ann was inducted permanently into our Blockhead Hall of Fame.

For over four years, that emergency call headed our list of inconsiderate client stunts. Fame, however, is a fleeting thing. Eventually, a new champion emerged from the ranks of my clientele. His name is Mr. Summons and he beat Ann Biguous by a mile.

He had called on Labor Day because his dog was having difficulty breathing. I arranged to see him as an emergency and met him at my hospital. He showed up with two dogs instead of one, but I wasn't surprised. I've learned to expect such things once in awhile. However, as I examined the first dog, another one of my clients, Mrs. Crony, showed up unexpectedly with two of her cats.

A moment later, Mr. Chum pulled into the lot with his dog. I told them I was not expecting them and asked if they had talked to the answering service.

"Oh, no, doctor," said Mrs. Crony. "We're friends of Mr. Summons. He knew that we had the day off from work due to the holiday. So, he called us and told us that you'd be here. We all figured it would be a good time to get our animals taken care of."

And so, we had a new champion. Mr. Summons moved into the No. 1 spot in the Blockhead Hall of Fame.

July 2000

Two rules to deal with salespeople: 'just say no', 'don't pay attention'

I was sitting in my office Wednesday morning when a very important question popped into my head. "Am I awake or asleep?"

There might have been a man seated on the other side of my desk talking to me. I wasn't sure.

However, after some serious concentration, I realized that I was neither awake nor asleep. I was "tuned out."

I had been using my particular skill to leave a conversation in which my input is not necessary and to mentally go elsewhere.

When in this state, I may appear to actually care about the subject at hand. My mind, however, has drifted back to my home planet.

Upon deciding that it was time for re-entry, the man in my office began to come into focus. He was yammering on about my family, the weather and the Philadelphia Eagles. It turned out to be Tom Hardsell, the Yellow Pages sales representative.

I'm not referring to the type of Yellow Pages that you get when training a puppy. I mean the kind where you pay an obscene amount of money for a tiny ad that they print once, but charge you for every month.

Tom had been going through the traditional chit-chat that all salesmen feel is necessary before getting down to business. Apparently, they are taught that some small talk will fool me into thinking that we are close friends and that, moments later, they need merely ask and I will be willing to donate a kidney.

At any rate, Tom had some distressing news for me. After an impartial review, he had determined that my Yellow Pages ad was not big enough. The only way to avoid deterioration of my practice would be to expand the ad at once.

It was my lucky day. A knight in shining armor had come to save my practice. His plan was simple and included upgrading to a full page display, adding color pictures and offering discount coupons. The cost? Why, when you compare it to the national debt or the Pentagon budget, it seemed like just peanuts.

I was about to sign on the dotted line when an attack of temporary sanity overtook me. I decided to risk the almost certain demise of my practice and leave my ad unchanged.

As it turned out, Tom was not the last person I would see on Wednesday who was full of advice designed to save me. Justin Case, the insurance salesman had an appointment to see me at 2 p.m.

A month earlier, he had offered to review my insurance coverages and make recommendations for any changes that might be necessary. The whole deal was free of charge. (What a guy!) His reason for today's appointment was to go over his findings.

Once again, I drifted into semi-consciousness while he prattled on about our "mutual" interests. (If you can't talk Harleys, don't talk at all).

I returned in time for the news. Guess what? He figured out that I need more insurance. (What are the chances of that?) Once again, I chose to throw caution to the wind and ignore the well-meaning advice of a good samaritan. (I like to live life on the edge.)

You can see from these examples that I have developed two rules for dealing with salesmen. Grab your pencil and write these down because they took me 50 years to develop and you can reap the benefits of my experience by simply reading them here.

Rule No. 1—"Don't pay attention."

Rule No. 2—"Just say no."

Practice these techniques when you have a spare moment. If you are married, you get plenty of opportunities to not listen and then say no. I do it all the time.

(My wife reads this column. As I said earlier, I like to live life on the edge.)

February 1998

The dreaded Double Whammy

There are two types of OOBs. And, you can believe me when I tell you, I hate them both. Just the sight of an OOB makes me think about retiring and getting out of this rat race.

It could be a pleasant day when all things seem to be going smoothly. Then, all of a sudden, I see it in my appointment book. An OOB has been scheduled. My attitude plummets.

You see, OOB is not a disease, it is a symptom. In your practice, you may know them by different names but, in my office, these two dreaded cat ailments are called UOOB (Urine Out of Box) and SOOB (Stool Out of Box).

There is, of course, a third entity that's even worse, the much feared SOOB & UOOB, known in my practice as the Double Whammy.

At any rate, there are few situations in practice where the history is so incomplete, the treatment is so unrewarding and the patient is so unimportant. By that, I mean that the frantic pet owner is often much more concerned about their rug than they are about my patient.

Such was the case when my old friend, Charlie Wingnut, called about his cat, Spooky.

"Mike, can you stop at my house on your day off and take a look at Spooky? He won't use his litter pan." (The Double Whammy).

Looking at the situation not as a house call but as an opportunity to sit down and have a few beers with an old friend, I wound up at Charlie's place the next afternoon.

Physically, the cat looked fine. I was just about to tell Charlie that, when it started. At first there was just a dull, distant roar. Then, as the noise grew louder, the cat clawed his way right out of my grasp. Through the floor, I could feel a slight vibration.

"I didn't realize your house was so close to the railroad tracks, Charlie," I told him. "Maybe Spooky's problem has something to do with the train noise."

"That ain't no train, Mike. That's my new litter pan. It cleans itself! I invented it after I saw one in a catalog for $200."

Moments later, I was treated to a demonstration of Charlie's pride and joy. The contraption was made of wood and took up a third of the room. It went off every 20 minutes whether the cat was in it or not. A mecha-

> *"That ain't no train, Mike. That's my new litter pan. It cleans itself! I invented it after I saw one in a catalog for two hundred dollars."*

nized comb scooped through the litter making a noise not unlike the start of Daytona.

"Don't worry about the comb, Mike," he said. "It's designed to be gentle."

I asked to borrow his bowling ball, and, after its reluctant delivery, placed it in harm's way and hit the switch. Had there been 10 bowling pins at the other end of the room, the litter pan would have gotten a strike.

There was no choice but to deliver the bad news. The mechanized pan would have to go. No cat in his right mind would go near the thing. Charlie was disappointed, but took my advice.

Not all clients who create their own problems are as quick to admit their mistakes. Take, for example, Mrs. Wifty. Just yesterday, she called in a panic because her new puppy was lame.

"Doctor, can I come right over? Sneakers can't walk right. He was fine this morning then, all of a sudden, he refused to walk. He shakes his feet as if they hurt, and he cries."

Moments later, as the pooch was led from the car to the clinic, I could see how uncomfortable he was. His high-stepping gait resembled that of a Tennessee Walker with sore feet.

I could also see the cause of his problem. He was wearing boots.

"Why yes, Doctor, I did put his boots on for the first time this morning. It's amazing that you could tell that. Anyway, it's a good thing I did. His feet seem to be bothering him so much that I'm glad they are protected by those boots. I hope we won't have to take them off to see what's wrong with him."

As you might guess, a happy, barefoot pooch was soon running around my office as if the entire incident never happened.

"I can't believe those boots were at fault," she said. "Somebody ought to invent boots that are more comfortable for dogs."

"Mother Nature already did," I assured her.

She vowed to return the boots to the pet store and exchange them for a more comfortable article of clothing. I know I'll be seeing Sneakers again soon.

May 1997